Translation into the Second Lang

APPLIED LINGUISTICS AND LANGUAGE STUDY

General Editor
Professor Christopher N. Candlin, Macquarie University, Sydney

For a complete list of books in this series see pages v–vi.

Translation into the Second Language

STUART CAMPBELL

LONGMAN
London and New York

Addison Wesley Longman Limited
Edinburgh Gate
Harlow, Essex CM20 2JE
England

and Associated Companies throughout the world

*Published in the United States of America
by Addison Wesley Longman Inc., New York*

First published 1998

ISBN 0 582 30188-2 Paper

British Library Cataloguing-in-Publication Data

A catalogue record for this book is available from the British Library

Library of Congress Cataloging-in-Publication Data

Campbell, Stuart, 1950–
    Translation into the second language / Stuart Campbell.
      p. cm. — (Applied linguistics and language study)
    Includes bibliographical references and index.
    ISBN 0-582-30188-2 (pbk.)
    1. Translating and interpreting. 2. Competence and performance
(Linguistics) I. Title. II. Series.
    P306.C296   1998
    418′.02—dc21   97–31003
                                                  CIP

Set by 35 in 10/12pt Ehrhardt
Produced through Longman Malaysia, PP

APPLIED LINGUISTICS AND LANGUAGE STUDY

GENERAL EDITOR
PROFESSOR CHRISTOPHER N. CANDLIN,
Macquarie University, Sydney

Strategies in Learning and Using a
Second Language
ANDREW D. COHEN

Errors in Language Learning and
Use: Exploring Error Analysis
CARL JAMES

Teaching and Language Corpora
ANNE WICHMANN, STEVEN
FLIGELSTONE, TONY MCENERY *and*
GERRY KNOWLES (EDS)

Communication Strategies:
Psycholinguistic and Sociolinguistic
Perspectives
GABRIELE KASPER *and* ERIC KELLERMAN
(EDS)

Language and Development:
Teachers in a Changing World
BRIAN KENNY *and*
WILLIAM SAVAGE (EDS)

Autonomy and Independence in
Language Learning
PHIL BENSON *and* PETER VOLLER (EDS)

Literacy in Society
RUQAIYA HASAN *and*
GEOFFREY WILLIAMS (EDS)

Phonology in English Language
Teaching: An International Language
MARTHA C. PENNINGTON

From Testing to Assessment:
English as an International Language
CLIFFORD HILL *and* KATE PARRY (EDS)

Language as Discourse:
Perspectives for Language Teaching
MICHAEL MACCARTHY *and*
RONALD CARTER

Language and Discrimination:
A Study of Communication in
Multi-Ethnic Workplaces
CELIA ROBERTS, EVELYN DAVIES *and*
TOM JUPP

Translation and Translating:
Theory and Practice
ROBERT T. BELL

Language, Literature and the
Learner: Creative Classroom Practice
RONALD CARTER *and* JOHN MCRAE (EDS)

Theory and Practice of Writing:
An Applied Linguistic Perspective
WILLIAM GRABE *and* ROBERT B. KAPLAN

Measuring Second Language
Performance
TIM MCNAMARA

Interaction in the Language
Curriculum: Awareness, Autonomy
and Authenticity
LEO VAN LIER

Second Language Learning:
Theoretical Foundations
MICHAEL SHARWOOD SMITH

Analysing Genre – Language Use in
Professional Settings
V.K. BHATIA

Rediscovering Interlanguage
LARRY SELINKER

Language Awareness in the
Classroom
CARL JAMES *and* PETER GARRETT (EDS)

Process and Experience in the
Language Classroom
MICHAEL LEGUTKE *and*
HOWARD THOMAS

An Introduction to Second Language
Acquisition Research
DIANE LARSEN-FREEMAN *and*
MICHAEL H. LONG

Listening in Language Learning
MICHAEL ROST

The Classroom and the Language
Learner: Ethnography and Second-
Language Classroom Research
LEO VAN LIER

Second Language Grammar:
Learning and Teaching
WILLIAM E. RUTHERFORD

An Introduction to Discourse
Analysis Second Edition
MALCOLM COULTHARD

Learning to Write: First
Language/Second Language
AVIVA FREEDMAN, IAN PRINGLE *and*
JANICE YALDEN (EDS)

Stylistics and the Teaching of
Literature
HENRY WIDDOWSON

Listening to Spoken English
Second Edition
GILLIAN BROWN

Observation in the Language
Classroom
DICK ALLWRIGHT

Vocabulary and Language Teaching
RONALD CARTER *and* MICHAEL
MCCARTHY (EDS)

Bilingualism in Education: Aspects of
Theory, Research and Practice
MERRILL SWAIN and JIM CUMMINS

Reading in a Foreign Language
J. CHARLES ALDERSON and
A.H. URQUHART (EDS)

Language and Communication
JACK. C. RICHARDS *and*
RICHARD W. SCHMIDT (EDS)

Error Analysis Perspectives on
Second Language Acquisition
JACK RICHARDS

Contents

Author's Preface   xi
Author's Acknowledgements   xii
Publisher's Acknowledgements   xiii

1 What is translation competence?   1
  The scope of this work   1
  The importance of a translator-centred view on translation   3
  Recent studies on translation competence   4
  Possible ways of conceptualizing translation competence   6
  Psychological modelling   6
  Translation quality assessment   7
  Translation pedagogy   9
  Translation competence and translation into a second
    language   11
  Translation competence in an interlanguage framework   12
  Some propositions about translation competence   18
  Some remarks on data in translation competence research   19
  Concluding remarks   20

2 Challenging the insistence on translation into the
  first language   22
  Aims   22
  Translation and immigration   22
  The supply/demand paradox in the Australian translation
    scene   24
  What is a second language?: Some problems of definition   25
  Educational needs of translators into a second language   26
  Translation labour market forces in Finland   27
  The importance of modelling translation competence in
    translators into the second language   28
  Concluding remarks   28

3   **A case study of candidates for translator education**   30
   Aims   30
   The setting of the study   30
   The language tests   31
      The test components   32
      Size of the candidature   32
      English competence   33
      Competence in the other languages   34
      Professed trilingualism   35
      Correlations between the test components   36
      The language tests in summary   38
   The questionnaire data   39
      The candidature as a whole   39
      The candidature summarized   41
      Arabic speakers   42
      German speakers   45
      Italian speakers   46
      Spanish speakers   49
      Vietnamese speakers   51
   Concluding remarks   54

4   **Translation into a second language and second language competence**   56
   Aims   56
   The difference between translation into a first and a second
      language   56
   Second language competence as an aspect of second language
      translation competence   58
   Translation and written language   59
   A case study approach to describing textual competence in
      translators into a second language   60
      Summary results   61
      The choice of analyses   63
      Implications of the case study   67
      Examples of the three competence levels   68
   Concluding remarks   70

5   **Translation competence and grammar**   72
   Aims   72
   The grammatical task of the second language translator   72
   Biber's multi-feature/multi-dimensional approach to genre
      variation   73

An outline of the use of the model 76
Relevant aspects of Biber's model 76
The target texts and their processing 80
Comparisons with Biber's norms 84
Nominalizations 84
Type/token 88
Word length 92
Agentless passive 93
Prepositional phrases 96
Concluding remarks 101

6 Translation competence and lexis 103
Aims 103
The disposition study 105
Persistent versus capitulating 107
Risk-taking versus prudent 107
Assessing disposition 107
The lexical transfers study 109
Choice networks 110
Lexical transfer strategies and textual competence 122
Concluding remarks 125

7 Monitoring translation performance 126
Aims 126
Issues in monitoring translation output 126
Quality of output: the assessment study 129
Under- and overestimation of translation competence 134
Differences in estimation among language groups 135
Summary of the assessment study 137
Monitoring ability: the editing study 138
Dimensions of editing 138
Profiling the editing of individual translators 141
The interpretation of editing data 142
Individual translator profiles 148
Concluding remarks 150

8 Towards a model of translation competence 152
Aims 152
Components of the model and their implications 152
Relative independence of the components 154
The developmental dimension 156

Describing the differences between the performance of
    different translators   157
Relationship of the model to other trends in translation
    research   158
Wider applicability of the model   160
    Different language pairs   160
    Different subjects   161
    Different genres   161
    Translation into the first language   161
Translation competence, pedagogy and assessment   162
    Students and translation competence   163
    Teachers and translation competence   166
    Accrediting authorities and translation competence   168
Concluding remarks   175

APPENDIX 1: Examples of target texts with varying
    combinations of textual competence, risk-taking and
    persistence   177
APPENDIX 2: Real-time edited texts   191

References   194
Index   199

Author's Preface

This book comes about after a decade and a half of puzzling over the problem of how translators learn to work into a second language. The book was written in many parts of the world and I should acknowledge the various universities and institutions that were generous enough to give me access to their libraries and, when they could, desk space. They are the University of Western Sydney Macarthur and the University of Sydney in Australia, Surrey University and the University of Westminster in the UK, York University (Glendon College) in Canada, and the Regional Language Centre in Singapore. Very many people have contributed directly or indirectly, and at the head of the list I put the hundreds of students at the University of Western Sydney Macarthur who have passed through my classes in translation, translation theory and linguistics. There are of course dozens of academic colleagues who have somehow had an impact, but I must mention several who had a direct role in making this book a reality: John Gibbons, Colin Yallop, Rifaat Ebied, Basil Hatim, Roger Bell, Chris Candlin. Finally, I am indebted to my early teachers, especially Peter Newmark, Salah El-Ghobashi and the late Izzat Abou-Hindia, who got me started in applied linguistics and Arabic at the Polytechnic of Central London.

Author's Acknowledgements

Acknowledgement is made of the contributions of the examination candidates whose texts form the data discussed in Chapters 4, 5 and 6. The candidates were referred to by code numbers so that I am unable to identify them individually. I should also acknowledge the National Accreditation Authority for Translators and Interpreters in Australia, who gave me access to the material. Likewise, the assistance of the students whose texts appear in Chapter 7 is acknowledged. Again, the individual names were replaced by code numbers so that I am unable to identify them individually.

Publisher's Acknowledgements

We are indebted to Cambridge University Press for permission to reproduce Table 5.3, extracts and adapted extracts from *VARIATION ACROSS SPEECH AND WRITING* (1988) by D Biber.

1 What is translation competence?

The scope of this work

This book asks a number of questions about translation, and tries to answer them in ways that relate to current key issues in applied linguistics. The special feature of this book is that it deals with translation into the second language, an area largely ignored by applied linguistics in general and by the literature of translation studies in particular. The problems that arise when an individual translates into a second language do not fit easily into the framework established by orthodox translation studies, which tends to assume that all translators work into their first language. Rather, they relate to four key issues in the wider field of applied linguistics. One is the issue of *second language acquisition*, and especially the acquisition of advanced skills and strategies in a second language; in very many cases an individual translating into a second language is still acquiring that language, so that it makes sense to think of learning to translate as a special variety of learning a second language. In fact, much of translation studies has ignored the issue of language development, tacitly assuming the existence of a perfectly bilingual translator. The second issue is that of *interlanguage*, the idea that the learner's output in a second language represents a stage in the acquisition of that language, rather than an imperfect variety of it; the output of a second language translator can be thought of as a special variety of interlanguage that is framed by the demands of the task of translation. An interlanguage perspective gives us a much more insightful way of looking at the 'errors' that second language translators make. The third issue is the *organization of language above the level of the sentence*, variously referred to as text-linguistics, discourse analysis or the study of genre. This issue is a key one since the translation discussed in this book is carried out not by rank beginners in the second language, but by those with substantial competence in the language; what translation challenges is their ability to produce stylistically authentic texts. Indeed, the stylistic difficulties of students translating into a second language have been the practical motivation behind the research reported in this book, and have determined my approach to investigating translation competence. One major element in this investigation is the development of textual skills in the second language. The findings of this research may also be applicable to translation into the first language; the acquisition of textual skills is not restricted to second language learners and is, of course, a staple ingredient of first language education in schools, whether it falls under the traditional descriptor of 'stylistics' or the more modern 'genre' approach. The fourth issue is the description of *levels of language competence*, the importance of which comes from the fact that translation is a profession with deep concerns about accreditation and the setting of standards.

These four issues form the landmarks which this book keeps in view in going about its central task – to explore how individuals develop the competence to translate into a second language, and to show that a key aspect – textual competence – is developed in a systematic way. In this way it makes a contribution not just to translation studies, but to the wider field of applied linguistics. The exploration of translation competence will leave us somewhat wiser about how second languages are acquired, about the nature of interlanguage, about the writing of texts, and about describing levels of language competence. The book proceeds along the following lines.

In Chapter 1, I lay the programmatic groundwork and place the research in the wider context of translation studies, translation competence studies and second language acquisition research. The main questions I ask here are 'What do we mean by translation competence?' and 'How have scholars dealt with it so far?' The chapter argues strongly for a translator-centred approach (rather than text-centred or system-centred ones), which sees the output of translation as interlanguage.

In Chapter 2, I argue that translation into the second language is inevitable in many situations because of the nature of immigration and the dynamics of the translation market-place. Because of its inevitability, translator educators need to understand it and develop appropriate strategies to teach it and assess it.

Chapter 3 supports the case for the inevitability of translation into the second language by analysing data on the candidature for an Australian university course in translation. This study shows in detail – possibly for the first time – the educational and linguistic profile of the clientele for a professional translation course in a state founded on immigration. The results reflect a complex and dynamic educational problem.

Chapter 4 presents a preliminary study that was carried out on a group of examination candidates for certification as translators from Arabic – their first language – into English. The results of this study suggest that there is systematic variation in the way the candidates were able to manipulate written genres, or, in other words, in their *textual competence*. The main result of this study is that the competence of such translators may be profiled as *substandard, pretextual* or *textual.*

In Chapters 5 and 6 I explore this notion further by analysing textual competence from the points of view of linguistic structure and lexis. Chapter 5 shows that in translators into a second language there appears to be a gradient from those whose grammatical usage is more like that of spoken language to those whose usage is more written in character. Chapter 6 looks at vocabulary choice and the extent to which translators look beyond the immediate sentence to the text itself; it also builds on the idea of translation competence by proposing the notion of *disposition* – that the vocabulary choices made by translators into the second language reveal tendencies of *risk-taking versus prudence* and *persistence versus capitulation.*

In Chapter 7 I examine the issue of the monitoring of translation performance as an aspect of translation competence: first, by comparing self-assessment of translation output quality in translators into their first and second languages, and secondly, by examining the systematic variation in monitoring strategies used by translators into the second language.

Chapter 8 summarizes the aspects of the model dealt with in this research, acknowledges omissions, and suggests wider applicability.

The importance of a translator-centred view on translation

It is a little ironic that the role of the translator has only recently become a concern in translation studies. Only 30 years ago the writings of Catford were concerned primarily with the match or mismatch between source and target codes; the translator was a more or less invisible instrument since the product of translation – not the process – was the focus of attention (Catford, 1965) (although some hints about individual working styles of medieval translators are available: Amos (1973)).

It has been where translation is discussed in a real-life framework that translators are considered at all. Nida and Taber (1969), for example, include an appendix on 'Organisation of Translation Projects' where Bible translators are advised how to establish project teams. It is suggested, for instance, that 'the native speakers in such cases are recognised as the real translators, while the foreigners who participate are exegetical informants and assistants' (Nida and Taber, 1969: 174). This was no doubt a radical statement at the time since it suggested that not all those in the translation team had to be perfect bilinguals. If the point was noticed at all by the mainstream world of commercial and government translation, it was considered a marginal phenomenon that arose because of the kinds of languages that Bible translators deal with. There are plenty of reasons to see translation into a second language as an activity as normal and possibly as widespread as translation into the first language.

More recently, the translation *process* has caught the interest of theorists, in line with an entire shift in thinking about language:

> During the last thirty years . . . the study of language has undergone radical changes: the focus of interest has widened from the purely historical to the contemporary, from the prescriptive to the descriptive, from the theoretical system to the concrete realization, from the micro-level of the sign to the macro-structure of the text. (Snell-Hornby, 1988: 7–8)

It is now accepted that merely to study target texts is insufficient: 'To study translations in isolation from the factors affecting their production is consequently to miss out an important dimension of the phenomenon' (Hatim and Mason, 1990: 13). Any conception of the wider context or process necessarily entails admitting the translator into the picture, for example, as a participant in a chain of communication or as the possessor of the linguistic and cognitive skills that make the act of translation possible. The translator can no longer be thought of as a ghostly perfect bilingual, but as a living being with a role and abilities that can be described and discussed; when the translator emerges, then translation competence begins to emerge as an important issue. Such a situation opens the way for views like that of Toury, who concedes that in translator training the development of bilingualism might be partially sacrificed for other abilities (Toury, 1984). Indeed, Bell (1991) develops a model of translating that uses proposals about translator competence as its foundation stone. The idea of the translator playing a key role reaches its apogee in Hewson and Martin (1991), where the Translation Operator is the core of the so-called Variational approach. One can only speculate about why it has taken the translator so long to emerge, but at the same time be thankful that a new viewpoint on the translation process is available.

Recent studies on translation competence

A number of authors have made explicit statements about translation competence. Toury (1984) suggests that bilinguals have an 'innate translation competence comprising bilingual and interlingual ability', as well as 'transfer competence' (Toury, 1984: 189–90). While Toury's focus is translation teaching, Bell's horizon is wider – he has a model of the process of translating in his sights – when he proposes three ways in which translator competence might be characterized (Bell, 1991).[1] One way is an 'ideal bilingual competence' characterization (p. 38), which would conceive of the translator as an idealized, flawlessly performing system, in much the same way that transformational-generative grammarians assume an ideal speaker–hearer and describe the competence, but not the performance, of that speaker–hearer. Another way is to characterize translator competence as an 'expert system' containing a knowledge base and an inference mechanism (p. 39). Finally, Bell suggests a 'communicative competence' characterization with four components, namely grammatical, sociolinguistic, discourse and strategic competence (p. 41), with clear affinities to Canale and Swain (1980). This last characterization resonates with the ideas of Kiraly (1990) who bemoans the product focus of translation teaching in general and the scant regard paid to the process of second language acquisition in teaching translation into foreign languages:

> . . . a great deal of time is spent 'learning' and virtually none is spent using the language for self-expression or communication. This is the result of the dominant paradigm in translation teaching, which can be called the 'equivalence' or 'linguistic transfer' paradigm. (Kiraly, 1990: 209)

Hewson and Martin (1991) also talk about competence while they are building a theory of translation (actually the title of their Chapter 3). Their theory is reflected in the types of competence they propose. 'Acquired interlinguistic competence' is fairly straightforward: '. . . competence in at least two linguistic systems and a certain knowledge of the L[anguage] C[ultures] associated with them' (p. 52). Next is 'Dissimilative competence', which includes: '(1) an aptitude to generate and dissimilate homologous statements and (2) an aptitude to define and recreate socio-cultural norms' (p. 52). Finally, there is 'Transferred competence' – not something possessed by the translator, but '. . . all the dissimilative competence which has been accumulated and committed to translation auxiliaries such as translation methods, dictionaries, data banks, and expert systems' (p. 52).

Nord (1992), in advocating text analysis as a translation teaching method offers a catalogue of competences that should underpin teaching:

> . . . competence of text reception and analysis, research competence, transfer competence, competence of text production, competence of translation quality assessment, and, of course, linguistic and cultural competence both on the source and the target side, which is the main prerequisite of translation activity. (Nord, 1992: 47)

Meanwhile Pym (1992), in an attempt to dissociate translation from linguistics, provides a definition of translational competence in a kind of behavioural framework:

1. The ability to generate a target-text series of more than one viable term (target text$_1$, target text$_2$ . . . target text$_n$) for a source text.
2. The ability to select only one target text from this series, quickly and with justified confidence, and to propose this target text as a replacement of source text for a specific purpose and reader. (Pym, 1992: 281)

Finally, some writers simply mention translation competence in passing, as if it were a given. For example, Farahzad talks of examination candidates' 'level of command of both source and target language as well as their level of translational competence' (Farahzad, 1992: 276).

It seems that the way translation competence is characterized has a great deal to do with one's purpose. Teaching has already been mentioned; in this case investigating translation competence ought to make for more effective intervention in the classroom. Theorizing about the translation process is another purpose, where investigating what translators have to *know* will lay the foundation stone of a description of what translating *is*. Indeed, it is difficult to imagine why one would want to investigate translation competence at all without some broader purpose in view. In the next section I will examine these purposes in some detail.

Possible ways of conceptualizing translation competence

There are a number of major areas of enquiry in translation studies that have an interest in translation competence. These can be termed *approaches* to investigating translation competence because they are quite distinct in their methodology and objectives. The three most important of these are *psychological modelling of the translation process*, *translation quality assessment* and *translation pedagogy*.

Psychological modelling

By psychological modelling of the translation process, I mean attempts to infer mental constructs from empirical data. The main examples are the works of think-aloud methodologists such as those reported in Faerch and Kasper (1987). One link with translation competence is to attempt to chart the development of such competence. This could be done by mapping the inferred mental constructs in translators of different levels of ability, or longitudinally in student translators. For example, a perennial issue in translation studies is the unit of analysis. Does one translate in words, phrases, sentences, or in larger units? Do professional translators translate at a different level of analysis from student translators? If the units of analysis were seen as a criterion of translation competence (see Gerloff, 1987), then one could design quite interesting experiments that measured the size of the 'chunks' that translators processed. If, as may be the case, student translators worked in smaller chunks than professional translators, one could make inferences about the different cognitive strategies used by each group.

Hölscher and Möhle (1987) begin with a model of planning and test it against think-aloud data. The data allow their investigator to make inferences about the type and extent of planning in which the translator engages. An approach like this could also be harnessed to translation competence; if the ability to plan were proposed as an aspect of translation competence, experiments could try to show how this ability develops over time.

Two comprehensive psychological approaches are found in Lörscher (1986) and Krings (1986). Lörscher sets out to investigate translation strategies in oral translation into the second language. From think-aloud data a range of strategies is detected, including 'Realizing a translational problem', 'Monitoring of SL- or TL- text segments', 'Rephrasing of TL- text segments', and others (Lörscher, 1986: 279–81). Again, this approach ought to be amenable to a translation competence orientation; cross-sectional or longitudinal data could be used to model the development of these strategies. Similarly, Krings develops a flow chart to illustrate his 'tentative model of the translation process' (Krings, 1986: 269). This includes such strategies as retrieval, monitoring, decision-making and others. Once again, to set this work in a competence framework could be to show experimentally in some way how the strategies developed over time.

What all these examples have in common, then, is that empirical data are used to infer mental constructs about translation; there is no reason why a model of translation competence cannot be built around these kinds of construct. However, this is not the only way. Translation competence can also be addressed from a translation quality assessment approach.

Translation quality assessment

In distinguishing these major themes in translation studies it is useful to consider the elements represented in each. At the core of the psychological models are the individual translators; the texts that they produce have the status of experimental data, and the readers of the texts are the processors of the data. In a translation quality assessment approach, the textual product is the core of any model and the individual translator is backgrounded, if considered at all; but the reader of the text, as the yardstick against which the text quality is measured, is very much in the foreground. The key feature of translation quality assessment is, in fact, its focus on the text itself. The superficial relevance to translation competence is that the quality of a translated text is a reflection of the translator's competence. Among the works that propose schemes for translation quality assessment are Hosington and Horguelin (1980), Fau (1990), NAATI (1993) and Cascallar et al. (1996). What each of these does is to describe quite complex methods of grading translated texts for the purpose of professional certification or student assessment.

One of the problems of translation quality assessment schemes is the question of their construct validity, that is the extent to which they are based on an appropriate model of competence or even of learning. I would argue that most translation quality assessment systems are not underpinned by theory at all, at least in any principled or even conscious way on the part of their designers. For example, a scheme that deducts marks for things like spelling errors, omissions, excessive literalness and so on is surely only valid if the error types reflect some set of beliefs about what ingredients go to make up a good translator. To be valid it must also omit error types that have been explicitly excluded from that set of beliefs. If, for instance, a marking scheme does not deduct marks for excessive text length, what is one to believe about the scheme? Was text length left out by accident? Was it not an issue? In the same way, the weighting of various error types (perhaps less deductions for misspellings and more for mistranslations) ought to have theoretical implications; does the underlying theory see mistranslation as somehow more crucial than misspelling, and why? Translation competence does, then, appear to be relevant to translation quality assessment schemes; a set of beliefs or explanations about what makes a good translator must inevitably be the blueprint for the assessment procedure.

One recent translation quality assessment proposal that at least begins to consider some aspects of translation competence is Cascallar et al. (1996). The paper surveys the translation assessment models recently proposed for use by the Federal Bureau of Investigations: a 1982 proposal described translation performance in terms of reading and writing ability (pp. 294–5), followed by a mid-1980s scheme which described translation performance according to the categories of 'grammatical accuracy' and 'thought conveyance'. This latter category was subdivided into 'lexical 'choice' and 'tone' (pp. 295–6). By 1992 a new scheme was proposed, which used the categories of 'interpretive information', 'expression' and 'accuracy' (p. 297). Having opened up the notion that translation testing might assess different types of ability, the writers go on to make the proposal that high-level reading and writing skills are no guarantee of effective translation performance: 'The glue which integrates these abilities would still be missing. Child (1990) calls that glue *congruity judgement(s)*: the ability to successfully match donor language features, characteristics or forms to their most suitable receptor language equivalents' (p. 299). They go on to discuss the skills of 'organization' and 'shaping', which appear to have some parallels with what linguists know as coherence and cohesion, then propose a typology of texts, namely 'orientational', 'instructive', 'evaluative' and 'projective'. These 'text modes' are then tied to performance levels with the not unreasonable claim that the more difficult text type will require a higher level of language competence (pp. 302–3). Lastly, a 'congruity scale' is proposed, which describes three levels of proficiency, namely 'professional', 'transitional' and 'pre-professional'.

It is easy to criticize the ingenuousness of much of this paper. It apparently draws on no particular discipline, and acknowledges little previous work. It makes blundering forays into well-researched realms such as textlinguistics and educational measurement theory. It somewhat naively puts forward the concept of congruity[2] to label the problem that it perceives but cannot describe. And of course it makes no systematic use of data to support its arguments. Despite all this, it does contain two important notions: it acknowledges that translation competence may have separate components and it hints at the idea of the development of proficiency by the use of the term 'transitional'. It incidentally illustrates the gulf of understanding between professional translators and academic linguistics.

Translation pedagogy

While psychological modelling foregrounds the individual, and quality assessment focuses on the relationship between the text and its reader, translation pedagogy does neither. Instead, it tends to foreground theories of teaching and learning, which it presents with varying degrees of persuasiveness, comprehensiveness and eclecticism.

There is a quite large body of writing that advises how translation should be taught. Among the hallmarks of many of these writings is that the advice offered is not arrived at through strictly empirical procedures. For example, one reliable way to find out the 'best' way to translate a particular term of construction would be to find a large number of translations in a text corpus. However, 'how to do it' texts seldom offer more than pseudo-empirical data (in the form of a few alternative renditions). Their use of theory is sometimes limited to using a theoretical standpoint as the jumping-off point for a pedagogical programme. Among the more convincing of the translation pedagogy works is Delisle (1980). Discourse analysis is recommended as the basis for a pedagogy of translation. The model is justified in statements such as:

. . . les théories de Ljudskanov, Catford et Nida ne facilitent pas beaucoup l'organisation de l'enseignement de la traduction français de textes pragmatiques anglais en raison de leur caractère trop abstrait (Ljudskanov et Catford) ou trop spécifique à un genre particulier de traduction (Nida).

[. . . the theories of Ljudskanov, Catford and Nida do not greatly facilitate the organization of teaching French translation of practical English texts because of their excessively abstract character or because they are too specific to a particular genre of translation.] (Delisle, 1980: 57)

The work provides practical exercises based on the model. Kuepper (1984) is a more modest example of this type. Although beginning from a theoretical standpoint of textlinguistics, 'on the level of developing practical translation strategies . . . the approach . . . must centre . . . around the question of how particular linguistic features function within the source text' (Kuepper, 1984: 145), practical advice is given on teaching strategies that focus mainly on exercises concerning coreference. Similarly, Neubert (1981: 143) argues that interpreters and translators need to be trained to be aware of intertextuality. A strategy for examining student translators is outlined that involves discussion of a worked text between student and teacher. Discourse structure in Arabic is discussed in Sa'addedin (1987) and recommendations made for the teaching of Arabic-English translation to Arabic native speakers.

Surprisingly Sa'addedin's is one of only a few recent works that explicitly discusses interference, presumably because Sa'addedin's subjects are working into a second language. Writers on translation often seem to share an extraordinary reluctance to admit the possibility of poor grammar or non-native style. I interpret this in two ways: on the one hand it may reflect the failure to recognize the translator as a significant part of the process, and on the other, an abhorrence of translation into the second language.

Another discourse-based work is Hatim's (1989) discussion of translation didactics, which recommends close text analysis and by implication supports the idea that textual competence is a crucial aspect of the ability to translate.

By contrast, some writers propose ways of training translators (and again imply something about the ability to translate) without recourse to any theoretical position at all. For example, Mareschal (1989) offers advice on training translators in technical terminology, noting points of difficulty such as polysemy and the overlap between everyday and specialized language, while Picht (1985) gives a more general treatment of terminology in translator education. Theory-free and highly practical is Vitale et al. (1978); hundreds of English texts are provided along with notes and hints for the guidance of student translators into French.

One of the most comprehensive didactic works is Larson (1984). Organized on the basis of *the lexicon, propositional structure, communication relations, texts* and *the translation project*, the book offers theoretical overviews, impressive arrays of examples from obscure languages, and practical exercises. Its provenance is the Bible translation movement whence comes its astonishing practicality and variety.

From the translation competence standpoint, then, these works tend to be text- or theory-centred, rather than student-centred. Their prescriptive nature automatically prevents them from being able to describe competence *per se*; what they describe is the anticipated results of the programmes that they espouse.

An insightful approach is that of Wilss (1976), where a 'pedagogical working hypothesis' is called for (p. 122), the basis of which is proposed to be 'the interplay between SL analyzing techniques, prospective (SL/TL) transfer strategies, and retrospective (TL/SL) testing procedures' (p. 123). Here, unlike in much writing on translation pedagogy, the notion of translation competence is acknowledged, and indeed defined as 'the ability to reproduce technical, common language and literary texts adequately in the target language [which] constitutes the overriding (pivotal) learning target on which all curricular components . . . are focussed' (p. 118). Wilss uses this working hypothesis to put forward a five-step operation for teaching translation which includes source text analysis, evaluation of translation difficulties, elimination of difficulties, assessment of equivalence, and back-translation.

Translation competence and translation into a second language

This book arises from a context for translation that differs from the one reflected in the canon of translation studies. The majority of writing on translation tacitly implies that translation is done into one's first language.

Yet for many parts of the world, translation into the second language is a regular and accepted practice. In virtually any post-colonial society in the developing world where a major European language still has a foot-hold, there will be people who regularly write and translate in that language as a second language. Similarly, in countries of high immigration, there will be second language speakers of the host language who write and translate in that language. Such a reality requires appropriate educational strategies such as curricula and testing regimes based on appropriate models of learning. If learning to translate into one's first language were no different a process than learning to translate into a second language, then there would be no need for different models. But the reality is that they are different, and that such students need to be taught differently. It is for this reason that we need a model of translation competence for second language translator education.

Translation competence in an interlanguage framework

I have already mentioned the growing focus in translation studies on the role of the translator. Here I want to sharpen that focus to the translator working into a second language, and that individual's dual role as translator and learner: any translator working into a second language is, by definition, on a developmental path with respect to that language. Accepting this notion immediately opens a number of viewpoints on translation competence which can all be conveniently placed under the umbrella of *interlanguage*. This notion, originally proposed in Selinker (1969), gives us a framework in which we can begin to discuss translation competence in a way that is systematic and that draws on related areas of research such as contrastive analysis, bilingualism and second language acquisition. My use of the word 'framework' is important here; Selinker goes to great lengths (1992: Chapter 8) to characterize the interlanguage hypothesis as 'a reasonable theoretical story' (p. 246). He summarizes the IL Hypothesis as follows:

(1) People create a (partly) separate linguistic system.
(2) In that system interlingual identifications and language transfer are central.
(3) One selectively uses the NL by context.
(4) One fossilizes at least parts of the IL.
(5) One selectively fossilizes differentially according to linguistic level and discourse domain.

(6) The IL one is creating is susceptible to the force of several types of language universals, as well as interlanguage universals.

(7) The IL one is creating is susceptible to the training and learning strategies that are adopted.

(8) The IL one is creating is susceptible to simplification and complexification strategies. (Selinker, 1992: 247)

Given this summary it is quite extraordinary that translation studies has virtually ignored the idea of interlanguage. There is the exception of Duff (1981), who, although writing outside the theoretical paradigm of interlanguage, does make some insightful claims that are worth a little discussion.

Duff's book carries the tantalizing title *The Third Language*. The broad premise is that interference often produces translations that are somehow midway between the source and target language: '. . . the translator who imposes the concepts of one language on to another is no longer moving freely from one world to another but instead creating a third world – and a *third language*' (Duff, 1981: 10). This third language, according to Duff, puts readers off. The poor reputation of translation in the English-speaking world is attributed to the fact that 'translation *does not sound like English*' (p. 124). Although Duff never delves very far into the phenomenon of interference, what is important about the book is that it broaches the subject of cross-linguistic influence at the level of style and that it is quite specific about the microlinguistic exponents of style. Alas, the tantalizing title leaves the applied linguist somewhat frustrated because a clear theoretical framework is never established. Ultimately, this is because the work takes the text rather than the translator as its focal point.

We find other occasional hints in the direction of interlanguage in the translation literature such as Nord (1992), when she speaks of 'a didactic progression which allows a reasonable and fair control of learning progress' (p. 47) and Wilkinson (1987), who begins from an interlanguage standpoint in his discussion of variability in information structure among student translators working from Dutch into second language English.

To return to Selinker's (1992) summary, the resonances with translation competence are extremely striking. It is quite easy to take statements 1–2 and 4–7 and to propose for each some anecdotal or informal way in which it could be relevant to translation competence:

(1) *People create a (partly) separate linguistic system.* This is at least intuitively felt by anyone who teaches translation; student translations often appear to be in neither the source language nor the target

language, and 'errors' often seem to be idiosyncratic. If teachers do not teach this 'in between' language, then presumably students construct it for themselves.

(2) *In that system interlingual identifications and language transfer are central.* The whole enterprise of learning to translate is to learn to establish interlingual identifications and to make language transfers.

(3) *One fossilizes at least parts of the IL.* Again, at least intuitively, translation teachers are familiar with students who seem to have intractable difficulties with a specific part of the target language system; teachers spend lots of energy trying to diagnose and fix these problems, perhaps expressed by the sentiment 'I don't know how many times I've told him, but he keeps getting it wrong'.

(4) *One selectively fossilizes differentially according to linguistic level and discourse domain.* Teachers of translation will be familiar with the student who speaks the target language 'like a native', but writes it 'like a foreigner'.

(5) *The IL one is creating is susceptible to the force of several types of language universals, as well as interlanguage universals.* This principle underpins the entire notion of a translation curriculum; if there were no commonality in the performance of translation students, then it would be pointless to attempt to teach translation in an organized way. Presumably, translation teachers have rejected such an idea, preferring to believe that the language behaviour of translation students is at least partly uniform, and is therefore amenable to some general curriculum principles.

(6) *The IL one is creating is susceptible to the training and learning strategies that are adopted.* Again, if teachers did not believe this, they would not attempt to teach translation.

While I do not intend to test each of these principles in a systematic way (or to tackle principles 3 and 8), the exercise of trying to recast them from a translation competence standpoint is valuable in that it gives us a setting for the remainder of this book – 'a reasonable theoretical story' around which the story of translation competence can be woven.

Interlanguage is our entry point to language acquisition theory. Larsen-Freeman and Long (1991) describe the historical development of approaches to second language acquisition analysis in which the notion of interlanguage has become central, and I use this framework below in an attempt to understand how translation competence can be considered from an interlanguage perspective.

In terms of the 'contrastive analysis hypothesis' (Larsen-Freeman and Long, 1991: 53), translation competence would reflect the translator's

ability to avoid transferring first language phenomena in their translations. For example, competence as a translator from native French into
English could be measured by the ability to avoid reproducing some
aspect of French grammar – for example, the determiner system – in
English. To describe an individual's translation competence would be to
quantify the source language interference in their translations. Such a
model would suffer from two problems. First, it is extremely difficult to
be sure about the motivation for errors in translations, and unambiguu-
ously to specify interference as the cause. Secondly, the model would
suffer from the same difficulty as any language acquisition theory based
on the contrastive analysis hypothesis, that is that second language learning difficulties (and by extension the development of the linguistic aspects of translation competence) cannot be predicted entirely on the basis
of contrastive analysis. Larsen-Freeman and Long (1991: 55–6) cite various studies that refute the contrastive analysis hypothesis. The complexity of the issue is illustrated by Selinker (1992), who carefully argues the
complex role of transfer in second language learning, concluding that
'Language transfer is best thought of as a *cover term* for a whole class of
behaviours, processes and constraints' (1992: 208).

A model based on 'error analysis' (Larsen-Freeman and Long, 1991:
56) would describe translation competence in terms of systematic deviation from the target norms; translation data into the second language are,
of course, often full of 'errors', and the model appears at first to be an
attractive one – so attractive that translation assessment systems are usually based on counting errors. However, judgements about what is right
or wrong in a translation soon become hard to make as one moves up the
scale of linguistic analysis. Any teacher of translation will testify to the
difficulty of marking student texts. At the level of morphosyntax, errors
are usually uncontroversial – a concord error is a concord error; at the
level of lexis things are less clear; and at the level of discourse, a dichotomy between right and wrong is a virtually pointless concept. Pym
(1992) evidently shares this opinion when he tries to distinguish between
binary and non-binary errors in translation.

Despite the limitations of error analysis as a technique, these comments by Corder are highly relevant:

A learner's errors, then, provide evidence of the system of the language
that he is using (i.e. has learned) at a particular point in time (and it
must be repeated that he is using some system, although it is not yet
the right system). They are significant in three different ways. First to
the teacher, in that they tell him, if he undertakes a systematic analysis,
how far towards the goal the learner has progressed and, consequently,

what remains for him to learn. Second they provide to the researcher evidence of how language is learned or acquired, what strategies or procedures the learner is employing in his discovery of the language. Thirdly . . . they are indispensible to the learner himself, because we can regard the making of errors as a device the learner uses in order to learn. (Corder, 1967: 167)

For us, Corder's statement provides a programmatic framework that we can adapt for our purposes. By systematically analysing what looks stylistically unnatural or wrong in translations, we ought to be able to discover what system the translator is using to construct texts. That knowledge ought to be useful to teachers of translation in that they will know what is still to be learned. The researcher will discover evidence about how textual skills develop and about the strategies being used in that process. For students of translation, these stylistic 'errors' will be indispensible in their learning to acquire textual competence.

In fact we will see in Chapter 7 a very fruitful use of error analysis in a study of translators' 'real-time' editing (that is editing done as the translator works) and what it can reveal about the capacity to 'monitor' translation output. I will propose that there are two main types of edit: a *correction* repairs a language error, and includes both *errors* and *mistakes* in Corder's terms (Corder, 1967); a *revision* is a change of mind about the way something has been translated.

What arose from error analysis was the concept of *interlanguage* (Selinker, 1969, 1972), and it is from this point that the second language acquisition framework starts to be applicable to translation competence. Felix (1977), in discussing Selinker's notion of interlanguage, describes the second language acquisition process as 'a successive chain of "interlanguages" whose grammatical structure is partly determined by features of the learner's mother tongue' (1977: 96). In such a framework, a description of translation competence would ideally involve determining the extent to which the individual's interlanguage approximated to the target norms, and describing the non-target language systems that were found. It would allow for a developmental dimension; the interlanguages of an individual at different points in time could be compared, and descriptions of any systematic changes made. This somewhat ambitious programme is not proposed as a practical project, but as further argument to support the shift to an interlanguage paradigm that will provide constructive solutions to the question 'what is translation competence?'.

If interlanguages form a successive chain, how does the study of second language acquisition resonate with translation competence? Can we propose that translation competence develops in a systematic way just as the developmental sequence investigations summarized in Larsen-Freeman and Long (1991: 63–5) attempt to show that grammatical competence develops systematically? An immediate issue for translation competence is that this kind of work has mainly concentrated on structural levels no larger than the sentence, and often as small as the morpheme. Indeed, Pienemann and Johnston's model is sentence-bound because of the theory of processing constraints on which it is based (Pienemann and Johnston, 1987). In practice, students of translation into the second language are assumed to be able to construct sentences in a native-like way, but to have difficulties in deploying those sentences to form authentic-looking texts. This is not to say that no student translator working into a second language ever constructs an odd-looking sentence – the target texts found in the Appendices contain many such sentences. Rather, I would say that the priority area of investigation is the acquisition of the ability to produce authentic-looking texts. Is this ability acquired in a systematic way? Can we find anything resembling developmental sequences? In general terms, we find positive answers to these questions as a result of the empirical studies reported in Chapters 3, 5 and 6.

Larsen-Freeman and Long (1991: 65–9) also discuss learner strategies as an aspect of performance analysis. One area of learner strategies in second language acquisition is that of formulaic utterances, prefabricated routines and prefabricated patterns. This has echoes of what might be called *matching* (see Chapter 8 for a brief discussion) as an aspect of translation competence; professional translators need to have a great store of formulaic transfers at their fingertips – *to whom it may concern, with reference to, acquired immune deficiency syndrome*, etc. For example, any study of metaphor in a translation competence framework would need to refer to this kind of strategy to account for the ability to identify metaphors that can be transferred and those that have to be reduced to sense. More interesting, however, is the idea of the broad strategy or approach that translators take – whether they take risks or not, whether they persist or give up easily. I call this aspect of translation competence *disposition* and will attempt to show in Chapter 6 how it varies systematically among translators. There are some parallels with risk-taking in second language acquisition research. Ellis (1992) discusses personality aspects of learners, and notes that while some second language students are wary of exposing themselves to risk, 'other learners are keen to try and feel no anxiety about risking themselves in public' (1992: 116). Ely (1986) is cited, where a study of adult learners of second language Spanish at university showed that classroom participation could be positively predicted by risk-taking (Ellis, 1992: 116).

The last approach to second language acquisition studies discussed by Larsen-Freeman and Long is discourse analysis. Conversational analysis may appear somewhat distant from translation, given the fact that translator and reader do not interact in the same time- or space-frame. On the other hand, if we characterize the writer and reader of a translation as interlocutors, we can begin to ask 'how learners learn to use the forms appropriately for a particular discourse function' (Larsen-Freeman and Long, 1991: 73). This brings me back again to my concern with text; the acquisition of higher level skills in a second language and the development of textual competence in translators are surely closely related.

Some propositions about translation competence

So far, I have argued that the approach to investigating translation competence depends on one's purpose. In the special circumstances of translation into the second language, the investigation should be strongly linked to second language acquisition theory and research. The task of this book is to produce a model of translation competence that will serve a pedagogical purpose, and at this point I should like to establish a set of propositions that will guide the work. The model has three practical purposes:

1. It should provide knowledge about the separate underlying components of translation competence, so that well-motivated curriculum objectives can be designed.
2. It should underpin the sequencing of the translation curriculum.
3. It should lead to assessment techniques that are valid because they are based on a well-motivated theory of learning.

These purposes can be recast as a set of propositions:

A model of translation competence should be able to do at least three things:

1. It should show whether translation competence is divisible into components, and, if so, describe those components and their inter-relationships.
2. It should be able to describe the developmental pathway taken in learning how to translate.
3. It should include means for describing the differences between the performance of different translators.

These propositions form the programme that underlies the remainder of this book, and I will return to them in Chapter 8.

Some remarks on data in translation competence research

Data analysis plays a key role in translation competence research, but I have said nothing so far about its nature. Discussion of the data is warranted for two reasons: to highlight the genuinely empirical nature of the work reported here, and to clarify the type of data used.

In a sense, any work on translation that is supported by examples is potentially empirical. However, the vagueness of many translation studies is in the confusion in the use of hypothetical and real examples. Catford (1965) presents a mix of both types. Malone (1988), on the other hand, uses a vast collection of citations. In the end, very little of this work is truly empirical since examples are not systematically collected, and the examples that do occur are usually cited to illustrate a predetermined theoretical point. A notable exception is Lindquist (1989), where a study of translation of English adverbials in translation into Swedish is based on a large corpus of literature.

Indeed, what translation studies is only beginning to develop is an experimental arm; the methodology of this kind of work is in its infancy, and is best represented at the moment in the work of the think–aloud or verbal data experimenters. Whether think–aloud data will eventually provide clues to the translation process that can inform a model of translation competence does, however, depend on the validity of the data collection model itself. Börsch (1986) provides a comprehensive and lucid discussion of verbal data methods, beginning with the suggestion that the historical roots of the method need to be well understood. While introspective methods originated in psychology, they have been long rejected and only recently revived in language learning and teaching research. Preferring to use the neutral term *verbal data*, given the specialized meanings of terms such as *introspection* in psychology, Börsch goes on to pose three crucial questions that the researcher contemplating this method needs to ask:

Which mental processes are accessible to verbal reports?
Does the instruction to verbalise change the process of thinking in its very nature?
How complete and correct can verbal reports be? (Börsch, 1986: 200)

The article concludes on a note of caution, arguing that the method is valuable but with limitations: its usefulness will depend on the type of research envisaged; verbalization will not access automatic thought processes; and verbalization may cease or be less complete when a heavy cognitive load is placed on the subject. This book uses linguistic data – translated texts – rather than verbal data. The reason for this is connected with the second language orientation of the work, which makes a focus on language development a priority over cognitive skills development. In this regard, genre is a key concern for translator training in Australia; I use translated texts to explore this aspect of language development, or *textual competence*, in the context of translation competence. However, what I will show is that data of this kind will also permit inferences about some psychological aspects of translation competence.

Concluding remarks

Translation studies has only recently become translator-centred, rather than centred on the target text or the languages themselves. This shift of perspective has run parallel to developments in applied linguistics concerned with the study of bilingualism, contrastive analysis, interlanguage and second language acquisition. What has barely happened, however, is any attempt to reconceptualize the phenomenom of translation in this configuration of topics.

At the same time, translation studies has virtually ignored the reality of translation into the second language, a natural and commonly occurring activity. The problems of translating into a second language beg to be answered in an interlanguage/acquisition framework. We are led inevitably to the translators and their competence; profound questions can be asked about the process of learning to translate because by reconceptualizing it in an interlanguage/acquisition framework we have ways to frame meaningful questions: is the ability to translate into a second language acquired in a systematic way? How can this knowledge help teachers and learners?

This reconceptualization carries with it the demand for systematic empirical research. Second language acquisition research is solidly data based; translation studies is occasionally data based, but usually not; mostly there is a thread of quasi-empirical thinking. What we will find in the remainder of this book, then, is somewhat revolutionary for a text on translation theory (but quite normal in many other areas of applied linguistics): conclusions about the nature of the translation process based on the systematic analysis of data.

Notes

1. Bell's term is *translator* competence rather than *translation* competence.
2. Cascallar et al. (1996) refer their readers to this apparently unpublished paper for the origin of the term congruity judgement: Child, James R. (August 1990) 'Language skills and textual norms across languages'. Paper presented at the annual meeting of the American Association of Teachers of Spanish and Portuguese, Miami, FL.

2 Challenging the insistence on translation into the first language

Aims

In Chapter 1, we pointed out four landmarks that this book will keep in view – second language acquisition, interlanguage, language above the level of the sentence, and levels of competence. In this chapter I want to point out another landmark that has already appeared but is such an important feature that it deserves some detailed discussion and justification. This is the issue of the inevitability of translation into the second language, which will be argued in this chapter with reference to the general situation of translation in Australia and Finland, and in Chapter 3 with reference to a detailed study in Australia.

Translation is, of course, a consequence of bilingualism; in a sense, it is the essential bilingual act, the moment when both languages are simultaneously in play. But bilingualism is not politically, socially or economically neutral – the world is not constructed in such a fashion that each language has equal status. Except for some notable examples where official language planning has conferred 'equal' status on two languages, for most bilinguals in the world one of their languages will be characterized as having lesser status in some sense. Similarly, the relationships between source and target languages in translation are seldom in balance except in those rare cases where 'equality' is legislated, such as the case of English and French in Canada. Apart from these cases, the political and social assymmetry of source and target language is guaranteed by the phenomena of immigration, colonialism, international trade and geopolitics. We begin by examining how immigration impacts on the dynamics of translation.

Translation and immigration

This imbalance between source and target languages in translation has been felt for some two decades in Australia, a country characterized by high immigration. A comprehensive history of the Australian translation movement is yet to be written, although a partial account appears in Ozolins (1991). A thumbnail sketch of the early years would show the following: Australia underwent a political and cultural upheaval in the early 1970s that coincided with the election of a Labor government after decades of conservative rule. One outcome of this upheaval was the emergence of a policy of multiculturalism, sponsored by governments at state and federal level. This policy trend was to be continued by Labor and conservative governments alike. The central philosophical foundation for this policy was that Australia's large immigrant community was no longer expected to assimilate into the host community and disappear. Instead, immigrant communities were seen to be making distinct contributions to the mosaic of society.

Just as they contributed in special ways, so they were seen to have special needs. One such need was for immigrants to have access to social and other services through their own languages, and with this impetus there quickly developed a community interpreting and translating industry.[1] By the end of the 1970s most Australian states had language services agencies providing free interpreting and translation. These services extended to parts of the private sector, so that it was not uncommon for the major banks in capital cities to offer in-house language services to cope with such things as housing loan applications.

Along with the services came training, at first in the form of short technical college courses, and within a few years as three-year degree courses. The degree courses tended to be offered by Colleges of Advanced Education, the poor relations in the 'binary' system of tertiary education that prevailed until the end of the 1980s. The established universities – the other side of the binary system – showed little interest. The establishment of the degree programmes in interpreting and translation coincided with a move to enrol tertiary students from the immigrant communities, and at the same time to increase participation in areas of the capital cities that had been traditionally starved of educational opportunities. The students who enrolled in these courses were almost entirely of recent immigrant background and often without the academic credentials to enter the established universities.

The 1990s brought new influences. Now the imperative was for Australia to look beyond its borders and, in particular, to find ways to articulate politically, economically and culturally with Asia. With this trend (and with the conversion of the old Colleges of Advanced Education to universities), interpreter and translator training took on a more international perspective. Conference interpreting techniques, for example, began to appear in training programmes.

Despite this recent internationalizing trend, the bulk of interpreting and translation in Australia is still carried out by immigrant language professionals serving the needs of other immigrants. For translators, this has led to a situation where many are expected to work into a language that is not their mother tongue.

While this book arises from an Australian setting, there is no reason why its conclusions cannot be generalized to many other settings around the world.

The supply/demand paradox in the Australian translation scene

The patterns of language use prevailing in Australia as the result of waves of immigration present a paradox in the labour market-place of translators able to work into English. This paradox lies in the fact that the communities most in need of translators are often those for which translators into English are least able to be found. At the stage in an immigrant community's life when the bulk of its members are newcomers to the country, it is inevitable that the source of supply of translators is that community itself. The result is that many of these translators will need to work into English, their second language. As ethnic communities become settled and produce second and third generations, language shift and language loss typically result in better skills in English and a corresponding reduction in the need for community translation services. At any one time, cities like Sydney and Melbourne contain a spectrum of ethnic communities that clearly illustrate this paradox.

The second generation presents a further difficulty; language shift leads to attenuated skills in the ethnic language or a restricted range of contexts in which the language is used. Australian translator educators frequently encounter second generation students who can use their parents' language convincingly in home contexts, but who cannot function in the language in an academic setting. In fact, there emerges a complex picture of individuals for whom a first or second language is often difficult to identify since their English and their other language serve in different contexts of use. While English is the language of schooling and of contexts outside the home and the ethnic group, the other language may be the language of preference within the ethnic group, or at least with older family members. The speakers may function as first language speakers of, say, Spanish, with their grandparents and of English with their brothers and sisters. The picture is further complicated by non-standard varieties, which may be the only code in the language available to some second-generation speakers. Many Italian Australians, for example, speak southern varieties of Italian, while most Arabic speakers use Lebanese dialect varieties. For the second generation, then, the mirror image of the situation with the first generation applies; first-generation speakers need to learn to translate into English, their second language, while second-generation speakers need to be trained to translate into an ethnic language which is a second language from the point of view of formal contexts of use.

A superficially simple solution would, of course, be a division of labour so that first-generation translators worked into the ethnic language and second-generation translators worked into English. Unfortunately, this is largely impossible because the translation market is too small and too varied for this kind of specialization. Australian translators are mostly freelancers who must be prepared to translate almost anything and in either direction.

For both first- and second-generation immigrants in major cities like Sydney and Melbourne, then, the supply/demand paradox makes translation education into a second language a virtual inevitability.

What is a second language?: Some problems of definition

The very notion of a 'second' language is a glib oversimplification. As I have said, in the second generation of an ethnic community, the identity of the second language is often difficult to pin down. In fact, the metaphor of a spectrum describes this kind of bilingualism better than a binary split between 'first' and 'second' languages. At one extreme are the first-generation immigrants with a genuine first language other than English – individuals who were born and brought up in, say, Chile, and have been schooled in Spanish. Typically, they have come to the host country as adults and studied English in special classes for immigrants. At the other end is the native English speaker who has studied a language formally from, let us say, secondary school. One way of describing these two extremes is as 'circumstantial' and 'elective' bilingualism (Valdés and Figueroa, 1994: 11–15); my Anglo students who learned French elected to do so, and my Lebanese students learned English because of the circumstances in which they found themselves. In the middle are all colours of the spectrum: receiving bilinguals who speak only English but understand much of the family talk in Armenian; balanced bilinguals who have had alternating periods of schooling between Australia and Germany; individuals who speak substandard varieties of both English and their parents' language; people literate in English and the other language, illiterate in both, or literate in just one. Clyne et al. (1997) put some order into this confusion by usefully classifying ethnic background students in Australian schools in seven categories:

B (i)   Recent arrivals: target language is the principal language of socialization/education.

B (ii)   Less recent arrivals: a strong background in the target language: most/all primary education.

B (iii)   Good knowledge of spoken language: pre-school development and limited further development.

B (iv)   Limited colloquial home background.

B (v)   Passive knowledge of spoken language only.

B (vi)   Limited active and/or passive knowledge of language based on direct input only.

B (vii)   Variety very heavily influenced by English. (After Clyne et al., 1997: 8)

Although Clyne et al.'s classification is intended to describe school populations, it serves the wider clientele of translator education. Most of the subjects discussed in the case studies in this book fall into categories B (i)–B (iii). While I will continue to use the term *translation into the second language* in the rest of this book, it should be regarded as a convenient label to cover all possibilities except translation into a genuine first language. Perhaps we should give Clyne et al. the last word: 'In the context of language acquisition and development in multicultural Australia, the terms "native" and "non-native speaker" have little significance' (1997: 5).

In Australian universities this spectrum of bilingualism has been observed since the early 1980s when translation education began. The range of languages spoken by translation course candidates at the University of Western Sydney Macarthur displays examples of the entire spectrum from mainly first language speakers of Vietnamese or Arabic at one end to mainly second language speakers of German at the other – the circumstantial to elective continuum. The middle part of the spectrum is occupied by Spanish and Italian speakers, who are largely circumstantial bilinguals.

Educational needs of translators into a second language

The bilingual and sociocultural spectrum, along with the supply/demand paradox, makes special demands on translator education in Australia, and no doubt in any other country with similar circumstances.

In the case of second-generation candidates, the main difficulty is likely to be in extending the control of the language other than English to wider contexts of use than informal contacts. A partly effective response to this problem is to convince students to go 'home' to the country of their parents for a year. In the case of Italian and Arabic speakers, the problem is often compounded by the fact that their use of the language other than English leans towards a non-standard variety, so that a degree of bidialectalism has to be learned. This complex of problems is not the focus of the present research, but certainly requires extensive investigation.

In the case of genuine second language speakers of English, the difficulty is that, assuming these individuals have control over the morphosyntax of English, they do not have control over a range of written genres. They are, in a sense, the advanced segment of the clientele for English as a Second Language teaching. Translator education for these individuals needs to incorporate the acquisition of high-level textual skills.

Translation labour market forces in Finland

Let me also put the matter of translation into the second language into a wider context. Translation into the second language is not limited to countries of migration. I have met translators working into non-native English from a number of countries (for example, the Soviet Union, Norway) where it is impractical to expect to find sufficient native English speakers able to do the job. Writing in *Language International*, a professional magazine, William Lise, President of the Japan Association of Translators, claims:

> Contrary to the common wisdom outside Japan, almost all of Japan's J–E translation is done by Japanese writing English as a foreign language, which is then the object of heroic damage-repair efforts by foreign rewriters. (Lise, 1997: 27)

From a Finnish perspective Ahlsvad (1978) argues that it may be not only necessary but desirable for translation to be done into the second language. Discussing the matter from the viewpoint of the translation of Finnish forestry texts into English, he cites four grounds on which it is unreasonable or undesirable to insist that translators work into the mother tongue. First, it is impossible to find sufficient foreigners in Finland able to work as translators, and in any case, foreigners seldom acquire a good enough passive command of Finnish. Secondly, in technical translation accuracy is more important than felicity of style. Thirdly, it is more important for the translator to know the subject matter than to be a native

speaker of the target language. Finally, Ahlsvad claims that proper training can produce competent non-native translators, whose work will be
checked by native speakers anyway. This theme is taken up by McAlester
(1992) who cites two recent surveys in Finland that show that for most
types of text, more translations are done into foreign languages; at the
same time, the Finnish Translators' and Interpreters' Association membership contains only 6% of practitioners whose first languages are not
Finnish or Swedish.

The importance of modelling translation competence in translators into the second language

The experience of countries of high immigration, like Australia, and
of countries where the use of a commercially or politically dominant
second language is necessary makes the insistence on translation into the
first language unrealistic. Vast amounts of translation take place into
second languages. Up to now, however, theories to explain translation
and curriculum models based on them have mostly ignored second language translation. What is needed is ways of describing translation competence that do not necessarily assume native control over the target
language. The failure to develop such models is to deny the realities of
the supply and demand complex in countries like Australia and elsewhere. It is open to challenge whether translation into the second language is the *norm*. If it is, then translation pedagogy is in serious trouble.

Concluding remarks

This chapter concludes by bringing us back to the landmarks that were
pointed out in Chapter 1: second language acquisition, interlanguage, the
organization of language above the level of the sentence, and levels of
language competence. In second language acquisition terms, translators
working into the second language, be they Finns in Finland or Vietnamese in Australia, inevitably produce language that is in some way different
from the target language norm, and may conveniently be described as
interlanguage. The matter of felicity of style, which Ahlsvad is prepared
to sacrifice to an extent, is the stuff of suprasentential linguistics. And the
assessment and accreditation of translation skills – levels of language
competence – will be crucial to the integrity of the profession in countries
like Finland and Australia.

Note

1. See Plimer and Candlin (1996) for a discussion of how women have fared in relation to language services in Australia.

3 A case study of candidates for translator education

Aims

I stressed in Chapter 1 that the focus on the translator, rather than the text or the code, was to be welcomed. This shift of focus opens up rich possibilities for understanding the nature of translation, among these being the potential to see the second language translator as an acquirer, rather than just a possessor, of the target language. And in both the preceding chapters, the crucial point was made that the second language translator is a reality because of the sociolinguistic consequences of immigration, colonialism, commerce and other factors.

So far, the second language translator remains no more than a silhouette, and in this chapter we will fill in some of the human detail. The chapter is based on a case study of candidates for an undergraduate programme in interpreting and translation in Australia and will provide some hard evidence for my claims about the supply/demand paradox and the difficulties of defining first language. Despite the Australian setting, it is quite likely that the picture I draw here would not be out of place in any country that has experienced recent immigration from a variety of parts of the world.

The setting of the study

A word or two about the social and geographical setting of the university will help to frame the case study. Some 30 kilometres inland from Sydney Harbour are the suburban centres of Bankstown and Liverpool. These are mostly working-class areas and part of what is known as Sydney's Western Suburbs, which are often compared unfavourably with the wealthier suburbs of the northern and eastern areas of Sydney. The Western Suburbs have long suffered from low provision of tertiary education institutions, public transport and hospitals. The area's low-cost housing has attracted immigrants and there are considerable concentrations of particular language groups. The University of Western Sydney is a new creation based on a number of colleges, and the Macarthur campus is located close to large Vietnamese, Latin American and Arab communities.

The university has a strong regional focus and has programmes to target local students who have academic potential but who may have suffered educational disadvantage.

The interpreting and translation programme, established in the early 1980s, was seen as a way to utilise the language resources of students of immigrant background in the Western Suburbs, a strategy that accorded well with the university's aim to make itself accessible to disadvantaged groups, and with the multicultural policies being espoused by Australian governments at the time. Unlike other degree programmes at the university, the interpreting and translation course did not use the general matriculation examination to select students. This was for two reasons. First, the course designers believed that language competence should be the primary factor in selecting students; they had little confidence that students who had passed matriculation courses in languages would have sufficient language competence for the course. Secondly, experience with subprofessional interpreting and translation courses which preceded the courses at university level around Australia had shown that the likely student body would be very mixed in age and backgrounds; it was likely that many applicants would have overseas qualifications that would be difficult to equate with the local matriculation examination. With these factors in mind the course designers decided to use a battery of language tests as the main selection tool. The tests form a unique record of the language resource of an Australian city during a period of vibrant multilingualism. More importantly for the topic of this book, the tests give a snapshot of the several hundred individuals available each year as potential translators into their second languages – the types of individual we need to have in mind in developing models of translation competence that do more than blithely assume first language competence in the target language.

The tests comprised a dictation and a modified C-test in each of English and the candidates' other language, and the case study considers the results of these tests over four of the ten years when they were used. A questionnaire was added in the fourth year to elicit data about language background and use. There are, then, two data sets – language tests that paint a picture of the bilingual profiles of the candidates, and a questionnaire that makes it possible to probe more deeply to discover how bilingual profiles relate to age, gender, education and so on.

The language tests

In late 1985, 1986, 1987 and 1988 candidates for professional language courses at the University of Western Sydney Macarthur (then known as

Macarthur Institute of Higher Education) were invited to sit a bilingual selection test. In 1985 and 1986 each candidate was tested in English and one of Arabic, German, Italian, Spanish or Vietnamese. Candidates were invited to the test by applying first through the Universities and Colleges Admissions Centre (UCAC) of New South Wales in response to that organization's annual directory of tertiary courses. The publicity for the course stated that candidates should be 'bilingual' in English and one of the languages mentioned above.

In 1987 and 1988 French was introduced into the test and candidates were advised in the UCAC publicity that they needed to be 'fluent' in English and one of Arabic, French, German, Italian, Spanish and Vietnamese. They were also advised that they could be tested in a third language if they desired.

The test components

The components of the test battery were:

(a)   A 50-item modified C-test in English, comprising three passages, each with the first sentence unmutilated and the last half deleted from every alternate word in the remainder of the passage; where the complete word contained an odd number of letters, the unmutilated part contained half the letters plus one.

(b)   A 50-item modified C-test on the model of the English test in each of Arabic, French, German, Italian and Spanish. The Vietnamese C-test presented some difficulties because of the largely mono-syllabic word patterns and the tone system; after some experimentation, the Vietnamese C-test was modified to comprise a text with the tone marks deleted in alternate words; candidates supplied the tone marks.

(c)   A 100-word tape recorded dictation passage in English.

(d)   A 100-word tape recorded dictation passage in each of Arabic, French, German, Italian, Spanish and Vietnamese.

Size of the candidature

The size of the candidature for each group (see Table 3.1) bore some relationship to the recency of settlement of the immigrant group. This was clearly demonstrated in the case of German, which had very few candidates – the heyday of German migration to Australia was in the immediate postwar period. Italian migration is of a slightly later vintage than German, and continued longer, and the figure of 159 candidates

TABLE 3.1   Candidates by year and language(s)

Year	1985	1986	1987	1988	1985–88
Arabic	39	30	32	44	145
French	—	—	14	18	32
German	15	14	12	19	60
Italian	38	32	56	33	159
Spanish	45	60	48	57	210
Vietnamese	40	28	28	33	129
French/Arabic	—	—	8	8	16
French/German	—	—	0	1	1
French/Italian	—	—	7	3	10
French/Spanish	—	—	5	2	7
French/Vietnamese	—	—	0	1	1
Italian/Spanish	—	—	5	1	6
German/Italian	—	—	1	0	1
Total candidates	177	164	216	220	777

reflects this. The Spanish group was the biggest, reflecting high recent migration and a concentration of Latin American immigrants near the campus. Arabic and Vietnamese migration are of approximately the same vintage as Spanish, although the candidatures are smaller. While this book is not concerned with the sociology of migration, we can hazard the guess that the smaller candidatures have something to do with educational choice and with educational background. On the whole, Vietnamese families do not see the language professions as highly desirable (it is very difficult, for example, to find Vietnamese willing to train as language teachers in Sydney).

English competence

The scores for the English component of the test (see Table 3.2, overleaf) reveal a gradation from the most recent to the oldest settled immigrant groups. Mean scores for the English C-test rank Arabic and Vietnamese as the lowest, followed by Spanish, then Italian, and German at the highest rank. The English dictation scores reveal a similar rank, although Vietnamese candidates are markedly below Arabic, presumably because of the characteristic difficulties of Vietnamese speakers with the phonology of English. Here, then, is concrete evidence of the paradox of translator supply and demand in the *émigré* context: the language groups in most need of language services are the least able to supply individuals to provide those services.

TABLE 3.2   Mean raw scores out of 50 on English tests, grouped by language
other than English

Year	1985	1986	1987	1988	1985–88
Arabic candidates					
C-test	16.6	19.1	17.5	18.8	18.0
Dictation	39.8	42.8	40.5	42.8	41.5
French candidates					
C-test	—	—	28.6	27.6	28.1
Dictation	—	—	47.3	47.4	47.4
German candidates					
C-test	33.5	39.5	36.8	34.3	35.8
Dictation	45.0	50.0	49.3	49.1	48.2
Italian candidates					
C-test	31.2	30.5	30.4	31.9	30.9
Dictation	47.7	47.5	48.7	47.9	48.1
Spanish candidates					
C-test	25.1	28.3	28.6	25.2	26.9
Dictation	42.0	40.7	45.3	43.9	43.0
Vietnamese candidates					
C-test	16.1	22.5	20.4	16.0	18.4
Dictation	34.9	37.9	38.2	29.8	34.9

Competence in the other languages

The tests for each language (see Table 3.3) are, of course, independent.
Strictly, one cannot make comparisons between the C-test in the various
languages because the differing morphological systems of the languages
mean that the C-tests do not necessarily measure the same thing. However, the dictation tests can perhaps be compared. Since all the dictation
passages were taken from general sources, it can be assumed that an
educated native speaker would get an almost perfect score whatever the
language – there is at least an upper benchmark. On this basis, the
languages rank as follows: Arabic candidates did best in their dictation
followed by Vietnamese, Italian, German, Spanish, French. Average scores
of 47/50 for Arabic and 32/50 for Spanish give an idea of the range:
47/50 indicates that there were six words in a 100-word passage with at
least one error; 32/50 indicates 36 words with errors. The French average score is even lower than Spanish, but it should be recalled that for
many French candidates this was a third language.

TABLE 3.3   Mean raw scores out of 50 on tests of languages other than English

Year	1985	1986	1987	1988	1985–88
Arabic C-Test	17.9	18.9	20.8	20.7	19.7
Arabic dictation	46.5	46.5	50.0	49.4	47.8
French C-Test	—	—	18.7	21.8	20.3
French dictation	—	—	19.8	28.9	24.3
German C-test	26.5	28.9	30.5	18.9	25.4
German dictation	31.8	37.8	40.5	34.4	35.8
Italian C-test	22.4	21.8	19.8	20.0	20.7
Italian dictation	42.0	42.1	36.8	36.4	38.8
Spanish C-test	26.2	26.0	22.4	26.1	25.1
Spanish dictation	32.6	33.6	29.9	31.9	32.0
Vietnamese C-test	38.9	41.4	39.2	37.4	39.1
Vietnamese dictation	47.8	48.4	47.0	46.3	47.4

Bearing in mind the difficulties of objectively comparing the scores for the languages other than English, we can say with some confidence that the English and non-English scores are more or less in complementary distribution.

Professed trilingualism

In 1987 and 1988, candidates were given the opportunity of sitting a test in two languages other than English. Course organizers predicted a large number of Arabic/French candidates because of the prevalence of French in some sectors of the Lebanese education system, and expected some Vietnamese/French candidates among older Vietnamese applicants. The Arabic prediction was borne out, with some applicants professing trilingualism (see Table 3.1). There was not, however, a flood of elderly French/Vietnamese/English trilinguals. In 1987, an initially encouraging number of professed trilinguals appeared in the other languages, but was not repeated in 1988. The dearth of trilingualism among these candidates points to an important feature of the Australian scene. The international conference interpreting and translation scene assumes that most practitioners are competent in three languages, reflected in the A, B and C designation for working languages. Except for the Arabic speakers, it would not be easy for these Australian candidates to market their skills internationally.

Correlations between the test components

Correlations across the test components offer some further insights into the bilingual profiles of the candidates and into the reliability of the test battery. For all languages other than English, C-test scores and dictation scores correlate highly. Nevertheless, there is some variation among the languages. At one end of the extreme, Arabic C-tests correlated with Arabic dictations with a coefficient of .58; at the other came French with a correlation of .80 (see Table 3.4).

TABLE 3.4   Correlation of dictation and C-test in the seven languages

	Ar.	En.	Fr.	Ge.	It.	Sp.	Vi.
Arabic	+.58						
English		+.64					
French			+.80				
German				+.66			
Italian					+.70		
Spanish						+.71	
Vietnamese							+.69

$p = <.001$ in all cases.

The choice of C-test and dictation was originally made so that a spread of language competence could be measured in at least two ways: it was thought that the two tests would measure different aspects of language competence in the same individual; and it was hoped that the dictation would discriminate well among weaker candidates, and the C-test better among stronger candidates.

Perhaps more revealing is the variation in correlations for the English tests by language groups (see Table 3.5). For all groups except German

TABLE 3.5   Correlation of English dictation and English C-test by language of candidates

	Ar.	Fr.	Ge.	It.	Sp.	Vi.
Arabic	+.65					
French		+.63				
German			+.30			
Italian				+.55		
Spanish					+.58	
Vietnamese						+.61

$p = <.001$ in all cases except 'German', where $p = <.02$.

speakers, the English C-tests and dictations correlated highly. For German speakers, barely more than a trend was observed. The strength of the correlations corresponds fairly closely to the ranks seen earlier for the English test raw scores, so that the Italian and German groups have a lower correlation and generally better English, and the Arabic and Vietnamese groups have a high correlation and generally poorer English. This is almost certainly due to the plateauing of dictation scores in the stronger groups so that many candidates are achieving near perfect scores; the poorer groups have a better spread of dictation scores to produce a correlation with a spread of C-test scores.

Somewhat of a puzzle is a group of correlations that appear not to be feasible at first sight. Correlations were calculated between the English tests and the tests in the other languages (see Table 3.6).

TABLE 3.6   Correlation of English dictation and C-test with languages other than English dictation and C-test

	English C-test	English dictation
Arabic dictation	−.09	−.12
French dictation	+.10	+.04
German dictation	+.34 (p = <.01)	+.22 (p = <.10)
Italian dictation	−.04	+.19 (p = <.05)
Spanish dictation	−.06	−.02
Vietnamese dictation	+.28 (p < .01)	+.27 (p = <.01)
Arabic C-test	+.04	+.07
French C-test	+.11	+.08
German C-test	+.15	+.30 (p = <.02)
Italian C-test	−.08	+.20 (p = .05)
Spanish C-test	−.08	+.06
Vietnamese C-test	+.36 (p = <.001)	+.43 (p = <.001)

In the case of the Arabic, French and Spanish groups, the lack of significant correlations between English and the other language tests showed that the competences tested were quite separate. In other words, one could be sure that candidates are good or bad at French or English, rather than good or bad at tests in general. The correlations found among the German, Italian and Vietnamese groups are dealt with one by one.

There is a high correlation between the English and German dictations. This may be partially explained by the high number of candidates for whom neither English nor German is a first language. For these candidates, dictation may be a measure of the ability to acquire a second language – bad learners learn both languages badly, good learners learn both languages well. It might also reflect some 'semilingualism' among second-generation German candidates. The same factors might underlie a weak correlation between the German dictation and the English C-test and between the German and English C-tests.

The English C-test correlates significantly both with the Italian dictation and the Italian C-test. The Italian candidature is predominantly second generation straight from high school, with some first-generation Italians who have finished school in Australia. These correlations may reflect a benefit of language maintenance; where Italian is well maintained, English benefits too, presumably reflecting the phenomena discussed in Cummins (1979 and 1981). The lack of a correlation with the English dictation is probably due to the Italian group ranking highest in English dictation; a plateau of near-perfect scores precludes a correlation with a spread of scores.

Finally, the Vietnamese candidates reveal high correlations among all four possible combinations of English and Vietnamese tests. This puzzling phenomenon seems at first sight to reflect an extreme example of test-wiseness; if the candidates are good at doing tests in English, then they are good at tests in Vietnamese. But a comparison with the Italian group suggests that the language maintenance phenomenon is operating. Recall that the English dictation of Italian candidates did not correlate with the Italian tests probably because of the plateau effect in the English dictations. The Vietnamese candidates' English dictations plateaued much less (mean = 34.92/50 compared with 48.07/50 for Italian candidates) and therefore permit a better correlation coefficient. But one needs to consider a different kind of language maintenance here – possibly linked with a general education factor for Vietnamese candidates – since unlike many Italian candidates, they are generally first-generation migrants for whom English is not the stronger language. Without the benefit of other information, the tentative hypothesis is that Vietnamese candidates who acquire English well also maintain their Vietnamese.

The language tests in summary

The language tests give us an initial picture of the reality that professional translator training faces in Australia and, it can be assumed, any country with large-scale migration. Recent immigrant groups with a high demand for translator services are the least able to supply candidates with high levels of competence in English. Subtle sociolinguistic influences on the bilingual profiles of these groups appear to operate. We now turn to the questionnaire data to paint in some of the detail.

The questionnaire data

In 1989 a questionnaire was administered along with the tests. The questionnaire elicited the following data: age, gender, postcode, country of primary and secondary education, language of instruction in primary and secondary education, languages studied in primary and secondary education, secondary qualification obtained, tertiary education undertaken, own, father's and mother's first languages, number of languages and proportions spoken at home and socially, special contexts of language use, relevant experience. It also asked whether candidates took the NSW Higher School Certificate at school in the current year (the local matriculation examination). Of these 126 expressed a first preference for the Bachelor of Arts in Interpreting and Translation (as opposed to other language courses offered), and this group is discussed here. Given that this was the only such course in the state of New South Wales, it can be claimed that the group was the total population available for undergraduate interpreter/translator education in Arabic, German, Italian, Spanish and Vietnamese in 1989.

The candidature as a whole

The striking feature of the candidature is its staggering heterogeneity. Translator educators in Australia, and we can surmise in other countries of migration, will not find homogeneous student groups of young individuals of similarly educated and monocultural backgrounds.

The age and gender profile shows extraordinary variation. Just under half the candidates (44%) were in the 17–20 age bracket; around a quarter (26%) were in the 21–30 range, and 14% were in the 31–40 range. Only a handful (3.2% and 0.8%) were in the 41–50 and 51–60 age ranges respectively. Eleven per cent of candidates declined to state their age. Females made up 63% of the candidates, and males 31%, while 6% declined to state their gender. Just over one-third (37%) were immediate school leavers.

Similarly, there was no homogeneity in educational background and achievement. Just over one-third (37%) of the candidates had their primary education wholly in Australia, while about 5% had their primary education in Australia and another country. The remainder were educated in 19 different countries, namely Abu Dhabi, Argentina, Canada, Chile, Colombia, Cuba, Egypt, Iran, Italy, Kuwait, Lebanon, Malta, Nicaragua, Peru, Portugal, Spain, Uruguay, Tunisia and Vietnam. The medium of primary education was English for 37% of the candidates and English in combination with one or more other languages for a further 13%. About 63% were schooled in one language of instruction only, about 30% bilingually, and about 3% trilingually. The study of languages at primary school other than the medium or media of instruction was sparse: 81% did not study a language.

Compared with primary education, slightly more candidates (43%) had their secondary education wholly in Australia and many more (13%) were secondary educated in Australia and one or more other countries. The remainder were educated in some 19 different countries, these being Abu Dhabi, Argentina, Chile, Colombia, Cuba, Egypt, Guatemala, Iran, Italy, Lebanon, Malta, Peru, Portugal, Spain, Tunisia, United Arab Emirates, Uruguay, USA and Vietnam. The medium of secondary education was English for 39% of the candidates, and English in combination with one or more other languages for about 25%. Over half (58%) had a monolingual secondary education, about a quarter (28%) a bilingual education, and 10% a trilingual education. Language study was more widespread than at primary school: about 58% studied at least one language other than the medium or media of instruction at secondary school, 21% studied two languages and about 6% studied three or more.

Continuity of education displayed some variation. Almost three-quarters (71%) had their primary and secondary education in the same country and 62% in the same medium. A further 17% had their primary and secondary education in partially the same countries and 22% in partially the same medium of instruction. Ten per cent had their primary and secondary education in different countries and different languages. There was little continuity of language study over primary and secondary education. About 6% studied language(s) at primary only, and 48% at secondary only. About 11% studied language(s) at primary and secondary school, 5% studying the same languages, 5% partially the same languages and about 2% different languages. One-third (33%) studied no languages at school other than the medium or media of instruction.

An apparently high proportion (47%) claimed some kind of post-secondary education. The questionnaire item was open-ended and therefore difficult to interpret. Allowing for some flexibility of interpretation, the kinds of post-secondary education were as follows: further education courses – 22% of candidates; nursing qualifications – 2%; teacher training – 3%; part of an undergraduate degree – 6%; a complete undergraduate degree – 9%. There was a miscellany of other types of post-secondary education or qualification, with one candidate each claiming accreditation as a language aide, 'missionary school', 'exchange student', and partial completion of a masters degree.

Language background and use reflect a very varied candidature. Just under one-third (30%) claimed English as their first language, but only

6% claimed that their father's and mother's first language was English. Just under three-quarters (72%) had the same first language as their father, and 75% the same as their mother. Nearly all (94%) said that their father and mother had the same first language. A small number (17%) came from monolingual homes, while 74% were from bilingual homes. Almost 9% came from homes where three or more languages were spoken. Asked what proportion of English was used at home, 33% claimed between none and 20%, 28% claimed between 21% and 40%. The proportions fell therefrom, with 13%, 6% and 10% claiming 40–60%, 61–80% and 81–100% respectively.

Candidates were asked how many languages were spoken with friends, and the responses were similar to home languages, with 10% having a monolingual social life, 73% a bilingual social life and 16% using three or more languages. English use was much higher than at home: only 6% used between none and 20% of English, 9% between 21 and 40%, 29% between 41 and 60%, 24% between 61 and 80%, while 19% used between 81 and 100%. Further analysed, the figures show that only 10% used more English at home, while 71% used less English at home. Four per cent claimed to use the same proportion at home as in their social lives.

Responses to the three open-ended questions on special situations of language use, experience with languages and other relevant experience tended to overlap so that the responses are here considered together. A large proportion (76%) responded to one or more of the questions with a vast array of experiences. Notable is that 19% gave church, mosque or prayer as a context of use, and 11% cited ethnic clubs. Other experiences included scouts, welfare work, tour guiding, nursing, master of ceremonies, school functions, bilingual shop work, flying instruction, accounting and others. Many cited interpreting and/or translation but these data are unlikely to be reliable given that candidates may have been gilding the lily in their applications. In some cases it was clear that candidates misunderstood the question since the examples given in the question were repeated by candidates. Nevertheless, a considerable number seem to have done informal interpreting and translation for relatives.

The candidature summarized

The candidature comprises first- and second-generation immigrants, somewhat above the average age of candidates for a standard arts degree. Indeed, these individuals tend not to be immediate school leavers and may have quite substantial post-secondary education. They are almost twice as likely to be female than male.

They are more likely to have had their primary education outside Australia than inside and will have mostly had a monolingual primary education. About half will have had English as at least one of the languages of instruction. Few will have studied languages at primary level. At secondary level, they are just as likely to be Australian educated as not, but more likely to have had English as one of the languages of instruction. Most will have studied languages at secondary school. On the whole they will have had good continuity over primary and secondary school in their country of education and medium of instruction. However, there is little continuity of language study since so few studied languages at primary school. Bilingual or trilingual education at primary or secondary level was the exception rather than the rule.

English is less likely to be the candidates' first language; most candidates are likely to share a first language with their father and mother. Bi-or trilingual home backgrounds are the norm, with English mainly used less than other languages. On the other hand, in their mainly bi- and trilingual social lives English is the major language. Most used more English in social life than at home. Candidates offered a great assortment of languages experience, with religious and ethnic club use being frequently cited.

Perhaps the most glaring feature of this overall profile of the candidature is the apparent lack of balanced bilingual and bicultural backgrounds. Almost all parents shared a first language so that there is virtually no possibility of 'one language, one parent' bilingualism. Bilingual schooling is the exception and language study seems to be of the academic high school variety; immersion-type bilingualism is probably rare in the candidature. The lack of correspondence between own first language and parents' first language in a quarter of the candidature points to possible language loss and a loss of identification with the parents' culture. Few candidates were able to achieve bilingualism through having their primary and secondary education in different countries.

We now focus on the language groups.

Arabic speakers

The Arabic-speaking candidates fell into two main age and gender groups. One is a group of young females mainly in the 17–21 and 21–30 age brackets, including the bulk of school leavers. The other is a group of males in the 21–30 and 31–40 age brackets.

Three-quarters of all the candidates (74%) had their primary education in Lebanon, and 90% in one Arabic-speaking country or another. Only 8% had an Australian primary education and a single candidate, representing 3%, had a primary education in Iran. It is clear from the secondary education data that the younger candidates' education was often disrupted through migration; 18% had their secondary education in Australia and Lebanon, and 13% were educated in Australia. All of these were in the 17–20 or 21–30 age groups, with the majority in the former. Eight per cent of the group had their primary and secondary education in different languages of instruction. The proportion claiming post-secondary education was high: 33% claimed university studies overseas, and 23% mentioned further education courses of one kind or another (mostly in Australia).

Most of the candidates (74%) had not studied languages at primary school other than as the medium or media of instruction. Almost as many (62%) had not studied languages at secondary school, although these figures need to be balanced against the high proportion (70% primary, 67% secondary) claiming a bilingual or trilingual education (French and Arabic being the commonest combination).

Despite the frequency of bilingual education and the almost one-third who had at least part of their secondary education in Australia, it was rare for candidates to claim other than Arabic as their first language. The three who did were a Farsi speaker, an English speaker with an Arabic-speaking father and English-speaking mother, and an English speaker with an entire Australian education but Arabic-speaking parents.

The bulk of the Arabic group (74%) came from bilingual homes, and 13% each from monolingual or trilingual homes. All of the monolingual homes were Arabic-speaking. The proportion of English used at home was predictably low, with the majority claiming 0–40% of English use. It is worth mentioning that this question probably caused some confusion because of the general way in which it was couched. Occasionally, candidates tried to be more specific, mentioning that English use was high with their children but low with parents. The percentages obtained are open to all kinds of interpretation, for example, English used with n% of family members, n% of time with all family members, etc., and need to be considered with caution. It should be remembered too that candidates had only a few minutes to make a gross assessment of a rather complicated situation, and may even have been motivated to exaggerate in one direction or another in order to bolster the image they aimed to put over in their applications. Perhaps their greatest value is in giving a general picture of the relative skew in home as opposed to social life. With friends, about half the Arabic group assessed their proportion of English use as between 41% and 80%. Indeed, 59% claimed to use more English socially than at home, while 5% claimed to use the same proportion. The number of languages used socially differed from home use in the very small number (2.6%) claiming a monolingual social life – in fact a single candidate who claimed only to use English with friends.

Arabic candidates were eager to talk of special contexts in which they used their language. Religious use was cited six times, and some kind of bilingual work (interpreting, translation, bilingual aide, teaching) was cited 24 times among the 39 candidates. This latter category also included ordinary jobs where the candidates claimed to use their languages, for example, shop assistant, flying instructor, hospital orderly.

Test scores for the Arabic candidature reveal that the 17–21 group score higher than the older groups in English but are somewhat poorer in Arabic. Cross tabulations appear in Table 3.7:

TABLE 3.7   Language test scores of Arabic candidates, cross-tabulated by candidate's age and range of scores

Score	<71	71–90	91–110	111–30
Age 17–21				
English test scores	0%	0%	28%	3%
Arabic test scores	8%	3%	15%	5%
Age 21–30				
English test scores	10%	13%	10%	5%
Arabic test scores	3%	0%	26%	10%
Age 31–40				
English test scores	—	5%	10%	0%
Arabic test scores	—	0%	3%	13%
Age not stated				
English test scores	—	10%	3%	0%
Arabic test scores	—	0%	10%	3%

While there is a promising cluster around the mean for both languages in the 17–21 groups, only a handful of Arabic candidates achieve scores in the 111–30 range for English, and none reach the >130 range. English for this group is in the middle range. A tiny proportion of the 21–30 group appear in the above average 111–30 cell for both languages. It would appear that the main possibilities for Arabic candidates are (a) older candidates with good Arabic and poor English or (b) younger candidates with poor to middle range Arabic and middle range English.

Although the subgroup of higher scoring candidates is small (n = 2), it may be instructive to examine the 21–30 age-group candidates who scored between 111 and 130 in one language and between 91 and 110 in the other, since these are apparently the most promising: one candidate is a male, educated entirely in Lebanon in French and Arabic. He claims a degree from France, is a first language speaker of Arabic, as are his parents, and has experience as a bilingual receptionist. While he does not state the proportion of English used socially, he claims to use 70% Arabic and 30% English at home. The other is also male, educated in English and Arabic in the Gulf (Kuwait – primary, United Arab Emirates – secondary). He does not cite any post-secondary education. He and his parents are first language speakers of Arabic, and while he does not mention the proportion of English used at home, he claims 70% Arabic and 30% English socially. He mentions his bilingual work as an operating theatre orderly. The common link is an uninterrupted bilingual education. The first candidate has undertaken higher studies while the second is unusual in having been educated in the relatively affluent Gulf, where the influence of British and American educational practice is high and EFL (English as a Foreign Language) teaching is well established.

In general, the Arabic candidature is rather cleanly split into two groups. First, the older, mainly male candidates generally have poor English and good Arabic, and tend to be well educated or at least to have had a second bite at education since coming to Australia. Secondly, the younger, mainly female candidates generally have middle-range English and Arabic and appear to have suffered from discontinuity in their school education. Only a handful of candidates approach educated, balanced bilingualism and none achieve it.

German speakers

A feature of this group is their small number (7) and their homogeneity. This discussion will cite raw numbers of candidates rather than percentages of the total German candidature. All of the German candidates were young, with only one in the 21–30 group. Four were direct school leavers and only one was male.

All had their primary and secondary education in Australia in the medium of English. Three mentioned some post-secondary education, namely a Japanese evening course, a further education course in management and a nursing qualification. None studied languages at primary school but all studied languages at secondary school. The combinations were German only (n = 3), French and German (n = 2), Chinese, French and German (n = 1), and French, German, Indonesian and Latin (n = 1).

All but one were first language speakers of English with English-speaking parents. One had Danish-speaking parents but claimed English as her first language. The Danish speaker used Danish, English and German at home and socially, while the remainder led entirely monolingual home and social lives. All but two cited some languages experience, including 'Japanese babysitting', 'school functions', 'exchange student' and 'working in Germany'.

All scored in the 111–30 band for English and were clustered around the mean for German. The one candidate who scored in the 111–30 band for German had worked in Germany.

Very little of significance can be said about the German candidature because of the small numbers except for its great difference from groups like the Arabic speakers; despite a large (although old in terms of migration) German-speaking community in New South Wales, German is clearly not seen as a professional asset to be exploited by that community. The 1989 candidates fit the category of keen high school modern language students, as evidenced by the range of languages studies. The group is not entirely representative of the candidature for previous years, which has included some native German speakers and a number of Hungarian, Yugoslav and Iranian candidates who have acquired German during periods of temporary residence in Europe in the process of migration.

Italian speakers

If the Arabic-speaking group is mainly first generation and the German-speaking group not of recent immigrant background at all, then the Italian group falls between the two; it is very much second generation. Although 89% of the candidates' fathers and 93% of their mothers are first language speakers of Italian, 81% give English as their first language.

Except for the German candidates, the Italian speakers are the youngest group with 70% in the 17–20 age bracket. The biggest age/gender group is composed of 17–21-year-old females (56%). There is a small group of older females (26%) and a smaller group of males in the 17–21 range (15%).

Most of the group (81%) had their primary education in Australia. Of the remainder, two (7%) were primary educated in Australia and Italy, two (7%) in Italy, and one candidate, representing 4%, in Malta. Only three (11%) claimed a bilingual Italian–English primary education. There was great continuity of primary and secondary education, with only one candidate (4%) educated in entirely different countries and in a different language. Given the low average age of the Italian candidates, it was not surprising that there was little mention of post-secondary education: one candidate had an Australian bachelor degree and one had partially completed such a degree; one was qualified as a nurse, and three had taken further education courses. In all, only 22% claimed some post secondary-education. In migration terms, most of the group is clearly one generation ahead of the Arabic speakers with none of the educational disruption experienced by that group.

Language study other than as the medium or media of instruction was sparse at primary school (85% did no language study) but was considerable at secondary school; all but one candidate studied between one and three languages.

Despite their usually Italian-speaking parents, most of the candidates gave English as their first language. Of the five (19%) who did not, two were first language speakers of languages other than Italian or English, namely Spanish and Maltese. The remainder nominated Italian. Of these, one was Italian-educated and over 40 years old and another was educated in both Italy and Australia and was over 30 years of age. Unaccountably, a single male candidate in the 17–20 age bracket claimed Italian as his first language despite a very similar background to the other second-generation candidates. An informal observation is that among current students, being Italian is seen to be rather stylish – perhaps the beginnings of an ethnic revival. These candidates may identify with the ethnic culture in a different way from the second-generation Arabic candidates, whose identification with it may stem partly from a desire for solidarity in a low-status migrant group. All but two candidates (93%) came from a bilingual home but only one trilingual home was reported, namely an English–Italian–Maltese environment. However, nearly a quarter (22%) claimed monolingual social lives. Despite the use of more than one language socially, the proportion of English was high, with more than half the candidates reporting that they used 81–100% English socially. Proportions of English used at home clustered around 21–40%. With frequent club and church use reported (see below), it is clear that Italian is restricted to family-oriented activities, but that English dominates in the outside world. A smaller proportion than the Arabic candidates mentioned special contexts of use, and often a single candidate mentioned several. Use in clubs was cited five times among the 27 candidates, and church use eight times. Some 14 varieties of bilingual work or work experience were mentioned.

The test scores in Table 3.8 (overleaf) reveal that three-quarters of the Italian candidates scored in the 111–30 range or higher for English, or at least half a standard deviation above the mean for the entire candidature. Candidates falling in the average band or below (< 71–110) for English were all in the 17–21 age group. In Italian, however, it was the older candidates who tended to score in the higher ranges. The younger group was clustered just below the mean, with the largest number in the 71–90 range. Eight candidates (22%) scored in at least the 111–30 bands for both languages. Of these, less than half were in the 17–21 age bracket.

TABLE 3.8   Language test scores of Italian candidates, cross-tabulated by candidate's age and range of scores

Score	<71	71–90	91–110	111–30	>130
Age 17–21					
English test scores	4%	4%	19%	44%	—
Italian test scores	7%	30%	22%	11%	—
Age 21–30					
English test scores	—	0%	—	15%	0%
Italian test scores	—	4%	—	7%	4%
Age 31–40					
English test scores	—	—	—	4%	4%
Italian test scores	—	—	—	4%	4%
Age 41–50					
English test scores	—	—	0%	4%	—
Italian test scores	—	—	4%	4%	—
Age not stated					
English test scores	—	10%	3%	0%	—
Italian test scores	—	0%	10%	3%	—

The main possibilities for this group, then, seem to be (a) older candidates with good Italian and good English or (b) younger candidates with poor to middle-range Italian and good English.

The common links among the eight candidates scoring in both languages in at least the 111–30 bands are as follows: four claimed a bilingual education at the primary and/or secondary stages; five were older than the 17–21 age bracket; all had studied languages in secondary school; four had undertaken post-secondary studies; six had some bilingual work experience. Less enlightening is the fact that only one claimed Italian as her first language (she was educated in Australia and Italy), while the one candidate who had her entire primary education in Italy cites English as her first language. A Maltese-English bilingual in this high-scoring group gives Maltese as his first language.

In general terms, this predominantly young second-generation candidature is Australian-educated and identifies linguistically with the host community. English is likely to be good but Italian rather poor since it is not formally maintained; the study of Italian tends to come in Australian high school where it is likely to be treated as one of the academic subjects. The sprinkling of older Italian-born candidates are likely to be more balanced in their bilingualism, especially where there has been a bilingual education.

The Spanish speakers

The Spanish speakers fall, in migration terms, midway between the Arabic and Italian speakers with a mix of first- and second-generation speakers. However, the second-generation candidates in this group, unlike the Italian speakers, are less likely to cite English as their first language; although 49% had at least part of their primary education in an English-speaking country, only 19% of the Spanish candidates claim English as their first language. The group is more heterogeneous than the others in age, although there is a largish group of young female applicants and a preponderance of females (70%) overall.

Because of the great variety of countries in which the Spanish candidates were educated, they are categorized here as follows: Australia; Spanish-speaking country/ies; a combination of English-speaking and Spanish-speaking countries; and non-English- or Spanish-speaking countries. Nearly half (38%) had their primary education in Australia, and a further 11% were educated in a combination of English- and Spanish-speaking countries. All the remainder were primary educated in Spanish-speaking countries with the exception of one Farsi-educated and one Portuguese-educated. About a quarter had a bilingual or trilingual primary education. However, the Spanish speakers were the second worst casualties of migration in discontinuity of education; 14% had their primary and secondary education in entirely different languages and countries. Post-secondary education was fairly high with 12 instances of technical college training, one complete bachelor degree, one incomplete bachelor degree and one trained teacher. Two candidates mentioned interpreting and translation courses and one 'missionary school'.

The pattern of infrequent language study at primary school was repeated; only 16% studied languages at primary school but the figure rose to 65% at secondary school. Interestingly, only five candidates (14%) studied Spanish (other than as the language of instruction) at secondary school. In other words, very few of the 43% who went to Australian high schools had or took the opportunity of formal study of their first language. The Italians did much better in this respect; 74% studied Italian at secondary school. This lack of formal language maintenance may explain the generally dismal dictation scores of Spanish candidates. The mean raw score over 1985–88 is 32/50, representing 36 not completely correct words in a 100-word dictation passage. The mean raw score for Italian is 39/50; the Spanish candidates appear to spell very badly.

Almost three-quarters of the group (73%) gave Spanish as their first language, despite the fact that 38% cited English as the sole medium of primary education and 35% had Spanish as the sole medium. Of the remainder, 19% cited English, 2.7% (a single candidate) gave Kurdish, and 5.4% did not state their first language. Eighty-six per cent and 89% gave their father's and mother's first language respectively as Spanish, with an English-speaking and a Kurdish-speaking household and a handful of mixed marriages accounting for the discrepancy. The non-Spanish-speaking parents spoke Chinese, Italian, Kurdish or Italian. About three-quarters of the candidates had the same first language as their fathers (73%) and their mothers (76%). Of the candidates who cited English as their first language, those in the younger age groups dominated and English was generally stronger than Spanish. Bilingual homes were the norm (76%) for this group, with 11% claiming a monolingual and 11% a trilingual home. A single candidate declined to answer the question. No candidate claimed a monolingual social life – exclusively English-speaking circles of friends, as observed among the Italians, are yet some way off, with 81% citing bilingual social lives and 16% trilingual social lives. Home use of English was concentrated at the lower end of the range with more than one-third in the 0–20% bracket and about a quarter in the 21–40% range. In their social lives, however, almost three-quarters reported a proportion of English use between 41% and 80%. Nearly all candidates mentioned some special context of use with a great variety of experiences, including interpreting and translation, journalism, student exchange, various kinds of teaching, tour guiding and congress organizing, and bilingual jobs such as secretarial, shop, bank, dental and waitressing work. Church use was cited 12 times, and club use eight times.

Over two-thirds of the Spanish candidates scored 111 or higher in English, comparable with the Italians (see Table 3.9). All of those scoring in the average band or below were younger candidates, in the 17–21 age bracket. Like the Italians, Spanish was stronger in the older candidates and poorest in the 17–21 age range, where over half were in the average band or below. Seven candidates (19%) scored above average in both English and Spanish; these were distributed over the higher age ranges with only one in the 17–21 bracket. Overall, the Spanish-speaking group are more heterogeneous in their bilingualism than the Arabic or Italian speakers, so that strong tendencies are difficult to observe. However, the expected Spanish loss in the younger candidates is a characteristic of the group.

The only commonality observed among the high-scoring candidates is that all but one were older than 20 and that all but one had studied a language at secondary school. There seemed to be a good range of contexts of language use, although the Spanish-speaking group as a whole cited many such contexts. Otherwise, a range of backgrounds was found:

TABLE 3.9   Language test scores of Spanish candidates, cross-tabulated by
candidate's age and range of scores

Score	71–90	91–110	111–130	>130
Age 17–21				
English test scores	4%	19%	44%	—
Spanish test scores	30%	22%	11%	—
Age 21–30				
English test scores	0%	—	15%	0%
Spanish test scores	4%	—	7%	4%
Age 31–40				
English test scores	—	—	4%	4%
Spanish test scores	—	—	4%	4%
Age 41–50				
English test scores	—	0%	4%	—
Spanish test scores	—	4%	0%	—
Age not stated				
English test scores	0%	—	4%	—
Spanish test scores	4%	—	0%	—

in some cases primary education was in English and secondary education
in Spanish; sometimes there was a single medium. Two of the seven had
had bilingual or trilingual education.

In general, the Spanish group is highly heterogeneous as regards age
and educational background. While English tends to be good and English
is a common educational medium, the group prefers to identify with
Spanish. Those approaching a balanced bilingualism tend to be older,
while there is evidence of loss of Spanish in younger candidates. A snapshot judgement of the group would be that they are cosmopolitan sur-
vivors of migration compared to the Italians with their settled second
generation and the Arabic speakers with their sharp split between older
monoculturals and first-generation products of disturbed education.

Vietnamese speakers

With only an emerging second generation, the Vietnamese-speaking group
is the least acculturated of the candidature and the least varied in country
of education, parenthood and first language. It finds itself at the opposite
end of the migration to the German-speaking group whose connections
with the 'home' country are virtually absent. Although the group is small
(n = 16), there appears to be a fairly sharp split into older male candidates

and younger female candidates, males being concentrated in the 21–40 range and females in the 17–20 range. Four candidates (25%) declined to state their age.

Most candidates (88%) had their primary education in Vietnam, with only one educated in Australia and another in both countries. Slightly more (25%) were secondary educated in Australia, but overall continuity of country of education was high, with 75% having had both primary and secondary education in the same country – Vietnam in all cases but one. This continuity was not reflected in the medium of instruction; only 31% of the candidates had their primary and secondary education in the same language, but this low figure was accounted for by the high level of bi- or trilingual secondary education, since 31% had their primary and secondary education in partially the same medium. Only three candidates (19%) had a bilingual primary education (French and Vietnamese), but at secondary level the proportion was higher: one candidate was educated in English and French, two in English, French and Vietnamese, two in English and Vietnamese and two in French and Vietnamese. The question on post-secondary education revealed that a quarter of the candidates (n = 4) had partially completed a bachelor degree, while three had taken technical courses and two were trained teachers. Only two candidates studied a language other than the media or medium of instruction at primary school, one taking Chinese and one French. At secondary school the figure was slightly higher – three took English and French – although this low figure should be considered with caution since bilingual secondary education was common.

All candidates cited Vietnamese as their first language, including the single Australian-educated candidate. All the candidates' parents were Vietnamese speakers. Three-quarters of the candidates reported bilingual home environments and one-quarter monolingual, the highest proportion of non-English-speaking households found among the language groups. The proportion of English used in the home was also the lowest with more than half the candidates (56%) reporting 0–20%, and 25% reporting 21–40%. All candidates, however, had bilingual social lives; the proportion of English was spread over the 0–80% range, with a surprisingly high concentration of 44% of the candidates in the 41–60% band. Most candidates (73%) used more English socially than at home. This group is distinguished by a low incidence of church use – only one candidate volunteered such use – and no club use, but a high degree of bilingual community work. Almost half the candidates mentioned some kind of community-oriented activity such as bilingual assistant, community worker, language aide. The picture that emerges is of a candidature that has found a niche where bilingual skills are in demand.

Below average English scores are clustered around the 21–50 age band, although there is not the expected concentration of average or above English in the younger age groups. In the 91–110 range, three young candidates appear as well as three whose ages were not stated. Judging by their post-secondary education and work experience, this modest trio was in the older age range. No Vietnamese-speaking candidate scored higher than in the 91–110 average band for English. More predictably, Vietnamese was stronger in the older age ranges and poorer in the younger. All candidates of 31 or older (if the category includes those who did not state their age) fell into the average or above average range for Vietnamese. The Vietnamese scores formed a neat implicational scale; Vietnamese improves with the age of the candidates. The language scores are shown in Table 3.10.

TABLE 3.10   Language test scores of Vietnamese candidates, cross-tabulated by candidate's age and range of scores

Score	<71	71–90	91–110	111–30
Age 17–21				
English test scores	6%	6%	6%	—
Vietnamese test scores	6%	6%	6%	—
Age 21–30				
English test scores	—	13%	13%	—
Vietnamese test scores	—	13%	13%	—
Age 31–40				
English test scores	13%	13%	0%	0%
Vietnamese test scores	0%	0%	19%	6%
Age 41–50				
English test scores	—	6%	0%	—
Vietnamese test scores	—	0%	6%	—
Age not stated				
English test scores	—	6%	19%	0%
Vietnamese test scores	—	0%	19%	6%

Only four candidates scored in the average band for English and Vietnamese, and once again some commonality was observed. Three did not state their age but can be reasonably assumed not to be school leavers, while one was in the 17–20 range. This young female candidate had her primary education in Vietnam and Australia, and her secondary education in Australia. Of the older candidates, one, a male, was schooled in Vietnam but reported a bilingual secondary education (English and Vietnamese); he works as a language aide and a bilingual assistant. Of the two older female candidates, one had a bilingual primary and secondary education (French and Vietnamese), while the other studied law in Vietnam for two years after a monolingual education; this latter candidate is a community worker. All three older candidates reported a high proportion of English in their social lives.

In general, English is poor, and Vietnamese apparently inadequately maintained in the younger candidates. There is little consolation to be found in the older group where Vietnamese, being the first language, is strong but English often weak. Those approaching balanced bilingualism are few and appear to have had a richer educational and work experience.

Concluding remarks

A case study like this one is, I believe, the strongest argument that can be put forward for developing models of translation competence that take into account translation into the second language. It is clear beyond doubt that countries like Australia are simply not in a position to demand that translation will only be done into the mother tongue. Unlike Europe, where national languages are of equal status, languages in Australia have to fit into one pecking order or another. English, the language of government and commerce, takes first rank; no translator can insist that they will not translate into English. Languages like Vietnamese fall far down the order in terms of university provision and attractiveness to the mainstream student population. There are few universities where Vietnamese can be studied and there is scant interest among native English speakers in a career as a Vietnamese professional linguist. As a result, Vietnamese translators must be sought from the immigrant community, where, as we have seen, younger students will have a deficit in Vietnamese and older students a deficit in English. Perhaps a language like Italian finds itself ranked a little higher; numerous Italian programmes are offered in Australian universities, and many non-Italian speakers have considered it worthwhile to study the language to a high level. But, as we have seen, the second generation of Italian speakers struggles to maintain good Italian skills.

My interest in translation into the second language was originally prompted when I faced classes of students like those described in this chapter and discovered that the field of translation studies had virtually nothing to say about them. What began to make a difference was to see them not as students attempting to mimic target language writers and failing; rather, they needed to be seen as learners constructing their own systems of target language use, with the prospect of developing those systems in the direction of the native-speaker system. This approach compels the researcher to examine target language texts in a detailed and systematic way, in just the same way that second language acquisition research has been largely data-based; it is very well to propose that some system exists, but only empirical study will begin to reveal its nature. Chapter 4 begins that process.

4 Translation into a second language and second language competence

Aims

This chapter is principally about textual competence. It is woven around several of the themes that shape this book, including the themes of discourse and levels of competence. A key argument is that one of the aspects of translation competence is competence in the target language, and specifically at the level of text or discourse; that is, part of learning to translate into a second language is learning to write in a stylistically authentic way. This chapter begins by developing this argument, relying on insights from the field of written versus spoken language. In essence, the concerns of translation competence studies are limited by the typical genres encountered by professional translators – official prose, administrative texts, and so on. A major element in the pedagogy of translation is to teach students to create texts like these in a second language. Textual competence is the element of translation competence that such pedagogy addresses.

The second part of the chapter deals with a case study that analyses the target texts of a group of translators working into English as their second language in an effort to describe textual competence. It is here that we find the link with the other major theme mentioned in the opening paragraph of this chapter – levels of competence. What I argue here is that it is possible to profile the textual competence of second language translators in a way that will yield useful normative and diagnostic judgements. The chapter ends with a preliminary attempt at profiling textual competence.

The difference between translation into a first and a second language

As I have discussed in Chapters 2 and 3, there is little doubt that much translation has been and will continue to be carried out into translators' second languages. This presents a serious problem for those responsible for training and accrediting such translators because the business of translating into a second language is clearly very different from translating into the first language.

The two activities are in a way mirror images. In translating from a second language, the main difficulty is in comprehending the source text; it is presumably much easier to marshal one's first language resources to come up with a natural looking target text. In translating into a second language, comprehension of the source text is the easier aspect; the real difficulty is in producing a target text in a language in which composition does not come naturally. It is probably wise to assume at the outset that perfectly balanced bilinguals are so rarely found that virtually all human translation activity falls into one of the two categories – into or from the second language.[1]

The benefits of one or the other can be argued, although it must be said that expert (and no doubt public) opinion favours translation into the first language. Neubert (1981) argues a case at the level of discourse, claiming that working into the mother tongue avoids the problem of lack of textual competence in the target language – in other words, native writers can manipulate all the devices that go to make up natural-looking texts. The same case could be argued at finer levels of linguistic analysis; first language writers are, presumably, less likely to make grammatical errors and unfortunate vocabulary choices than second language writers.

In theory this is fine, but in practice it poses some difficulties since the supply of translators into particular languages may not match the demand, so that translation sometimes (or perhaps even often) has to be undertaken into the second language. I have already mentioned that Ahlsvad (1978) makes virtue out of a necessity by claiming that translation into the second language may even be preferable in some circumstances. The necessity in this case is the near impossibility of finding English speakers who can translate from Finnish. The virtue is found in the claim that non-native readers of English are accustomed to and comfortable with reading technical texts written in second language English, and that accuracy is more important than stylistic felicity.

In Australia, a glance at the *Directory of the National Accreditation Authority for Translators and Interpreters* will show that many translators are accredited to work in two directions, and that few Anglo-Saxon names appear as accredited translators at all. There is nevertheless plenty of translation done in Australia into and from English. The inescapable conclusion is that despite the advantages of having translators work into their first languages, there will always be the need for many to work into the second language (notwithstanding the difficulties of identifying the second language among second-generation speakers of languages other than English). If such translators are to be trained in their craft, it is clear that the process of acquiring competence must be different from that of translators learning to work into the first language; the major focus with the former must be on learning productive skills, while with the latter it must be on learning comprehension skills.

In a country like Australia the position is further complicated by the fact that translators are most likely to be drawn from the migrant population, and that the migrant population itself is subject to language shift (towards English). As a result, depending on the maturity of a language community and its rate of language shift, the available translators may be first language speakers of the migrant language or of English. Generally speaking, in a recently settled community the available translators will be able to work best into the community language, while in a long-settled community they will be able to work best into English. In Australia, the Vietnamese and German communities represent the two extremes, as was seen in Chapter 3.

Second language competence as an aspect of second language translation competence

Let us assume that translation competence into the second language is somehow tangled up with second language proficiency. It is, however, a very special variety of second language proficiency: the second language translators have to work within the limitations of their second language repertoire, and the stages of individuals' language development must be reflected in the quality of their translation. But the translators also have to work within the limitations of the source text, and it is this that makes translation into the second language a very special variety of second language writing.

One aspect of this is that translation closely circumscribes writers' output, reducing their ability to produce optimum quality output. Writers of primary texts are free to a greater or lesser extent to control the content in accordance with their productive ability. For example, if I write a business letter in a second language, I am free to avoid or underplay certain aspects if my second language competence is insufficient to express them; I am free to make the letter long or short, to show off my second language competence or modestly express only the very minimum. In theory, I can hide my shortcomings by tailoring the text to suit my abilities. If I translate a business letter I am forced to reveal my shortcomings to an extent because I may be forced to write something that I cannot express properly. The source text writer has decided the meanings I have to express and therefore exposed me to risk. Indeed, it is difficult to think of a writing task that constrains the writer as much as translation does.

Translation and written language

Another aspect is the special character of written language itself, and the fact that high levels of second language proficiency in writing reflect control over these special features of written language. I will assume, for the purposes of this discussion, that much of what is professionally translated is at the more formal end of the stylistic scale, and that the ability to produce language more characteristic of writing than speaking is a built-in requirement for translators.

Chafe and Tannen (1987) review the literature on the differences between written and spoken language. The first part of the review deals with the structural differences between the two modes, while the second treats the contextual influences on their use and creation. Chafe's survey of research into structural differences shows that writers have tended to characterize each mode as containing more or less of a particular structural feature or bundle of features. For example, there is a degree of agreement that written text has more diverse vocabulary, more nouns, more adjectival constructions, more passives, and denser text. Using such measures, one could certainly describe the second language proficiency element of translation competence; the higher an individual's competence, the more one would expect his/her text to contain features of written rather than spoken language. The nature of the translation task itself, however, limits the number of such features that can be used in such a description and may even suggest different interpretations to those made as the result of other tasks.

An example of different interpretation is lexical diversity (type/token ratio). A writer composing freely on a topic can increase lexical diversity by simply wandering into conceptual by-ways and backwaters. For a translator, lexical diversity can only be increased by giving several alternatives for the same source text term or by decreasing the proportion of function words (with their limited number of types) and increasing the proportion of content words (which may be of a great number). Thus, in a composition task, high lexical diversity may be interpreted as a rich lexical repertoire, but in a translation task as the grammatical ability to use lexicalizations. The rather artificial example that follows illustrates the principle:

A. We will not put up with people destroying our property. We have
    put up with it for a long time . . .
B. We will not permit the destruction of our property. We have long
    tolerated it . . .

Version A contains 16 types and 20 tokens, which yields a lexical variety
ratio of $16/20 = .80$. Version B has a higher lexical variety ratio of .92,
with 12 types and 20 tokens. The higher ratio in B is achieved by using
two equivalents for *put up with*, that is *permit* and *tolerate*, and by decreasing the proportion of function words; the lexicalized versions of *put up
with* eliminate four instances of prepositions, and the recasting of *for a
long time* as an adverb *long* eliminates a preposition and a determiner. It
is also apparent that B is more characteristic of written rather than spoken
language.

Despite these difficulties it seems quite apparent that one element of
translation competence into the second language is the ability to deploy
a highly specialized variety of second language writing. At this point
I should also mention the characterization of written and oral language
as 'involved versus detached' (Tannen, 1982) or 'decontextualized and
contextualized' (Snow et al., 1991). The translation task is doubly decontextualized since the translator is not responsible for the content of the
original. The translation of run-of-the-mill tasks such as administrative
letters, reports, formal speeches and so on, is perhaps the most decontextualized language task that a human can perform. One would have to
acknowledge that literary translation is a different matter; the relationship
between a great literary translator like William Weaver and a great writer
like Umberto Eco is clearly of a different order.

A case study approach to describing textual competence in translators into a second language

With these thoughts in mind, I present below a case study with the
general aim of obtaining a broad profile of the competence of a group of
translators, and the more specific aim of obtaining a profile of the *textual*
component of the translators' second language competence. I will use the
term textual competence repeatedly in the remainder of this book, with
the understanding that I intend it to mean the capacity to deploy grammar and lexis above the level of the sentence. This is not very distant
from Bachman's definition of the same term:

> Textual competence includes the knowledge of the conventions for
> joining utterances together to form a text, which is essentially a unit of

language – *spoken* or *written* – consisting of two or more utterances that are structured according to rules of cohesion and rhetorical organisation. (Bachman, 1990: 88)

At the same time, I believe that my usage of textual competence may also be extended to include what Bachman calls 'sensitivity to differences in register' and 'sensitivity to naturalness', which are aspects of his sociolinguistic competence (pp. 94–5).

The case study was based on the translations of 38 candidates for a public examination in translation in Australia. The candidates were all native speakers of Arabic, and each translated the same passage, called here *Unemployment*, of 130 words from Arabic into English. The marks awarded by the examining authority were used to grade the candidates into four ability groups, which were compiled with two criteria in mind: they should be roughly equal in size; and they should each comprise a cluster of grades with a fairly clear break between one group and the next (see Table 4.1).

TABLE 4.1   Ability groups of the translation examination candidates

	Range of scores	Number of candidates
Group 1	0 –3.5/50	6
Group 2	14.5–25/50	10
Group 3	27.5–35/50	12
Group 4	38 –44.5/50	10
Total		38

Nine analyses were chosen in an attempt to profile the competence of the candidates. These were:

- Text length (TL)
- Lexical variety ratio (LVR)
- Tokens misspelt (TM)
- Average word length (AWL)
- Words directly translated (WD)
- Words shifted (WS)
- Words omitted (WO)
- More verbs (MV)
- Content/function words (CF)

Summary results

The raw scores are shown in Table 4.2.[2] The final column 'TEST' includes the score out of 50 given for the translation by the accrediting

TABLE 4.2   Results of analysis of *Unemployment* target text analyses

Subject	TL	LVR	TM	AWL	WD	WS	WO	MV	CF	Test
51	178	0.56	3.37	4.8	85	0	10	20.3	0.67	18.5
52	167	0.59	10.20	4.8	70	15	15	10.6	0.80	29.5
53	155	0.60	1.94	4.7	45	25	10	10.4	0.68	42.0
54	132	0.64	5.30	4.7	45	20	25	13.6	0.80	1.0
55	142	0.65	2.82	4.9	65	10	5	24.0	0.86	38.0
56	143	0.64	2.80	5.0	70	10	10	46.6	0.99	20.0
57	152	0.62	0.00	4.8	60	25	10	51.5	0.90	32.0
58	184	0.55	4.35	4.5	55	20	10	67.1	0.66	20.0
59	134	0.72	0.75	5.2	50	20	10	51.5	0.94	39.5
60	172	0.54	2.91	4.7	70	10	5	45.2	0.83	0.0
61	146	0.58	7.53	4.8	70	5	20	20.1	0.91	0.0
63	173	0.60	9.83	4.9	60	5	0	25.6	0.74	0.0
64	142	0.66	0.70	4.9	50	25	10	66.7	1.00	39.0
65	139	0.61	4.32	4.8	75	15	5	37.7	0.90	34.5
66	155	0.65	1.29	5.0	70	5	10	23.4	0.78	41.5
67	137	0.63	2.19	4.8	60	15	25	28.8	0.89	3.5
68	144	0.65	0.69	5.0	60	15	0	27.0	0.95	43.0
69	153	0.59	3.92	4.5	80	5	10	44.6	0.78	14.5
70	148	0.66	2.70	4.9	65	15	10	33.7	0.92	41.5
71	142	0.64	2.11	4.8	65	10	15	16.9	0.83	44.0
72	146	0.65	1.37	4.9	45	25	5	66.7	0.87	35.0
74	147	0.67	8.16	4.8	55	15	20	20.5	0.79	33.5
75	131	0.65	16.00	5.2	55	5	30	6.8	1.08	0.0
76	161	0.58	1.24	4.9	55	20	5	20.5	0.87	35.0
77	147	0.63	2.04	4.8	70	15	5	38.6	0.73	44.5
78	158	0.63	0.63	4.9	65	15	10	6.8	0.83	40.5
79	166	0.59	4.82	4.8	70	15	5	45.5	0.73	24.5
80	151	0.65	5.30	4.6	70	15	5	38.6	0.84	25.0
81	155	0.57	1.94	4.8	70	5	15	27.3	0.78	16.0
82	156	0.59	0.64	5.0	45	15	10	43.2	0.80	28.0
84	181	0.60	4.97	4.8	85	5	0	22.7	0.88	30.5
85	175	0.55	1.14	4.8	75	15	5	54.6	0.80	34.0
86	150	0.63	5.33	4.9	60	15	15	59.1	0.80	23.0
87	138	0.59	1.45	5.2	60	15	20	34.1	0.96	20.5
88	170	0.62	2.94	5.0	50	25	10	31.8	0.80	27.5
89	161	0.58	4.97	4.8	60	10	5	34.1	0.76	18.5
90	148	0.58	4.05	5.0	55	20	10	43.2	0.83	31.0
91	143	0.58	4.90	5.0	80	5	0	20.5	0.95	34.5
Mean	153	0.61	3.73	4.9	63	14	10	33.7	0.84	26.5

Key:
TL = Text length, LVR = Lexical variety ratio, TM = Tokens misspelt,
AWL = Average word length, WD = Words directly translated, WS = Words
shifted, WO = Words omitted, MV = More verby, CF = Content/function
words, TEST = Translation test score

body's markers. For the purpose of comparison in the following sections, the results of the analyses in Tables 4.3–4.11 are expressed as z-scores rather than raw scores, that is the mean is zero and the standard deviation is one.

The choice of analyses

Text length was chosen as a broad measure of translation competence which would reflect at least two facets. First, it was reasoned that very poor translators would produce shorter text because they would omit to translate difficult parts. Secondly, it seemed that better translators would produce denser and therefore shorter text because they would use more lexicalizations. Both suppositions were largely borne out by the analysis: as Table 4.3 shows, mean text length was low for Groups 1 and 4, and high for Groups 2 and 3; poor translators and good translators produced shorter text, while mediocre translators produced longer text. Text length was measured by simply counting the number of tokens, that is individual words, in the text.

TABLE 4.3   Text length expressed as z-scores: positive values indicate longer text, negative values indicate shorter text

Group 1	−0.34
Group 2	0.33
Group 3	0.28
Group 4	−0.46

The *lexical variety ratio* analysis was obviously intended to reflect candidates' vocabulary repertoire, but, as I have mentioned, in translation texts this analysis needs to be treated carefully; it is likely to reflect the use of multiple equivalents and / or the ability to write dense text by using lexicalizations. Table 4.4 shows that the lexical variety ratio of the poor and mediocre groups was similar, while in the good group it was much higher. Lexical variety ratio was calculated using the TEXTANA programme (University of Duisburg).

TABLE 4.4   Lexical variety ratio expressed as z-scores: positive values indicate more varied lexis, negative values indicate less varied lexis

Group 1	−0.08
Group 2	−0.38
Group 3	−0.17
Group 4	0.98

The *tokens misspelt* analysis was included as a general measure of written language competence and as rough confirmation of the composition of the four ability groups. As one would predict, the poor group had most misspellings, the mediocre groups were around the mean, while the good group had least misspellings. Table 4.5 illustrates the results.

TABLE 4.5   Tokens misspelt expressed as z-scores: positive values indicate poorer spelling, negative values indicate better spelling

Group 1	1.10
Group 2	0.03
Group 3	−0.02
Group 4	−0.67

Average word length was intended to reflect at least two facets: on the one hand, a higher score ought to reflect a lower proportion of function words, which are generally short words in English; and among content words it ought to reflect longer and probably more Romance than Germanic words. The analysis, shown in Table 4.6, shows an interesting profile. Average word length is moderate in poor translators, drops sharply in the lower mediocre group, then rises through the next two groups. Group 1 is the most interesting. The explanation for the higher word length than Group 2 is that the poor translators omit function words because of their lack of syntactic ability, producing 'telegraphic' type texts. Average word length was calculated using the TEXTANA programme.

TABLE 4.6   Average word length expressed as z-scores: positive values indicate longer words, negative values indicate shorter words

Group 1	−0.1
Group 2	−0.44
Group 3	0.15
Group 4	0.31

The *words directly translated* analysis was meant to reflect the extent to which candidates adhered to the lexical structure of the source text; did they try to maintain the match between a source text word and its meaning, or were they prepared to distribute the meaning of a source text word over several words in the target text? An example of such paraphrasing is Subject 54's *not long ago* for *ḥattā waqt qarīb* ('since time near') where a direct translation of *waqt* is not to be found. As Table 4.7 shows, the poor candidates were less likely to translate words directly, but the lower mediocre group was very likely to do so. There is then seen a sharp

TABLE 4.7   Words directly translated expressed as z-scores: positive values
indicate more direct translation, negative values indicate less direct
translation

Group 1	−0.28
Group 2	0.45
Group 3	−0.05
Group 4	−0.23

decrease in the number of direct translations until Group 1's score is
almost the same as Group 4's. The interpretation of this is that the poor
candidates omit or radically recast the source text meaning because of
their poor productive skills; the mediocre candidates play safe with translations that stick close to the source text; the good candidates are prepared to redistribute source text meaning over target text word boundaries.
Words directly translated were calculated by hand on a random sample of
20 source text words.

The *words shifted* analysis is meant to show the extent to which the
candidates were prepared to change the syntactic structure of the source
text. It identifies those words that have undergone a shift in their grammatical category during translation. According to this analysis, shown in
Table 4.8, the poor candidates make few shifts, sticking closely to the
original. There is a sharp increase in shifts, with a plateau or even a slight
decrease in the good candidates. This seems to demonstrate an increasing
ability to manipulate the syntax of the target language. Words shifted
were calculated by hand on a random sample of 20 source text words.

TABLE 4.8   Words shifted expressed as z-scores: positive values indicate more
shifts of grammatical category, negative values indicate less shifts

Group 1	−0.56
Group 2	−0.41
Group 3	0.42
Group 4	0.25

The *words omitted* analysis, shown in Table 4.9, overleaf, reflects the
fullness of the translation relative to the source text by counting the
number of source words for which there appears to be no direct or
indirect equivalent in the target text. The poor group has many such
omissions, reflecting gaps in target language lexical repertoire, while the
three higher groups have rather fewer. Words omitted were calculated by
hand on a random sample of 20 source text words.

TABLE 4.9   Words omitted expressed as z-scores: positive values indicate more source words not translated, negative values indicate less source words not translated

Group 1	1.01
Group 2	0.03
Group 3	−0.33
Group 4	−0.25

The *more verbs* analysis was an attempt to examine syntactic shift from a different viewpoint. This analysis measured the extent to which candidates adopted a more 'verby'[3] style in their translations and, since the source text was highly nominal, the extent to which they had departed from the source text structure. The poor group produced syntactically substandard text with few verbs to code the relationships between nouns, while the lower mediocre group's style was more verby (see Table 4.10). As ability increased, so the candidates were more able to use nominalizations. The *more verbs* analysis was carried out as follows. First, the verbal/nominal ratio of the source text was calculated by dividing the number of verbs by the number of nouns. This yielded a figure of 17/43, which was corrected to 19/43, or .40 to account for two copula verbs, which generally do not occur in the present tense in Arabic. Next, the same operation was carried out for each target text. A set of rules was developed for the sake of consistency to deal with anomalies. These were: Quantifiers (*many, a lot*, etc.) and pronouns were not counted as nouns. Similarly, nouns used adjectivally (for example, *unemployment* benefit) were not counted. However, gerunds (in *finding* a job) were counted as nouns. In the case of verbs, the entire complex, including modals and auxiliaries, was counted as a single verb, as were discontinuous verbal complexes (for example, *can never have*).

TABLE 4.10   More verbs expressed as z-scores: positive values indicate more 'verby' style, negative values indicate less 'verby' style.

Group 1	−0.62
Group 2	0.48
Group 3	0.10
Group 4	−0.23

In every case, the verbal/nominal proportion was higher in the target text. The final step was to calculate the percentage by which each subject's text was higher than that of the source text.

The *content/function words* analysis was intended to determine the extent to which candidates relied on lexicalizations as opposed to function words. In this case, Group 1 produced many content words, while Group 2 had many function words. Groups 3 and 4 tended towards higher proportions of content words. The clear interpretation of this is that the poor candidates produced telegraphic text that lacked function words because of their poor second language ability; mediocre candidates produced syntactically strung-out text, while the better candidates' text was grammatically dense because of the use of lexicalizations. See Table 4.11. There is, of course, a relationship here with word length since content words tend to be longer than function words. This is explored in some detail in Chapter 5.

TABLE 4.11   Content/function words expressed as z-scores: positive values indicate more content words, negative values indicate more function words

Group 1	0.39
Group 2	−0.48
Group 3	0.10
Group 4	0.13

To calculate content/function words, for each target text the numbers of content and function words were counted, and the number of content words divided by the number of function words to give a proportion. For example, a candidate who used 75 content words and 86 function words scores 75/86 which equals 0.8.

Implications of the case study

The analyses of translations of the *Unemployment* text point strongly to a range of textual competence among the candidates. In most of the measures, it is found that Group 1 presents English that is structurally substandard. While the structural standard of English improves in Groups 2 and 3, a degree of textual competence emerges in Group 4. This progression can be seen more clearly in Tables 4.12 and 4.13 (overleaf). In Table 4.12 I have grouped the analyses that seem to give a broad picture of textual competence, reversed the signs of some of the criteria and renamed them to reflect the favoured choice. Thus *average word length* becomes *longer words*, *more verbs* has its sign reversed and becomes *more nominal*, *content/function words* becomes *more content words*, *more direct translations* is reversed in sign and becomes *more indirect translation*, and *words shifted* becomes *more grammatical shifts*.

In Table 4.13 I have grouped the analyses that seem to indicate general language competence – at the subtextual level – as well as the translation

TABLE 4.12   Measures of textual competence

	Group 1	Group 2	Group 3	Group 4
Longer words	−0.06	−0.44	0.15	0.31
More nominal	0.62	−0.48	−0.10	0.23
More content words	0.39	−0.48	0.10	0.13
More indirect translation	0.28	−0.45	0.05	0.23
More grammatical shifts	−0.56	−0.41	0.42	0.25
Mean	0.13	−0.42	0.12	0.23

TABLE 4.13   Measures of general language competence

	Group 1	Group 2	Group 3	Group 4
Accurate spelling	−1.10	−0.03	0.02	0.67
Text fully translated	−1.01	−0.03	0.33	0.25
More varied vocabulary	−0.08	−0.38	−0.17	0.98
Examination test score	−1.84	−0.46	0.41	1.07
Mean	−1.11	−0.42	0.15	0.74

examination score, which is based very much on marking target language errors. *Tokens misspelt* has its sign reversed and becomes *accurate spelling*, *words omitted* is also reversed to become *text fully translated*, and *lexical variety ratio* becomes *more varied vocabulary*.

I propose, then, that among second language translators it may be possible to describe three main levels of competence. At the most basic level are those with *substandard competence* – in the case study represented by Group 1. The next level might be called *pretextual competence*, cutting in in Group 2 and extending well into Group 3. For this group, English competence is as yet bounded by the sentence – the effort of constructing a well-formed sentence from whatever components come to hand demands all their powers. The third level could be called *textual competence*. This begins towards the upper limits of Group 3 and extends through Group 4. These three levels are summarized in Table 4.14 with their defining characteristics.

Examples of the three competence levels

The examples below epitomize the three levels of competence in that each translator received the optimum combinations of scores typifying his/her level.

TABLE 4.14   Defining characteristics of the three levels of competence

Level of competence	Characteristics of text at this level
Substandard	Spelling is very inaccurate; source text is not fully translated and target text is short; function words are often omitted so that text contains high proportion of content words, especially nouns; translation is rather indirect because of efforts to cope with poor target language repertoire.
Pretextual	Spelling is accurate; source text is fully translated; text is long and strung-out because of use of function words rather than lexicalizations; vocabulary is not varied; translation is structurally very close to the source text; style is more 'verby'.
Textual	Spelling is accurate; source text is fully translated; text is short and syntactically dense through the use of lexicalizations; style is more nominal, and words are longer and more varied; the text is structurally more distant from the original because of grammatical shifts and indirect translation of source text words.

Substandard competence: Subject 61

The unemployment considered as the worst problem facing the world seldom a country dosn't suffer from this problem in the mean time. Even alto of people untill recent time think that in some country you never find unemployed people there because the rich & wealth of that country or the result of economic system with that country practise. The social unemployment result is worth than the unemployment itself by the time we see the developing country provindind the benifit for the unemployed to assist them to find a better employment. In the next side we find a lot of social problems and self desease which very hard and difficult for the specialist to valuate that result in long term and suburbs which the high level of financial and social people live will deffinily be effected from the result which caused unemployment in the othe suburbs.

Pretextual competence: Subject 58

Unemployment is regarded one of the most difficult problem, whic faces the world these days. It is hard to find a country which do not suffer from this problem in these days despit the fact of many believers thought recently that in some country do not exist this problem and that due to the weath which benefit these cuntries or due to the conomic system which they carry out The social consequence of the unemployent problem is far more worse than the problem itself. On one hand we saw the of the well-advanced countries providing unemployment-benefits to the people who have no jobs until they get the suitable ones but we find on the other hand that a group of social and psycholigical sickness has risen and emerged out which makes the experts hardly to estimate the The top government official have said that they are sure about the people who live in the areas which enjoy a social and economic high standard of living will be effected with the consequences of the unemployment problem which exist in the other places.

Textual competence: Subject 68

Unemployment is regarded as one of the worst problems facing the world. As there is hardly a country which does not suffer from this problem in our present time, This is despite the believe held by many people until recently that some states can not have unemployed people, either because of the wealth enjoyed by those states, or as result of the economical regimes they adopt. The social consequences of unemploy-ment are much harder than unemployment itself Because while we see that developed states provide benefits to help the unemployed until they can find suitable jobs, we see on the other hand a number of psychological and social diseases which experts find difficult to estim-ate their costs on the long run. Officials emphasise that areas of high social and economical standard residents will inevitably become affected by the consequences of unemployment in other areas.

Concluding remarks

What this chapter has shown is the fruitfulness of an interlanguage/ acquisition approach to second language translation. By conceiving of textual competence as a continuum, it is possible to hypothesize that the ability to translate into a second language develops in a systematic way. Although cross-sectional data of the kind presented here cannot properly test a developmental hypothesis, we can nevertheless mount a strong indirect case to support the notion that textual competence develops systematically.

One of the aims of this book is to identify the components of transla-tion competence, and the preliminary study confirms that target language competence is an important element. It particularly points to the fact that translators into the second language exhibit a range of ability in deploying language at the level of the text. Finally, it opens up useful avenues for exploring levels of competence in translation. Where much translation assessment operates by describing the deficiencies of the target language text, we can now propose a method that describes the competence of the producer of the text. The groundwork is thus laid for further exploration that is reported in subsequent chapters, where, in particular, the roles of lexis and grammar are investigated in the context of textual competence.

Notes

1. See Chapter 3 for discussion of what constitutes first language or second language among a typical group of translation course applicants; identifying first language and second language is often far from easy.
2. In Tables 4.3–4.11 it will be seen that the mean scores of the four groups form U-shaped curves on some analyses. In such distributions, the significance of differences among groups obviously cannot be tested because the differences between groups at the points of the U are cancelled out. When the Kruskal–Wallis test is applied, the values of H obtained for the nine analyses are 5.26, 24.68, 12.62, 3.29, 2.92, 5.63, 6.26 and 3.29. A cursory check with Tables 4.3–4.11 will show that trends or significant values are not obtained for U-shaped curves. A value of at least 7.82 is required at the 0.05 level of significance (df = 3).
3. The term 'verby' is used in preference to 'verbal' to avoid ambiguity – it means, of course, 'having more verbs' rather than 'spoken'.

5 Translation competence and grammar

Aims

This chapter draws on the resources of genre and second language acquisition theory in at attempt to come to an understanding of the way that grammar is deployed by second language translators to make texts. The central proposition is that a target language system can be identified and used as a yardstick against which the developing competence of translators can be measured. The yardstick is based on the work of Douglas Biber, to which I will devote a fairly solid introduction later.

Towards the end of Chapter 4, I gave samples of target translations that represented the three levels of textual competence suggested by the case study. The kind of writing in these samples will be familiar to any reader who has taught translation or English writing to second language speakers of English. The reader might also be familiar with the feelings of apprehension when, as a teacher, one has to provide constructive feedback to the writers. The instinctive reaction is to mark the individual errors, and I am sure that legions of translation students have pored over red-scored assignments with feelings of gloom about their rate of progress, and with little global understanding of how their writing compares with that of a native speaker. The field of translation studies has not, unfortunately, given us a method to respond in a way that reflects an understanding of how textual competence develops.

The grammatical task of the second language translator

Let us briefly review the grammatical task faced by the second language translator. The first challenge is to get the mechanics of the target language grammar more or less correct at the sentence level – matters of concord, word order, inflectional morphology, and so on. At the level I call pretextual, translators have achieved this. The next challenge is to deploy the target level grammar for a particular text type in a way that mimics the performance of a native writer; translators at the textual level are able to do this. In the case study presented in Chapter 4, I addressed the question of text type only in a casual fashion. The Arabic source text used for the study was more formal than informal, and definitely written rather than oral in mode. These are, however, fairly rough and ready labels for the text type. The present chapter focuses much more precisely on text type. Fundamentally, it compares the grammatical features of target texts of second language translators with the grammatical features of authentic English text types to ask the question 'how faithful are the target texts to similar texts written by native speakers?'

Now, in order to make such comparisons, we need to know something about how grammar is deployed in authentic text types – we need a set of norms. The most comprehensive attempt to describe the norms of English text types is to be found in Biber (1986, 1988), and I will rely heavily on the latter work. Biber's work is, of course, closely related to, and indeed originates from, earlier work that tried to describe the differences between spoken and written English.

What we will see is that translators into English as a second language systematically vary in their use of certain structural features and that this inter-subject variation resembles the variation between informal spoken and formal written English genres. At this point we can propose a working definition of textual competence: *translators demonstrate textual competence when their target texts have the structural features of formal, written English; they fail to demonstrate textual competence when their output resembles informal spoken English.*

The data used in this chapter will be the target texts of a number of aspiring translators who sat for public accreditation examinations in Australia. The source texts are pieces of formal Arabic typical of that found in editorials and discussion in the press.

Biber's multi-feature/multi-dimensional approach to genre variation

It is worth spending a little time describing Biber's multi-feature/multi-dimensional approach to genre variation as described in Biber (1988). The model provides a powerful tool for quantifying the features associated with certain genres in English[1] by establishing norms for the microlinguistic exponents of those genres. A range of written and spoken texts is analysed for some 67 linguistic features that are considered to signal stylistic variation. This pool of features is derived from a wide review of earlier authorities on the topic. Factor analysis is used to generate seven 'dimensions', the salient features of which are shared to a greater or lesser extent among the dimensions. This multi-dimension solution precludes the possibility of declaring that there is a sharp break between the linguistic features of written and spoken English. Instead, the dimensions form an intertwined network. The seven dimensions and their titles are shown in Table 5.1.

TABLE 5.1   Stylistic dimensions in Biber's (1988) multi-feature/ multi-dimensional approach to genre variation

Dimension 1:	Informational versus Involved Production (p. 107)
Dimension 2:	Narrative versus Non-narrative Concerns (p. 109)
Dimension 3:	Explicit versus Situation-dependent Reference (p. 110)
Dimension 4:	Overt Expression of Persuasion (p. 111)
Dimension 5:	Abstract versus Non-abstract Information (p. 112)
Dimension 6:	On-line Informational Elaboration (p. 114)
Dimension 7:	This dimension is not defined: 'The factorial structure of Factor 7 is not strong enough for a firm interpretation.' (p. 114)

To give a flavour of the genre types characterizing each dimension, the genres at the extremes of each dimension (extracted from Biber (1988), Figures 7.1–7.6) are shown in Table 5.2.

TABLE 5.2   Genres at the extremes of stylistic dimensions

Dimension	Genres
1	telephone conversations < > official documents
2	romantic fiction < > broadcasts
3	official documents < > broadcasts
4	professional letters < > broadcasts
5	academic prose < > telephone conversations
6	prepared speeches < > mystery and adventure fiction

The multi-dimensional nature of the model is evident in the way in which certain features are salient for two or more dimensions. Thus, word length has a high loading for both Factors 1 and 2; longer words are typical of both Informational Production and Non-narrative Concerns. On the other hand, private verbs[2] load highly for Factor 1 in Involved Production, but not for Factor 2 in Narrative Concerns, while past tense verbs load highly for Factor 2 in Narrative Concerns, but not for Factor 1 in Involved Production (see Biber, 1988: 102–3, Table 6.1).

The model goes on to compute Factor Scores and to test the statistical significance of each dimension (see Biber's Chapter 7). This procedure serves to 'indicate the importance of each dimension in distinguishing among the genres' (p. 126). All six dimensions (the seventh undefined dimension is discarded) have strong, but different capacities to predict genre distinctions. The relative predictive strengths of the dimensions are illustrated in Table 7.2 (p. 127), reproduced here as Table 5.3.

TABLE 5.3   Capacities of dimensions to predict genre distinctions

Dimension	F value	Probability (p)	R*R (%)
1	111.9	p < .0001	84.3
2	32.3	p < .0001	60.8
3	31.9	p < .0001	60.5
4	4.2	p < .0001	16.9
5	28.8	p < .0001	58.0
6	8.3	p < .0001	28.5

Source: Biber, 1988: 127.

While Biber states that 'the present study makes no simple two-way distinction between texts produced as speaking and those produced in writing' (p. 160), he concedes that 'it is meaningful to discuss the typical or expected types of discourse in each mode, associated with the typical situational characteristics of speaking and writing' (p. 161). From this standpoint, Dimensions 1, 3 and 5 can be considered 'oral/literate dimensions' (p. 162). Before I go on to outline how I will use this model, I will briefly expand on the nature of these three dimensions.

In the case of Dimension 1, two parameters are involved. On the one hand, the primary purpose of the writer or speaker will be at issue – is it 'informational' or 'interactive, affective and involved' (p. 107)? On the other hand, are the circumstances in which the text is produced – 'careful editing possibilities . . . versus circumstances dictated by real-time constraints' (p. 107). The main structural features that mark the Informational extreme on this dimension are a high proportion of nouns and prepositional phrases, longer words and varied vocabulary. Dimension 3 'seems to distinguish between highly explicit context-independent reference and nonspecific, situation-dependent reference' (p. 110). Relative clauses (WH relatives on object and subject positions, and pied-piping relatives) are the main structural feature marking the highly explicit extreme. Dimension 5 has to do with the distinction between abstract and non-abstract information. Passives are the main structural feature that typify the abstract extreme of this dimension.

An outline of the use of the model

Biber's model gives structural norms for specific genres. I have suggested that one measure of the textual competence of translators into English as a second language is the extent to which their target texts reflect the norms of primary texts of the same genre. For example, does the individual's translation of an official document adhere to the stylistic norms of an authentic official document in English? Or does it more closely correspond to the norms of face-to-face conversation? In Cummins's (1991) terms, we are assessing the extent to which the translators demonstrate in their translations Academic versus Conversational Proficiency. Similar distinctions are made by Tannen (1982) (involved versus detached) and Snow et al. (1991) (decontextualized and contextualized).

In practice, we can use Biber's model to describe this aspect of textual competence in the following way:

(a)   A corpus is gathered of translations by different subjects of texts representing a specific genre.
(b)   The translations are analysed for some of the linguistic features that characterize the genre.
(c)   The results of the analyses for each subject are compared with the norms for the genre.
(d)   The subjects' textual competence is described in terms of the similarity or difference between their performance and the norms.

Relevant aspects of Biber's model

The use of Biber's model needs to be limited to a number of aspects that impinge on translation. First, I propose to use only Dimensions 1, 3 and 5 since they allow us to focus on the oral/literate dimension. Secondly, I propose to restrict the number of genres to one which is typical for the selection of source texts in these data. This genre is *press editorials*. While many of the other genres are represented in the materials of translator training courses, this type seems to predominate and is very typical of accreditation examination scripts.

While the analytical power of the model is clearly a great advantage, a problematic feature is that it takes both a *structural* approach and a *semantic* approach. For an analysis of translations, the syntactic aspect seems to be more relevant because the translator has no real say in the creation of the ideational meaning; this job has been done by the source text writer. The second language translator's task with press editorials is to repackage meaning in a fashion that corresponds to the stylistic norms of native writing, but not to create new meaning; the source text writer is largely responsible for ideational and interpersonal meaning, while the translator is responsible for textual meaning.

The central point here is that one needs to distinguish between Biber's structural features, which offer the translator a choice, and semantic features, which do not because they are constrained by the meaning of the source text. Let us take a little time to make this point clear.

If a source text contains a private verb (or its semantic equivalent in another grammatical guise), such as *think* or *consider*, then a private verb or its equivalent will be required in the target text. If the source text says something like 'the president believes . . .', the translator is not at liberty to change the ideational content by rendering the text as 'the president declares . . .'. The choice, or rather lack of choice, is dictated by the meaning of the source text. On the other hand, if the source text contains a relative clause that can be glossed as 'the speech which the president delivered . . .', the translator has the choice to translate the full relative clause or a reduced relative clause (Biber uses the term WHIZ deletion). The target text could read 'the speech which the president delivered . . .' or 'the speech the president delivered . . .'. The translator could even passivize the verb to render either 'the speech which was delivered by the president . . .' or 'the speech delivered by the president . . .'. The ideational content of the original will not be compromised by either syntactic choice. It is in the deployment of these optional structural strategies that Biber's model is most insightful.

In fact, the model lacks the delicacy for it to be used to analyse stylistic aspects of lexis in translations, and for that reason I have taken a different approach with the question of lexis in Chapter 6. To return to the matter of private verbs, for instance, the only choices available to the translator here are among different lexical manifestations, for example, *believe* versus *reckon* versus *guess*, each of which might be more typical of one genre or another (*believe* in academic prose, *reckon* and *guess* in telephone conversations?). The only feature that Biber's model offers that could make stylistic distinctions among words like these would be *word length*; on the whole, one would expect Romance-derived words to be longer than Germanic-derived words, but this would be a very blunt instrument.

The full list of features used in Biber (1988: 223–45) is given in below:

Tense and aspect markers
1. Past tense
2. Perfect aspect
3. Present tense

Place and time adverbials
4. Place adverbials
5. Time adverbials

Pronouns and pro-verbs
6. First-person pronouns
7. Second-person pronouns
8. Third-person personal pronouns

Impersonal pronouns
9. Pronoun *it*
10. Demonstrative pronouns
11. Indefinite pronouns

Pro-verbs
12. Pro-verb *do*

Questions
13. Direct WH-questions

Nominal forms
14. Nominalizations
15. Gerunds
16. Total other nouns

Passives
17. Agentless passives
18. *By*-passives

Stative forms
19. *Be* as main verb
20. Existential *there*

Complementation
21. *That* verb complements
22. *That* adjective complements
23. WH-clauses
24. Infinitives

Participial forms
25. Present participial forms
26. Past participial forms
27. Past participial WHIZ deletion relatives
28. Present participial WHIZ deletion relatives

Relatives
29. *That* relatives on subject position
30. *That* relative clauses on object position
31. WH-relative clauses on subject position
32. WH-relative clauses on object positions
33. Pied-piping relatives
34. Sentence relatives

Adverbial clauses
35. Causative adverbial subordinators: *because*
36. Concessive adverbial subordinators: *although, though*
37. Conditional adverbial subordinators: *if, unless*
38. Other adverbial subordinators (having multiple functions)

Prepositional phrases
39. Total prepositional phrases

Adjectives and adverbs
40. Attributive adjectives
41. Predicative adjectives
42. Total adverbs

Lexical specificity
43. Type/token ratio
44. Word length

Lexical classes
45. Conjuncts
46. Downtoners
47. Hedges
48. Amplifiers
49. Emphatics
50. Discourse particles
51. Demonstratives

Modals
52. Possibility modals
53. Necessity modals
54. Predictive modals

Specialised verb classes
55. Public verbs
56. Private verbs
57. Suasive verbs
58. *Seem/appear*

Reduced forms and dispreferred structures
59. Contractions
60. Subordinator-*that* deletion
61. Stranded preposition
62. Split infinitives
63. Split auxiliaries

Coordination
64. Phrasal coordination
65. Independent clause coordination

Negation
66. Synthetic negation
67. Analytic negation: *not*

Of these, a selection was made using the following criteria:

(a)   Those that distinguish written from spoken genres.
(b)   Those that offer syntactic choices but are not concerned with the ideational meaning of the source text.
(c)   Those that occur frequently enough to yield statistically useful data.

The five features that met these criteria were: Nominalizations, Type/token, Word length, Agentless passives and Prepositional phrases.

The target texts and their processing

Fifty subjects' examination scripts were available. Each subject had been asked to translate two out of three Arabic passages into English. Of the 50 subjects, 34 were discarded. The 16 remaining had chosen the same two texts (*Africa* and *Finance*) and had completed both (in the sense that they had translated to the end of both). The discarded subjects had either not finished at least one text, or had chosen a third passage (*Einstein*). This provided a corpus of about 650 words of target text for each of the 16 subjects. The 32 handwritten target texts were transcribed with a word processor.

The algorithms described in Biber (1988: 222–45) were applied to the word-processed texts, with the various word-processor facilities employed to do the analyses semi-automatically.[3] The scores for each feature (except Type/token) were standardized to 1000 words so that they would be compatible with Biber's norms. An example follows:

Subject X's target text is analysed for agentless passives. Nineteen such constructions are found. The length of subject X's text is 367 tokens. Standardized to 1000 words, the agentless passive score is $19/367 \times 1000 = 51.77$.

The scores for the subjects are summarised in Tables 5.4 and 5.5 . In the tables, three columns are given for each feature. The first column shows the number of occurrences of the feature, standardized to 1000 words where appropriate. The second column gives a rating of L(ow), M(id) and H(igh): L is given for any score that is more than one standard deviation below the mean for that feature; H is for more than one standard deviation above the mean; and M is for more than any score that is within one standard deviation of the mean. The third column is the rank. On the extreme right of the table are two more columns: MEAN RANK is self-explanatory: it is the mean of the ranks of each feature. PROFILE is a listing of the ratings for each feature.

As I have mentioned, two texts were available from each subject. The reliability of the analysis clearly requires that similar scores are obtained for each subject across the two texts. In order to determine this, correlations were calculated between the *Africa* and *Finance* texts for each feature, and are shown in Table 5.6.

As can be seen in Table 5.6, Word length correlates best between the two texts, with a significance of less than $p = .005$. Agentless passive and Prepositional phrases are next, with correlations just higher than the .05 level. These three features, then, can be said with some confidence to be consistently used by subjects across the two texts. Next is Nominalizations, where no more than a trend can be claimed. Finally, Type/token appears to correlate very poorly across the two texts. However, there is one outlier (Subject 12) who scored 45.58 on *Finance* and 69.29 on *Africa*. If this subject is removed, the correlation coefficient is .59, which is significant at the 0.02 level (df = 13). It can be said, then, that, but for this one subject, there is a good correlation between the two texts on the Type/token feature. The texts for Subject 12 indicate substandard target language competence and some wide deviation from the ideational meaning of the *Africa* source text. Further discussion of the nature of the Type/token measure is taken up later in this chapter.

Finally, the profiles on the right of Tables 5.4 and 5.5 (pages 82 and 83) reveal considerable consistency across the features. In the *Finance* text, only two subjects (11 and 50) have ratings of H and L in their profiles; only four in the *Africa* text (12, 21, 31, 37) have H and L ratings. All other subjects have ratings in one category or two adjacent categories.

From this overview of the summary data it can be said with confidence that the analysis reveals systematic variation among the subjects. I now turn to the nature of that variation.

TABLE 5.4   Summary scores for five linguistic features: *Finance* text

Subject	N_NOM /1000	N_NOM Rating	N_NOM Rank	TYPETOKN t/t	TYPETOKN Rating	TYPETOKN Rank	WRDLNGTH n	WRDLNGTH Rating	WRDLNGTH Rank	AGLS PSV /1000	AGLS PSV Rating	AGLS PSV Rank	PREP /1000	PREP Rating	PREP Rank	MEAN RANK	PROFILE
8	21.80	M	6	49.32	M	6	5.00	M	8	13.62	M	13	108.99	M	4	7.4	MMMMM
9	13.51	L	1	52.03	M	9	4.90	M	4	10.14	M	9	101.35	L	3	5.2	LMMML
11	34.25	H	13	57.19	H	16	5.43	H	16	3.42	L	3	109.59	M	5	10.6	HHHLM
12	18.77	L	4	45.58	L	2	4.90	M	4	2.68	L	2	117.96	M	7	3.8	LLMLM
19	31.34	M	11	52.14	M	10	5.06	M	10	8.55	M	6	142.45	H	15	10.4	MMMMH
21	38.27	H	16	50.00	M	7	5.10	M	11	12.76	M	12	147.96	H	16	12.4	HMMMH
28	31.85	M	12	56.69	H	14	5.23	M	13	6.37	M	4	133.76	M	11	10.8	MHMMM
31	20.41	M	5	53.06	M	12	5.02	M	9	10.2	M	10	127.55	M	10	9.2	MMMMM
36	18.13	L	3	46.22	L	3	4.81	L	2	0	L	1	96.68	L	1	2	LLLLL
37	34.36	H	14	56.01	H	13	5.33	H	15	13.75	M	14	134.02	M	12	13.6	HHHMM
38	25.56	M	8	53.04	M	11	4.94	M	7	9.58	M	7	115.02	M	6	7.8	MMMMM
43	16.23	L	2	44.48	L	1	4.92	M	6	9.74	M	8	100.65	L	2	3.8	LLMLL
45	35.09	H	15	57.02	H	15	5.22	M	12	17.54	H	16	118.42	M	8	13.2	HHMHM
47	30.03	M	9	48.35	M	4	4.90	M	4	12.01	M	11	138.14	H	14	8.4	MMMMH
49	30.99	M	10	50.99	M	8	5.25	H	14	8.45	M	5	138.03	H	13	10	MMHMM
50	24.06	M	7	48.40	M	5	4.80	L	1	16.04	H	15	120.32	M	9	7.4	MLHMM

TABLE 5.5 Summary scores for five linguistic features: *Africa* text

Subject	N_NOM			TYPETOKN			WRDLNGTH			AGLS PSV			PREP			MEAN RANK	PROFILE
	/1000	Rating	Rank	t/t	Rating	Rank	n	Rating	Rank	/1000	Rating	Rank	/1000	Rating	Rank		
8	13.93	L	1	56.82	M	5	4.94	M	8	11.14	M	11	133.7	M	3	5.5	LMMMM
9	27.19	M	10	54.68	M	3	4.95	M	9	9.06	M	6	145.02	M	7	7	MMMMM
11	25.50	M	8	56.09	M	4	5.14	H	14	8.5	M	4	135.98	M	4	6.8	MMHMM
12	25.00	M	7	69.29	H	16	4.96	M	10	0	L	1	178.57	H	16	10	MHMLH
19	22.79	M	5	58.40	M	10	5.04	M	13	17.09	H	14	159.94	M	13	10.9	MMMHM
21	19.56	L	2	54.03	L	2	4.94	M	8	12.22	M	13	163.81	H	15	7.9	LLMHM
28	36.10	H	14	63.18	H	15	5.20	H	16	10.83	M	10	137.18	M	5	12	HHHMM
31	21.98	M	4	60.07	M	12	4.80	L	1	18.32	H	16	142.86	M	6	7.8	MMLHM
36	20.36	M	3	51.91	L	1	4.91	M	4	2.54	L	2	132.32	L	2	2.4	MLMLL
37	38.22	H	16	61.15	M	13	4.99	M	11	3.18	L	3	159.24	M	12	11	HMMLM
38	23.67	M	6	58.58	M	11	4.91	M	4	8.88	M	5	118.34	L	1	5.4	MMMML
43	26.76	M	9	58.19	M	9	4.93	M	6	10.03	M	7	160.54	M	14	9	MMMMM
45	30.93	M	11	61.86	M	14	5.15	H	15	10.31	M	9	147.77	M	8	11.4	MMHMM
47	32.45	M	12	57.52	M	7	4.90	M	2	17.7	H	15	156.34	M	11	9.4	MMHMM
49	32.91	M	13	57.97	M	8	5.04	M	13	10.13	M	8	151.9	M	10	10.3	MMMMM
50	36.41	H	15	57.42	M	6	4.91	M	4	11.2	M	12	148.46	M	9	9.2	HMMMM

TABLE 5.6   Correlations between feature scores on *Africa* and *Finance* texts

Feature	Correlation coefficient
Nominalizations	.30
Type/token	.13
Word length	.71
Agentless passive	.42
Prepositional phrases	.40

df = 14
p = 0.05 at .426 (one tailed)

Comparisons with Biber's norms

The next step is to compare the norms for the translators with the norms for the genres analysed by Biber. To do this two genres were selected at the extreme ends of the written versus spoken spectrum, namely *face-to-face conversations* and *press editorials*. The minima, means and maxima for each feature were compared with those for the *Africa* and *Finance* translations. Each feature is discussed in the following sections.

Nominalizations

The minimum proportion of nominalizations found in the translations of *Africa* and *Finance* corresponds almost exactly to the minima in press editorials (see Table 5.7) at around 13.5/1000, as do the means at about 27/1000. Both the minima and means in the translations are well above those for face-to-face conversations. Maxima in the translations around 27/1000 are well above that for face-to-face conversations, and somewhat below that for press editorials. It can safely be said that the translations have a very similar distribution to the target genres. However, it should be remembered that the variation in Biber's genre scores is among *different texts*. In the translations it is among *different translators* working from the *same text*. In other words, on this feature the translators' ability to

TABLE 5.7   Minimum, mean and maximum scores for Nominalizations

	Minimum	Mean	Maximum
Face-to-face conversation	2.0	9.2	25.0
Press editorials	14.0	27.6	45.0
Translations of *Africa*	13.9	26.8	36.4
Translations of *Finance*	13.5	26.5	38.3

produce text resembling the target genre was distributed within the range found in authentic texts.

In his discussion of nominalizations (that is words that end in -tion, -ment, -ness, -ity) Biber cites their use 'to expand idea units and integrate information into fewer words' and to '[convey] highly abstract . . . information' (Biber, 1988: 227). Can the same interpretation be used to differentiate among translators of the same text? Let me turn to the second of Biber's points first. The abstractness or concreteness of a translation is primarily a function of the ideational meaning of the source text. If the source text contains an abstract notion like 'liberation', then an acceptable translation will have to contain an abstract counterpart. Similarly, a concrete notion like 'oil' will have to be translated concretely. This use of nominalizations, then, is not likely to account for major variation in translations.

The matter of integrating information into fewer words is less related to the ideational meaning of the source text; for example, the nominalization 'incarceration' has the same ideational meaning as the string 'putting somebody into prison', which contains no nominalization. One would expect, then, that among the translators the major source of variation would be in the ability to pack information into fewer words.

This is more or less borne out by an examination of three *Finance* translations, although the picture is by no means clear cut. Subjects 37, 38 and 9 scored high, average and low respectively on the Nominalizations feature. A number of strings of text are shown below, where at least one subject used a nominalization. With each string is shown a gloss, designated 'G'.

String A
9   the people of the colonies
38 the colonial people
37 the colonized [N_NOM nations]
G   peoples – colonies

String B
9   thes countries failed
38 they have not a remedy
37 The latter were losing the [N_NOM ability]
G   loss – these – states – the-ability

String C
9   by spending
38 by the [N_NOM government] spending
39 through [N_NOM government] expenditure
G   by-means – expenditure – government

String D

9   To achieve full [N_NOM production], whether materialistic or humaine

38 To activate the [N_NOM production] using human and other resources

37 To achieve full [N_NOM employment] of human and material resources

G   for-realisation – the-employment – the-full – of-the-system – the-productive – the-material – and-the-human

String E

9   and [N_NOM revelutions] bursted

38 changed into social uncontrollable explosions

37 have turned into enormous explosions

G   change – to – explosions – social – wide

String F

9   To compensate the indepent countries

38 To compensate the newly independent countries

37 To compensate the newly-independent [N_NOM nations]

G   for-compensation – the-countries – the-liberated -from – the-colonisation

String G

9   the loss which they excersied during the [N_NOM occupation]

38 from their long [N_NOM exploitation]

37 for years of economic looting

G   for-the-looting – the long

String H

9   the developed countries

38 the rich countries

37 the developed [N_NOM nations]

G   the-countries – the-advanced

String I

9   and sometimes the truth hidden behind opposit to a theory

38 most of the time the [N_NOM realities] standing for them opposes what they say at the first glance

37 Often the facts behind them are contrary to what may be suggested by a superficial [N_NOM examination]

G   often – be – the-facts – the-hidden – behind-them – opposite – to-what – they-say-it – from – look – superficial

String J
9 and [can] not be understood
38 could not be understood and comprehended
37 Their meaning and [N_NOM implications] cannot be understood
G and-not – is-possible – understanding-them – and-knowledge – meanings-their

Several different phenomena are evident from these data. First, Subject 37 uses *nations* in Strings A, F and H, a word that is not a nominalization but is nevertheless captured by the algorithm. The word *government*, used by Subjects 38 and 37 in string C, is of the same type.

Secondly, there are nominalizations that represent abstract notions in the source text. One is to be found in String B, where only Subject 38 produces the reasonably faithful translation *losing the ability*. Another is to be found in String D, where Subjects 9 and 38 incorrectly produce *production*, and 39 produces *employment*. In String G, a similar situation occurs, but with the additional problem of a metaphor. Subjects 9 and 38 used the nominalizations *occupation* and *exploitation*, evidently to reduce a metaphor to sense; Subject 37 was more confident about transferring the metaphor and successfully used an English gerund to do so. String E is similar; Subject 9 seems to feel uncomfortable with the metaphor *explosions* and attempts to use *revolutions*.

Yet another phenomenon occurs in String I. Here the source text requires an abstract noun; of the three, Subject 38 uses a nominalization *realities*, but either of the alternatives would have done the job.

Finally, Subject 37 uses two nominalizations for integrating information in Biber's sense. One is in String I, where the subject repackages the source text with a passive and the nominalization *examination* for *look*. The second is an elegant piece of translation that warrants a close look. In String J, there are two source text verbal nouns, which can be glossed as *understanding* and *knowledge*. The object of *understanding* is *them*, and the object of *knowledge* is their *meanings*. This part of the string contains three content words. Subject 37 seems to be uncomfortable with the closeness in meaning of the two verbal nouns, but has preserved the three-word arrangement by translating one verbal noun into a passive *be understood*, and splitting *meanings* into the two terms *meaning* and *implication*, this last being a nominalization.

To summarize, then, of the occasions where nominalizations are found, perhaps three are not nominalizations at all, another five or six reflect abstract notions in the source text, and two (used by one subject only) are used to repackage information. This is largely in line with the prediction at the beginning of this section: abstract notions in the source text are likely to turn up as nominalizations in the target text, and their occurrence will not necessarily demonstrate the ability to use a formal written genre; but their use to repackage information is likely to vary from one translator to another and be an indicator of textual competence.

Type/token

This feature is discussed together with Word length in Biber (1988: 238– 9) as a measure of lexical specificity. In Table 5.8, it is clear that the Type/token means for the translations resemble those for *press editorials* and are considerably higher than those for *face-to-face conversations*. Minima and maxima also resemble those for *press editorials*.

TABLE 5.8   Minimum, mean and maximum scores for Type/token

	Minimum	Mean	Maximum
Face-to-face conversation	39.0	46.1	60.0
Press editorials	48.0	54.4	62.0
Translations of *Africa*	54.0	58.6	69.3
Translations of *Finance*	44.5	51.3	57.2

In his discussion of Type/token, Biber claims that lexical specificity 'truly correlates with the production differences between speaking and writing' (p. 238), and discusses its use by many earlier researchers. 'Longer words' claims Biber, 'also convey more specific, specialized meanings than shorter ones' (p. 238).

In translations, one would again expect two sources of variation in lexical specificity. The source text itself ought to have an influence on the Type/token ratio; the bigger the number of separate ideas expressed in the text, the higher the ratio is likely to be. For example, a discursive text where the same ideas are discussed from different standpoints should have a lower ratio than a progressive one where new subject matter unfolds. This should not be a significant source of variation among different translators of the same text, and ought to happen only under these circumstances:

(a)   Where a translator uses a number of target language synonyms of a single source text notion, for example, *nation, country, state* for *dawlah*.

(b)   Where a translator uses a single target word to render several near-synonyms in the source text, for example, *country* for *dawlah* and *waṭan*.

I believe that these two sources of variation are likely to be of very little significance in the texts used here. The texts contain virtually no near-synonyms; the only occurrence of (b) was the use of the synonyms like *country* and *state* in a handful of subjects. This aspect will not be pursued further.

The other source ought to be the translator's capacity to package information in longer and fewer words. In turn, this ought to be related to the proportion of content versus function words; one might expect higher Type/token ratios in texts with a high proportion of content words and lower ratios in texts that depend on function words to string semantic content together. This is because the number of types of function word is limited and relatively small. Indeed, one might argue that the function words are typically among those that 'become shorter as they are more frequently used and more general in meaning' (Biber, 1988: 238). One should, however, bear in mind the U-shaped distribution that was found in the exploratory study in Chapter 4. Here I suggested that in 'substandard' subjects one would find telegraphic text where function words were omitted, in 'pretextual' subjects one would find strung-out text rich in function words, and in 'textual' subjects there would be denser, more lexicalized text.

To summarize, then, variation in the Type/token ratio among the subjects may occur as follows:

(a)   Ratios may be lower where more function words are used.
(b)   Ratios may be higher where fewer function words are used.
(c)   The tendency described in (b) ought to be observed both in subjects with substandard language competence and subjects with textual competence.

To test these proposals I examine the *Africa* texts of Subjects 36, 50, 49, 37 and 28 whose Type/token scores are distributed from low to high. The proportions of function words and content words for each text were calculated; these can be found in Table 5.9. To calculate function words, a count was made of all determiners, prepositions, demonstratives,

TABLE 5.9   Function words in target texts of varying Type/token ratio

Subject	36	50	49	37	28
Type/token	51.91	57.42	57.97	61.15	63.18
Content words	53.18%	51.26%	53.00%	54.29%	56.68%
Function words	46.19%	48.74%	47.00%	45.71%	43.32%

complementizers (for example, *to*, *that*), conjunctions, pronouns, auxiliary verbs, modal verbs, WH-words, as well as all forms of *do*, *have* and *be*. All the remaining words were classed as content words.

Table 5.9 partly confirms the prediction: Subjects 50 and 49 have moderate Type/token ratios and high proportions of function words; Subjects 37 and 28 have high Type/token ratios and low proportions of function words. Subject 28 has substandard target language skills and has produced dense, telegraphic text. The odd person out is Subject 36.

Suspicions about Subject 36 are raised when some of the subject's other scores are examined. First, the subject scores lowest on Word length; secondly, he/she has produced a very long text. Subject 28 has almost the opposite pattern, with the highest word length score and very short text – the perfect descriptor of telegraphic text. Both subjects are, then, on the margins of the group, albeit at opposite ends.

The explanation for Subject 36's low Type/token ratio is to be found in the interactions of content and function types in the Type/token measure itself, and here we need to embark on a little theoretical discussion.

Function words (as operationally defined here) differ from content words in two important ways. First, they form a closed class and are therefore finite in their number of types; in fact around 45 types are found in the *Africa* texts. Secondly, because they are generally part of the syntactic building blocks of sentences, they must start to appear from the first sentence of a text. For these two reasons their separate types will have mostly occurred in the beginning of a text; as the text proceeds, only a few additional types will occur.

Content words form an open class, and their occurrence in a text is a function of the intentions of the writer, rather than sentence-level rules. For these reasons, their number of types will generally be higher, and will continue to increase after the bulk of the function types have occurred. The only reason for the number of types to dwindle as text length increases is semantic discursiveness.

In an idealized plot of function types and content types against text length, function types flatten out rapidly, and content types steadily increase. If the total Type/token ratio is plotted at various points in the unfolding of the text, the Type/token ratio continues to decrease even after the proportion of function words has flattened out – the continual decrease is caused by the steady increase in content types. The reason that Subject 36 scores relatively low on the Type/token ratio appears to be that the subject's text length has passed a critical point where there is no further increase in function types, but a continued increase in content types. The analysis of Subject 36's text in Table 5.10 shows precisely this. New function types occur rapidly until around 120–40 words into

TABLE 5.10   Cumulative occurrence of new function and content types

Cumulative word count	Function types – first occurence	Cumulative count of function types	Content types – first occurence	Cumulative count of content types
20	7	7	13	13
40	4	11	10	23
60	4	15	6	29
80	4	19	7	36
100	7	26	5	42
120	3	29	10	52
140	2	31	8	60
160	0	31	8	68
180	3	34	11	79
200	0	34	7	86
220	0	34	9	95
240	2	36	9	104
260	2	38	5	109
280	2	40	12	121
300	2	42	7	128
320	1	43	4	132
340	1	44	10	142
360	0	44	5	147
380	0	44	9	156

the text, and thereafter occur slowly, if at all. Meanwhile, new content types steadily increase throughout the text.

To return briefly to the difference between Subjects 36 and 28, each represents an extreme of translator behaviour: 36 is verbose and needlessly inventive; 28 is overly concise and gives in easily. In Chapter 6 I will introduce the notion of *disposition* to explore these behavioural facets of translators.

I conclude this discussion of Type/token with a brief summary. The subjects' translations had Type/token scores of a similar order to Biber's norms for press editorials. The variation among the translators' scores are related to their ability to package meaning in dense nominal strings or looser less nominal strings; in general, subjects with high Type/token scores may use less function words, while those with low Type/token scores use more function words. The Type/token analysis does, however, require caution. Subjects with substandard target language skills may also have high Type/token scores which reflect telegraphic text that omits function words. And where a text is very long but contains a high proportion of function words, the Type/token ratio is likely to be low because of the different rates of occurrence of new function and content types as the text unfolds; there is an interaction between text length and the Type/token ratio.

Word length

Word length is, as I have mentioned, considered a measure of lexical specificity and as such is said to mark the difference between spoken and written English (Biber, 1988: 238). The subjects' translations are both well above the norms for Biber's press editorials genre and very much higher than the face-to-face conversations (see Table 5.11). There appears to be no explanation for these high scores other than the nature of the semantic content of the source text. However, one suspects that the Standard Arabic found in press editorials may be highly nominal – this would be the subject of a separate study – and that this characteristic is transferred in translation.

TABLE 5.11   Minimum, mean and maximum scores for Word length

	Minimum	Mean	Maximum
Face-to-face conversation	3.8	4.1	4.3
Press editorials	4.4	4.7	4.9
Translations of *Africa*	4.8	5.0	5.2
Translations of *Finance*	4.8	5.1	5.4

The variation in word length among subjects is closely related to the Type/token ratio, and in turn to the proportions of content and function words, the latter being generally shorter than the former. This can be easily shown by correlating Word length with Type/token scores. For the *Finance* text, the correlation coefficient is very high (0.79, $p = <0.0005$); Word length undoubtedly increases with Type/token. For the *Africa* text, the correlation coefficient does not reach a level of significance (0.26). However, it is interesting to note that if the outlying Subject 12 is removed, then the correlation coefficient just approaches the 0.05 level of significance (0.42). If one accepts that Subject 12's data are anomalous, these correlations help to confirm the earlier conclusion that Type/token variation is closely linked with proportions of content and function words.

The clustering of subjects supports this interpretation. Three clusters can be identified, namely a cluster of subjects who score highly on both criteria on both texts (Subjects 37, 45 and 28), a mid-scoring cluster comprising Subjects 49, 19, 38 and 31, and a low-scoring cluster with 36, 21, 9, 8, 50 and 47. Three subjects – 11, 12 and 43 – behave inconsistently and cannot be grouped.

Agentless passive

Agentless passives, according to Biber,

> have been taken as one of the most important surface markers of the decontextualized or detached style that stereotypically characterizes writing. . . . In passive constructions, the agent is demoted or dropped altogether. (Biber, 1988: 229)

The translators' scores for Agentless passive are very similar to those for Biber's press editorials and much higher than those for face-to-face conversations (see Table 5.12), and I now turn to the possible reasons for this distribution in translated texts.

TABLE 5.12   Minimum, mean and maximum scores for Agentless passives

	Minimum	Mean	Maximum
Face-to-face conversation	1.0	4.2	11.0
Press editorials	7.0	11.7	19.0
Translations of *Africa*	0.1	10.1	18.3
Translations of *Finance*	0.1	9.7	17.5

The first observation is that this feature is much more closely related to the meaning of the source text than the features already seen; if the agent is absent in the source text, then one would expect it to be absent in the target text. Viewed simplistically, Agentless passives ought to occur in equal numbers in the target texts of various translators if they all convey the meaning of the source text.

This simple outcome would obtain presumably if there were a one-to-one correspondence between the Agentless passive construction and its counterpart in Arabic. However, although the Agentless passive is available in Arabic (for example, the *kutiba* form of the model verb *kataba* – *it was written* versus *he wrote*), there is a range of other structures which can yield an Agentless passive in English. Equally, there are alternatives to the Agentless passive in English. It is this potential structural asymmetry between source and target language structures that permits variation.

It also seems that variation in Agentless passive use is less systematic than other features. In the profiles in Tables 5.4 and 5.5, it is found that in most cases where there are non-adjacent ratings in a subject's profile, Agentless passive is anomalous: In *Finance*, Subject 11 has an anomalous low rating; in *Africa*, Subjects 12 and 37 have anomalous low ratings and 21 and 31 have anomalous high ratings. One can probably conclude that the variation in Agentless passive is motivated by a number of factors, among which textual competence may be just one.

In Table 5.13 the distribution of Agentless passives is shown for the *Africa* text. At the head of the columns target text glosses of source text strings are shown; a gloss is given whenever at least two subjects translated the source string with an Agentless passive. The Xs placed in the cells of the matrix indicate that an Agentless passive was used by the subject. The column marked *unique* contains the number of Agentless passives used by subjects that were not used by any other subject.

Two immediate observations can be made. First, if the unique instances are ignored, an implicational scale is beginning to emerge. Secondly, at least one subject – 31 – uses Agentless passives very idiosyncratically. Evidence for idiosyncratic use is also seen in Subject 37, whose very low score is at odds with high scores on other features.

Let us deal with two of these points, namely, the possible reason behind the emerging implicational scale, and Subject 37's low score. In the nine contexts that yielded Agentless passives in Table 5.13, the Arabic source text structures were noun + possessive pronoun (1), adjective (3), passive verb (3), active verb (1) and prepositional phrase (1).

No very obvious pattern emerges from these source language structures, but the matter is worth a little more exploration. The crux of the problem is that there is no simple correspondence between Arabic and English verb forms. While syntactically passive forms of active Arabic verbs can be constructed (for example, *kutiba*), syntactically active verbs of some conjugations are semantically closer to English passive forms in that their syntactic subjects may take the semantic role of patient. An example is the conjugation known as Form V by western Arabists, which is often referred to as mediopassive. Examples are *tajammada*, glossed in the Hans Wehr dictionary as *to freeze, become frozen*, etc., and *ta'aqqada*, glossed as, among other things, *to be or become intricate or complicated*. What is likely is that the choice of Agentless passive in a translation owes a great deal to the translator's ability to match source language structures with anisomorphic target language structures. For example, part of the general language competence – not textual competence – of an Arabic–English translator is to know that a common option for translating Form V verbs is an English Agentless passive.

But if translators do not use Agentless passives, then what do they use instead? Subject 37 is a good example. His/her renditions are shown below in italics:

to be sold (to Moscow): *for sale to Moscow*
(what) is required: *what is required*
(which) was held (in San Francisco): *held in San Francisco*
(which) was complicated: *after the complication*

TABLE 5.13 Distribution of Agentless passives for translations of the *Africa* text

	to be sold	is required	was held	was complicated	was intended	are flooded with	is strangled	is limited to	is concerned	unique
47	x	x	x				x			
19	x	x						x		
21	x	x	x	x	x	x	x	x		
31			x	x		x				4
8	x									1
9	x		x							1
50	x		x		x	x				
49	x			x						
11				x	x					
45	x	x		x	x	x				1
38		x		x					x	
28	x	x				x				
43		x	x		x					
36										
37		x							x	
12										

(which) was intended (to be sold): *planned for sale*
(stores) are flooded with: *the siloes are flowing*
(life) is strangled: *life is suffocating*
(the answer) is limited to: *(omitted)*
(as far as the international market) is concerned: *on the international sphere*

What Subject 37 has done is to implement a number of grammatical shifts such as nominalization and reduced relative clause. The upshot is that Subject 37's renditions are less faithful to the structure of the original – the subject has been prepared to take some risks and to create a translation that owes more to the semantics of the source text than its grammatical structure. This suggests another facet of translation competence that I touched on earlier in this chapter – that of *disposition* – to attempt to explain the difference between a very verbose and a very concise translator. This facet will be raised in Chapter 6, where we will see evidence of a different kind to show that Subject 37 displays a *risk-taking* disposition.

To summarize, then, the Agentless passive feature may reflect textual competence, but it is likely that its use is more closely related to two other phenomena. One is the competence to match source language structures with appropriate target language structures – a question of language competence. The other is the phenomenon of disposition; it may be that more prudent translators prefer the safety of an Agentless passive compared to risk-takers who are prepared to focus on meaning at the expense of reflecting source language structure.

Prepositional phrases

The final linguistic feature is Prepositional phrase, said to be 'an important device for packing high amounts of information into academic nominal discourse' (Biber, 1988: 237). Table 5.14 shows that Prepositional phrase scores were on the whole higher than those for press editorials and much higher than for face-to-face conversation.

TABLE 5.14   Minimum, mean and maximum scores for Prepositional phrases

	Minimum	Mean	Maximum
Face-to-face conversation	64.0	85.0	112.0
Press editorials	101.0	116.3	138.0
Translations of *Africa*	118.3	148.3	178.6
Translations of *Finance*	96.7	121.9	148.0

To examine the relevance of Biber's claim from the standpoint of translated text, one can compare the highest and lowest rating subjects (21 and 36) for Prepositional phrases on the *Finance* text. The two target texts are listed segment by segment below, with a running commentary. Prepositional phrases are marked in bold type.

21 Perhaps the limited number **of years for the American reserve** To become deplete according **to expectations**, have passed,
36 Is it possible that the expected years **for using** up all the petrol have gone

Here, Subject 21 includes material not included by Subject 36 (*for the American reserve* and *according to expectations*), and expands *years* to *number of years*.

21 and the catastrophe does not seem To loom **in the horizon**.
36 and the crisis hasn't started yet.

In this segment, 21 uses a Prepositional phrase instead of 36's adverb.

21 As **to the price of oil**, it started again To fall
36 The price **of the petrol** is devaluating

Subject 21 uses an additional Prepositional phrase as a result of the focusing of the subject with *as*.

21 and the oil exporting countries are almost losing the ability To stop and resist this decline.
36 and it appears that those countries who export the petrol cannot stop or resist that devaluation.

Neither subject uses a Prepositional phrase in this segment.

21 How did this hapen, and what are the changes, **in the future** that will occur related **to the role of oil** along side other sources **of energy**?
36 How did that happen? What are the changes that the future will bring to **those countries** exporting petrol?

Here, Subject 21's adverbial *in the future* appears as a subject in 36; 21 has additional material in *sources of energy*.

21 What are the new plans To develop the energy sources **in the world of tomorrow**?
36 What are the new plans **in developing** the resources **of energy in the future**?

In this segment, the use of different complementizers gives 36 an additional Prepositional phrase (*in developing*); the additional Prepositional phrase in 21's rather grand *in the world of tomorrow* is compensated for by 36's clumsy possessive construction in *the resources of energy*.

21   What would the impact of these plans be on the relations between the countries and the peoples of the world?

36   and the effect of that all between all the countries of the world?

Here 21 has additional material in *on the relations*.

21   in the fifties and sixties peoples of the colonies were able To achieve political independence.

36   in the fifties and the sixties all the people who lived under foreign colonies have gained their independence.

In this segment, 36's *under foreign colonies* is not captured by Biber's algorithm; however, its occurrence is a result of a verbal construction (*who have lived*) not used by 21.

21   The process of national economic construction has started with energy and enthusiasm,

36   Those people have started building their own countries with great energy and enthusiasm.

Here 36's text is more verbal, with *building* for 21's *construction*.

21   coupled with the emergence of a socio-economic crisis in developed capitalist countries,

36   in the meantime a sociable and economical problems have started in the most advanced capitalists countries.

Again, 36's text is more verbal than 21's nominal rendition.

21   and the loss of their ability To treat this crisis with their own economic means.

36   These countries have failed To solve the crisis with their own economical means.

This segment reveals a similar contrast between 21's nominal construction and 36's verbal construction.

21   The present policies, based on the artificial encouragement of the international demand, by means of public expenditure

36   The actual policies of the most advanced countries aim To encourage the local demand with the government help

In this segment, 36 uses the verbal *to encourage*, while 21 uses the nominal *encouragement*. Similarly, 36 has an early main verb *aim*, while 21 modifies *policies* with a participial construction, delaying the main verb until a later segment.

21   To achieve the full employment **of people** and the economy,
36   To achieve full employment **to everyone.**

Here, both subjects use Prepositional phrases to essentially the same effect.

21   are exhausted and its accumulated negative aspects started To be transformed **into large-scale social eruptions** inside the capitalist countries.
36   These capitalists countries have used completely its own resources and that was the result **of a full explosion.**

Again, both use Prepositional phrases, although 36 has begun a new clause. Subject 21's *inside the capitalist countries* (not captured by the algorithm) appears in the guise of a subject in 36.

21   **For this reason,** the objective **of economic liberation** which was imposed **by third world national movements** and revolutions,
36   The free economy, that was rejected **by the movements** and revolutions **of the third world,**

Subject 36 has omitted material here, although the subject gains an additional Prepositional phrase by the possessive construction *the movements and revolutions of the third world.*

21   and the emergence **of voices** seeking the introduction **of radical changes into the international economic system**
36   also the voices that were asking **for new economical [ILLEG-IBLE]** aimed To achieve better life **to the countries**

In this segment, 36 has additional material in *the emergence.*

21   **in order** To compensate the liberated countries **from colonialisa-tion, for the long-standing theft to which** they were subjected **in order** To support their its own efforts
36   [OMITTED]

Subject 36 omits an entire segment here.

21   To narrow the gap **between themselves** and developed countries,
36   who [ILLEGIBLE] also To shorten the distance **between the new development** countries and the most advanced countries, which are threaten **by these movements.**

It is Subject 36 who adds material here in *by these movements.*

21 all these measures are considered To be a sign **of a problem by the capitalist countries** which are looking **for new methods for economic domination.**

36 The capitalists always try To find the way To rule economically.

Subject 21's passive yields a Prepositional phrase, while 36 omits material.

21 It's a big mistake To transform the changes which are happening **in the world into mere silent numbers.**

36 It is a big mistake To alter all the changes happening **in the world to only silent numbers.**

In this segment, both subjects produce structurally similar strings.

21 For numbers do not explain themselves **by themselves,**

36 Figures do not mean anything

Subject 36 omits material here.

21 and often the truth which are hidden behind them, run contrary **to what they say at face value.**

36 as **on most of the time** facts do not reveal the true story **of what is happening** behind the scene:

This time, 36 uses a Prepositional phrase instead of an adverb.

21 The numbers themselves need an explanation, and one could not understand them and comprehend their meaning **except through the essence of current changes** which are undergoing **in the international and social life.**

36 We need To explain these figures we cannot understand these figures unless we understand the real changes **in the social life in all the world.**

Finally, 21 has additional material in *except through the essence of current changes.*

   In summary, there are two major sources of difference in the quantity of Prepositional phrases. One is the omission or addition of material; Subject 21 has approximately 13 additional pieces of material framed as Prepositional phrases, while Subject 36 has two. The other major source is verbal as opposed to nominal text; about eight of 36's Prepositional phrases are motivated by verbal constructions which occur as nominal constructions in 21. Some differences in the use of Prepositional phrases also occurred because of such constructions as *of* possessive, adverbials framed as Prepositional phrases, and *by*-passives.

Biber's description of the stylistic function of Prepositional phrases is, then, largely vindicated for the target texts; they do indeed pack more information into a text, and they do reflect more nominal discourse.

Concluding remarks

In this chapter, we have seen that the occurrence of certain structural features varies systematically among the target texts of translators into the second language. This variation is fundamentally in line with the variation that occurs among different genres of English as described in Biber (1988). The analysis reveals that in translations of a text that can be located in the genre of *press editorials*, the distribution of structural features used by the subjects varies between that found in the genres of *face-to-face conversations* and *press editorials*. This variation can be said to reflect textual competence; this competence increases with the ability to produce text that is structurally closer to the target genre. In other words, it is possible to describe textual competence on the basis of an analysis of structural features.

We also saw that in translations there are often special motivations for variations in the distribution of structural features. For high ratings of nominalizations, the integration of information was a more frequent motivation than semantic abstractness. Variation in the Type/token ratio was related to the ability to package information into longer and fewer words; a common device to package information densely was the use of content rather than function words. Variation in Word length confirmed this claim, in that function words are generally shorter than content words. Variation in Agentless passive was found to be less related to textual competence. Here I suggested that it reflects the ability to match target and source language structures on the one hand, and on the other the disposition to produce text that is more or less faithful to the grammatical structure of the original text. Finally, variation in the use of Prepositional phrases was motivated by two factors: first, there were more such phrases where extraneous information was packed into a text; secondly, they occurred more frequently with nominal text and less frequently with verbal text.

Let me return to the question I framed towards the beginning of this chapter: how faithful are the target texts of second language translators to similar texts written by native speakers? We are now able to answer this question with some confidence: they vary in their resemblance to authentic texts, but not in a random way. Rather, the variation is systematic. In attempting to produce texts of the editorial discussion type, second language translators produce a range of versions that vary from those that have the structural features of formal written language to those that are structurally like spoken language. We have, then, clarified our understanding of at least one aspect of textual competence in second language translators and with this understanding at our disposal are a little closer to being able to design well-motivated syllabuses and testing instruments. We are also closer to being able to see a developmental pathway in second language translators which involves moving from the ability to produce written language based on the norms characteristic of speech to the ability to learn and deploy the norms of writing.

Notes

1. The terms genre and text type are used more or less interchangeably here.
2. Private verbs, according to Biber, 'express intellectual states (e.g. believe) or nonobservable intellectual acts (e.g. discover)' (1988: 242).
3. For example, Type/token is easily calculated by the following steps: replace each single space in the text with a carriage return to obtain a list; sort the list alphabetically; print to a file to obtain the word count (=tokens); manually delete duplicate words; obtain a new word count (=types); divide types by tokens.

6   Translation competence and lexis

Aims

In Chapter 5 I showed that textual competence in second language translators varied systematically. That chapter was confined largely to examining the deployment of grammatical devices, and said very little about lexis. In this chapter I will discuss textual competence in second language translators from the point of view of word choice, or lexical transfers. Again, the chapter is built around a case study which employs the same data used in Chapter 5; but this time I submit it to a quite different kind of analysis, which breaks some new theoretical and methodological ground. My examination of lexis will take us a little beyond the matter of the translator's deployment of the target language; it will start to probe the psychological motivations behind those choices. I hinted at this area of investigation in Chapter 5 when I mentioned disposition.

The fundamental aim of the case study is to discover whether second language translators differ systematically in their textual competence as manifested through word choice. The data, it will be recalled, was a set of Arabic to English translations undertaken in a public examination. The basic analytical procedure was to take a sample of words in the source texts and to compare the way the translators rendered them. This yielded two kinds of data, which in turn allow us to make proposals about two facets of translation competence.

First, there were purely quantitative data such as the number of candidates who left a word untranslated. Some translators made many more omissions than others, and it seems reasonable to describe this variation as a matter of *persistence* as opposed to *capitulation*: A persistent translator is one who omits as little as possible, while a capitulating one gives up when difficulties are encountered.

Another type of quantitative data was the degree of similarity among individual translator's renditions. If we examine the way 16 translators translate a specific word, a number of patterns emerge. Sometimes all or almost all produce the same version. In other cases there is one favourite and a number of runners-up, and sometimes there is little agreement at all. By comparing each translator's version of each word with every other translator's version it is possible to build up a purely mathematical picture of the similarity among them; some translators perform overall very close to the norms for the whole group, while some produce unusual translations. This variation can be described as a matter of *risk-taking* as opposed to *prudence*: prudent translators make choices close to the norm; the risk-takers produce unusual translations.

These quantitative data can, then, be used to build up a profile of each translator's *disposition* – the point at which the translator falls along the two axes of *persistent* versus *capitulating* and *risk-taking* versus *prudent*. In fact, when the translators were plotted on a grid, the *disposition profile* of each was found to be a useful way of characterizing their performance. I should add here that I do not make any strong theoretical claims about the nature of disposition and its relation to personality. As Berry (1993) has shown, links between language test performance and personality have not been especially evident, possibly because of the failure of researchers to use properly validated measures of personality. Investigating the correlation between disposition and independent measures of personality is beyond the scope of this book, but certainly begs to be done.

Secondly, there were qualitative data that could be found in the lexical transfers. I used this data to come to conclusions about the translators' textual competence, that is their ability to write translations in a way that reflected an ability to manipulate English stylistically. It was reasoned that since English was the second language of the translators, one would find a great variety of textual competence among them, ranging from those who simply translated sentences without regard to the style of the original, to those who showed almost native ability to write in the required style.

The basic method employed was to compare the different translations of each word and to decide whether one or other versions demonstrated textual competence. Textual competence here is defined as a choice that was apparently influenced by factors beyond the immediate sentence. An example of such a choice is where a translator uses an equivalent that carries a connotation that supports the overall tone of the text, such as *affluent* rather than *rich* – this example is discussed in detail later. A range of such strategies is described towards the end of this chapter. Of the 16 translators, two used strategies that showed that they looked beyond the sentence in making their choices. These were, incidentally, superior to most of the group on other grounds such as grammar and spelling. A third translator managed to use some textual strategies but was poor in grammar and made drastic changes to the sense of the source text.

In summary, then, the analysis of lexical transfers gave important insights into translation competence by providing a profile of translators' disposition, and by determining which translators were able to make choices using information beyond the immediate sentence. A detailed account of the investigation follows.

The disposition study

The data was the same corpus used in Chapter 5. A section from each text was chosen for analysis, the aim being to select about 40 source language words and their target language equivalents for each subject. Two criteria were used in selecting the passages:

1.   The section was to be at the beginning of the text in the belief that the subject would be 'fresher' and perform optimally; and that the words encountered would, naturally, be the first occurrence so that one did not have to be concerned about previous attempts, or attempts at the same word in different contexts.
2.   The section was to be syntactically straightforward in the sense that it did not call for difficult grammatical shifts.

In the event, the first paragraph of *Africa* yielded 20 semantically 'full' words. The first part of *Finance* contained a troublesome structure requiring grammatical shifts which, in most cases, led to subjects having to distribute the meaning of one source text word over several target language words. The third paragraph was more straightforward and yielded 19 suitable words.

Each subject's rendition of each word was entered on a table. In entering the renditions, the grammatical category was ignored, and a citation form of the word entered, usually the infinitive verb, singular noun or a root (for example, econom-). This procedure was followed because of the variety of grammatical guises in which the target versions found themselves; in listing the versions it was possible to control for grammatical category. In a few cases, a whole phrase was entered, or its head word if more than one subject had produced the same or a very similar phrase. Where a subject did not translate the source text word, that is no target language element could be found that represented its meaning, a blank was entered, and the number of omissions for each subject was counted.

A dissimilarity matrix (Woods et al., 1986: 252–4) was constructed by comparing the entries of each subject with every other subject. Matches and mismatches were counted, and a dissimilarity count was made by calculating the proportion of mismatches, for example, 10 mismatches and 10 matches gave a dissimilarity count of $10/20 = .50$. The calculations were entered into a dissimilarity matrix (see Table 6.1). The total

TABLE 6.1 Dissimilarity matrix for lexical transfers – *Africa* and *Finance* texts

	Mean dissimilarity	8	9	11	12	19	21	28	31	36	37	38	43	45	47	49	50
8	6.611825	0.00															
9	5.194176	0.34	0.00														
11	4.991378	0.50	0.21	0.00													
12	7.155128	0.67	0.44	0.45	0.00												
19	5.353258	0.34	0.31	0.28	0.55	0.00											
21	6.196384	0.49	0.34	0.34	0.60	0.24	0.00										
28	5.113712	0.35	0.38	0.26	0.36	0.33	0.39	0.00									
31	6.96439	0.50	0.48	0.44	0.40	0.48	0.55	0.42	0.00								
36	5.860054	0.48	0.30	0.28	0.52	0.37	0.38	0.44	0.46	0.00							
37	6.306971	0.51	0.43	0.39	0.60	0.29	0.39	0.44	0.54	0.37	0.00						
38	5.90111	0.50	0.28	0.28	0.30	0.38	0.50	0.26	0.43	0.35	0.48	0.00					
43	5.653977	0.36	0.38	0.38	0.45	0.36	0.42	0.35	0.35	0.36	0.28	0.48	0.00				
45	6.103116	0.38	0.43	0.40	0.43	0.42	0.48	0.39	0.46	0.47	0.34	0.44	0.36	0.00			
47	5.246395	0.42	0.32	0.21	0.48	0.33	0.31	0.24	0.50	0.32	0.35	0.35	0.35	0.37	0.00		
49	5.709379	0.46	0.34	0.32	0.41	0.31	0.36	0.29	0.44	0.39	0.44	0.50	0.38	0.34	0.39	0.00	
50	5.307829	0.31	0.21	0.26	0.48	0.34	0.39	0.21	0.50	0.39	0.44	0.36	0.40	0.39	0.30	0.32	0.00

dissimilarity count for each subject was calculated by adding the scores in the rows and columns for each.

Finally, the omission and dissimilarity scores were converted to z-scores and plotted against each other on a scattergram. Since z-scores have a mean of zero, the axes of the scattergram intersect at the centre of the graph, giving four quadrants. I use the term *disposition grid* to describe this graph, which we will see a little later.

Persistent versus capitulating

The omission score of each subject reflects their persistence, that is the extent to which they try to find equivalents for every source text item. A subject with high omissions is described as *capitulating* and one with low omissions as *persistent*. Although the number of omissions may reflect the subject's English repertoire, even quite poor subjects do persist and produce equivalents, even if they are inappropriate ones.

Risk-taking versus prudent

For most words, there appears to be an unmarked equivalent, defined operationally as the equivalent chosen by at least half of the subjects who offered an equivalent. The dissimilarity score reflects the extent to which a subject's choices resemble those of the group as a whole and, by implication, the unmarked equivalents. Subjects with a low dissimilarity score are described as *prudent*, that is they take the safest path. The interpretation of a high dissimilarity score depends on the subjects' English repertoire. Subjects with poor English are more likely to have a high dissimilarity score because they cannot even produce the unmarked equivalents. A subject with good English and a high dissimilarity score is one who knows the unmarked equivalents, but is willing to take a risk with unusual equivalents – a *risk-taking* translator.

Assessing disposition

The disposition of a subject is assessed by examining how the qualities of persistence and risk-taking interact. The four main categories are:

1. *Persistent and risk-taking*

Subjects in this category translate as fully as possible, and use unusual equivalents: Subject 8's English is very poor, whereas Subject 37's is good:

Subject 8
During the fifties and sixties many imperialized countries could achieve their Political dependence. And the scheme of national and economic building has begun with actively and enthousiastically. This happened side by side with the beginning of the Economic Social Crisis in the advanced Capitalism countries

While life in the African Continent is over suffering under the burdain of starvation and the creeping litus and the poisons of Volcano gases and the burning Civil War (The Sudan-Angola), The stores of the rich countries are flooding with extra grains.

Subject 37
In the fifties and sixties, the colonized nations were able to achieve their political independence. The task of building the national economies commenced with energy and enthusiasm. Meanwhile, the socio-economic crisis was surfacing in the developed countries.

While life in Africa is suffocating under the pressure of famine, locusts, poisons of volcanic gases and the flames of civil wars (Sudan-Angola), the siloes of wealthy nations are overflowing with huge grain surpluses.

2.   *Capitulating and risk-taking*

These subjects give up easily, and the equivalents they produce are more likely to be unusual ones.

Subject 31
In the fifties and sixties the occupied countries were able to regain their independency politicaly and started to build their economy nationaly with enthansiastic side by side with the obvious of the problem of the economy

While the life in Africa has been destroyed by some severe problems, famine, the attack of [. . .], gases from [. . .] and the national wars (Sudan-Angola there is an extra wheats in the storage rooms of the rich countries more than their needs.

3.   *Persistent and prudent*

Subjects of this type translate fully, using 'standard' equivalents.

Subject 50
In the 50's and 60's the people of the colonization could achieve their political independence, the operation of the national economy building

started actively and enthusiastically it occured with the rise of the socio-economy crisis in the advanced capitalized countries

When the Africa continent are suffering from starvation locus attacks, posinous volcanoe gases, civil war fires (Sudan & Angola) the rich countries' stores are surplus of a huge reserved quantity of grains.

4. Capitulating and prudent

These subjects also give up easily, and the equivalents they produce are 'standard' ones.

Subject 28
In fifties and sixties, people of colonies achieved political independence and started – actively and enthusiastically – to build their national economy. In the same time that advanced countries faced social and economical crisis

When African continent dies from hangar and volcanic gaz and national wars (Sudan, Angola) the rich countries warehouse are flooded with grains reserves and surpluses.

Subject 43
In the fifties & the sixties the undeveloped countries achived there political independence, and [. . .] building there national economy with great enthusiasm. Unfortunately they could not solve there economic problems.

While live is very harsh in Africa because of famine dies to invasion of loctus, poisonous volcanic gases and national wars. In other parts of the world silos have excess of grain for human consumption.

The disposition grid is shown in Figure 6.1 (overleaf), with each subject's position marked by their idenitification number. By locating a translator on the grid, we have a powerful and easily interpreted diagnostic of this aspect of translation competence.

The lexical transfers study

Here I examine the lexical choices made by the subjects and the way in which those choices reflect their textual competence. This analysis used the same set of data that was used to profile disposition. As mentioned previously, with some source text words there was little or no disagreement among the subjects over their translations. Clearly, the translations of these words are of no interest. I have, therefore, only examined in detail those cases where there was considerable disagreement among the

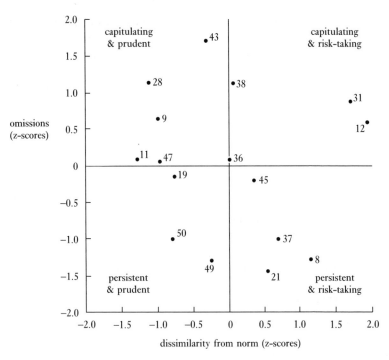

FIGURE 6.1   The disposition grid

subjects. For example, a word like *ḥurūb*, which all subjects translated as *wars*, is not considered.

The method used here is quite eclectic. Indeed, the analyses of each word reflect a process of trial and error. In essence, the alternative translations for each word are examined, and evidence is looked for that the word has been chosen using judgements based on factors beyond the sentence. Then, a network of choices is constructed for each word. Finally, a composite network is built up, and a number of strategies identified. In the following section, I present the choice networks for a number of lexical transfers. Judgements on meanings and equivalents in this analysis were checked against the *Hans Wehr* dictionary.

Choice networks

Source word: *takhnīq*

This word was by no means straightforward to translate, as the distribution of renditions shows; no rendition meets the definition of an unmarked choice:

suffocate	5/16
suffer	3/16
die	2/16
strangle	1/16
destroy	1/16
harsh	1/16
choke	1/16
stifle	1/16
run out	1/16

The first difficulty is that the root *ḵnq* denotes *throat*, so that *taḵnīq* can denote both the act of squeezing the throat and the act of cutting off the airway, that is *strangle* and *suffocate* respectively. The second difficulty is the metaphor of *strangling* or *suffocating life*. Eight of the 16 subjects chose to transfer the metaphor, three decided to reduce it to sense, and five used a different metaphor. Of those who chose to transfer the metaphor, seven chose the *suffocate* sense, and one the *strangle* sense. Of the *suffocate* sense, five used *suffocate*, one *choke* and one *stifle*.

Each of the three who chose to reduce the metaphor to sense used a different solution, and indeed a different sense, that is *harsh*, *destroy*, and (*life has*) *run out*. Of those who changed the metaphor, three used *suffer*, and two used *die*.

The strategies can be represented as a network of choices:

transfer metaphor
  SUFFOCATE: *suffocate, choke, stifle*
  STRANGLE: *strangle*
change metaphor
  suffer, die
reduce to sense
  harsh, destroy, run out

Note that in this network and those that follow, target words are written in italics, for example, '*choke*', and the names of strategies, for example, '*change metaphor*' in plain type. Upper case is used to indicate senses, for example 'SUFFOCATE'.

Source word: waṭ'

Again, there is not a clear unmarked choice, and there is considerable reluctance to translate the word at all:

pressure	3/16
impact	2/16

burden	1/16
threat	1/16
omissions	9/16

Waṭ' is an interesting example of anisomorphism. The *Hans Wehr* dictionary gives to its verbal root the sense of *tread (something) underfoot* and to the noun *waṭ'* the meaning *low ground, depression*. So much for non-metaphorical senses. The primary sense of *waṭ'* is listed by *Hans Wehr* as *pressure*, while the secondary sense is *oppression, coercion, compulsion, force*. What is found, then, is a metaphor in the source text word. The word *waṭ'*, by the way, is not used as an equivalent to *pressure* in such affectively neutral contexts as *blood pressure*, or even in the metaphorical context of *the pressure of public opinion*. Instead, the word *ḍagṭ* is used. *Waṭ'*, then, has a negative connotation that is not conveyed by *pressure*; and indeed those subjects who used *burden* and *threat* have tried to convey it by changing the metaphor.

I tentatively suggest this network of choices:

preserve sense
  choose equivalent without regard for connotation: *pressure*
shift sense
  choose equivalent without regard for connotation: *impact*
  choose new metaphor to reflect connotation: *burden, threat*

Source word: majāʿa

Three equivalents appeared, with *famine* the unmarked choice:

famine	9/16
hunger	5/16
starvation	2/16
omissions	0/16

This is a fairly straightforward case: Arabic has two words *jūʿ* and *majāʿa* derived from the same root, and denoting *hunger/starvation* and *famine* respectively. The network of choices looks like this:

preserve sense: *famine*
shift sense: *hunger, starvation*

Source word: zaḥf

There were three renditions of this word, and many omissions, with no unmarked choice:

attack	3/16
invasion	2/16
creep	1/16
crawl	1/16
raid	1/16
omissions	8/16

The source word is used non-metaphorically, that is it can be glossed as the *creeping/crawling* of locusts. Two main strategies have been used by the subjects. The first is to preserve the sense of *zaḥf* and render it as *creep/crawl*. This produces a poor translation, a fact recognized by those who took the second strategy – to use a military metaphor, that is *invasion/raid/attack*. Of these, *raid* and *attack* have a more intensive and violent sense than *zaḥf* and *invasion*. This is the network of choices:

preserve sense: *creep, crawl*
create military metaphor
ATTACK: *raid, attack*
INVASION: *invasion*

Source word: ahlīya

Every subject translated this word, with the majority choosing *civil*, so that there is an unmarked choice:

civil	11/16
national	5/6
omissions	0/16

The word occurs in the source text in the collocation *ḥurūb ahlīya* the translational equivalent of which is *civil wars*. In other contexts, *ahlīya* can have the sense of *popular* and *civil*; those who chose *national* here simply did not know the equivalent English collocation. The network of choices is as follows:

familiarity with equivalent collocation: *civil (wars)*
unfamiliarity with equivalent collocation: *national (wars)*

Source word: ṭarīya

All but one subject translated this word, with the majority choosing *rich*, the unmarked choice:

rich	9/16
wealthy	5/16

affluent   1/16
omissions   1/16

In this case, the source word *tarīya* can be translated as any one of *rich*, *wealthy* and *affluent*; indeed, the *Al-Mawrid* dictionary gives it as a definition for all three. The differences in English are largely related to context, although it could be argued that there is a difference of degree between *affluent* and the other two: hence, *I'm just affluent, but he's wealthy/rich*, but not *I'm just rich/wealthy, but he's affluent*.

Similarly, *affluent* may connote the style of life resulting from wealth, rather than the wealth itself, since one does not usually specify the source of affluence: hence, *mineral wealth* but not *mineral affluence*, and so on. This leads me to another subtle connotational difference: the word *rich* carries the potential for a negative (possibly envious) judgement by the speaker, thus *stinking rich, filthy rich* but not *stinking wealthy, filthy affluent*. The reason for this may be connected with the closer association of *rich* with cash. Lottery winners are more likely to shout 'I'm rich!', rather than 'I'm wealthy!' or 'I'm affluent!'.

For these subjects, the choice is very difficult. The text itself takes an accusatory line against the West, and one would expect a competent translator to reflect this attitude in their lexical choices where there is an opportunity to do so. In this case, the potential negative tone of *rich* (perhaps connoting *grasping, crass*, etc.) would seem to do the job, while the use of *wealthy* could reflect a neutral attitude. On the other hand, one could argue that the descriptions of the daily calamities of African life – civil war, locust plagues, poison gases – would contrast with the 'lifestyle' flavour of *affluent* (perhaps evoking images of modern cars, good housing, hygienic food, etc.). Finally, it may be that among the poorer subjects, *rich* is the first and only word to come to mind. The network of choices might be constructed like this:

only equivalent available: *rich*
alternative equivalents available
  reflect attitude of writer
    accusatory connotation: *rich*
    neutral connotation: *wealthy*
  contrast with African life: *affluent*

Source word: makāzin

The unmarked choice *store* is one of five versions offered by the subjects:

store   10/16
silo   3/16

container   1/16
warehouse   1/16
storage room   1/16

The marked choices seem to fall into two categories: those who used *silo* may have done so because they anticipated the contents of the *makāzin*, that is grain, which is mentioned towards the end of the sentence. This tactic is a risk-taking one that supplies more meaning than occurs in the source text.

The second category comprises subjects who chose equivalents that had the wrong range of application, that is container (too small), warehouse (not for bulk goods), and storage room (too small). These are the choices available to the subjects:

preserve sense
     translate at word level: *store*
     supply more meaning from text: *silo*
shift sense: *container, warehouse, storage room*

Source word: lahīb

Only half of the subjects translated this word:

flame   3/16
burn   1/16
zest   1/16
disaster   1/16
fire   1/16
omissions   8/16

The direct translational equivalent of *lahīb* is *flame*. The problem for the subjects was that it was used metaphorically. Their first dilemma was whether to transfer the metaphor on the lines of *the flames of civil war*. Three did so, and three more transferred the metaphor not with the translational equivalent but with the slightly different images of *burn, heat* and *fire*. One subject reduced the metaphor to sense with *disaster*, and one produced the odd *zest*. The choice network can be represented like this:

transfer metaphor
     translational equivalent: *flame*
     change image: *burn, heat, fire*
reduce to sense: *disaster*
mistranslate: *zest*

Perhaps the real puzzle here is why so many subjects simply omitted to translate an apparently easy metaphor. One possibility is that more prudent translators into the second language tend to avoid metaphors unless they are quite sure of their acceptability.

Source word: tafyīḍ

There was little apparent agreement here, but just a small number of omissions:

flood	4/16
overflow	3/16
full	2/16
omissions	2/16

The root *fyḍ* from which *tafyīḍ* is derived, is used to form words meaning *flood*, *deluge*, and so on; *tafyīḍ* has the primary sense of *overflow* and *flood* of rivers, which is extended in the text to refer to grains. The equivalents *overflow* and *flood*, then, preserve the sense, although *overflow* collocates with *siloes* better that *flood*. The subjects who offered *full* have missed part of the sense or perhaps shifted the sense; an equivalent for *tafyīḍ* needs to include the notion that the vessel cannot hold what is being poured into it – it must be *full to overflowing* and not just *full*. The choice network is shown below:

preserve sense: *overflow, flood*
shift sense: *full*

Source word: ḍak̲āma

This word ought to have been be fairly straightforward to translate (*Hans Wehr* gives *bigness, largeness, greatness* as the primary senses), but the large number of omissions testifies to the contrary:

huge	4/16
extra	2/16
excess	1/16
enormous	1/16
whole	1/16
large	1/16
omissions	6/16

Those who did translate it chose one of two main strategies. The first was to use an equivalent in the 'very large' semantic field, thus *huge*, *enormous* and perhaps *large*. The second strategy was to use an equivalent

that carries the rather different notion of 'more', thus *extra, excess.*
Underlying this second strategy may be an interference factor; Arabic
does not have a ready equivalent of *too*, and many Arabic speakers produce sentences such as *I have read too many books* rather than *I have read
a great many books*, apparently merging the notions of *very* and *excess.*
One subject mistranslated with *whole.* Here we suggest a network of
choices:

VERY LARGE: *huge, enormous, large*
VERY + EXCESS: *excess, extra*
mistranslation: *whole*

Source word: iḥtiyāṭi

There were few omissions with this word, and a clear unmarked equivalent in *reserve.* Hans *Wehr* gives *precautionary* as the primary sense:

reserve	8/16
surplus	3/16
more than	1/16
stocks	1/16
excess	1/16
omissions	2/16

Again, subjects chose one of two main strategies. One was to take the
sense of 'in reserve for future needs', hence *reserve, stocks.* The other was
to take the sense of 'more than is needed', hence *surplus, more than, excess.*
The choice network is as follows:

IN RESERVE FOR FUTURE NEEDS: *reserve, stocks*
MORE THAN IS NEEDED: *more than, excess*

Source word: hubūb

This word was relatively straightforward. While most agreed on *grain*,
three subjects missed the mark with *cereal* (too general), *wheat* (too
specific) and *crops* (too general):

grain	12/16
cereal	1/16
wheat	1/16
crops	1/16
omissions	1/16

Here is the resulting network of choices:

translational equivalent: *grain*
AGRICULTURAL PRODUCE
    too general: *crops, cereal*
    too specific: *wheat*

Source word: istaṭā'a

There were subtle choices to be made here. While *can* is ambiguous with its senses of *ability* and *permission*, *istaṭā'a* has only the sense of *ability*. Against this background, subjects fell into three groups:

able	5/16
can	3/16
manage	1/16
omissions	7/16

One group used *can* and risked (or were not aware of) ambiguity. The second avoided ambiguity by using *able*. The third can be seen as a subgroup of the second in that he/she has chosen an equivalent *manage* that connotes *positive achievement*, in line with the sentiment of the text, in which the ex-colonies' efforts are seen as laudable. The choices available were:

risk ambiguity: *can*
avoid ambiguity
    no connotation of positive achievement: *able*
    connotation of positive achievment: *manage*

Source word: ṣu'ūb

People was the unmarked choice here, with *country* offered by a large minority:

peoples	1/16
people	8/16
country	4/16
population	1/16
nation	1/16
omissions	1/16

Despite the popularity of *people*, in all but one case, the choice was faulty because of the inability to deploy the word as a countable plural; *ṣu'ūb* is a plural form corresponding to *peoples*, while its singular form *ṣa'b* corresponds to *people* as a singular or a mass noun. Eight of the nine used *people*, while one used *peoples*. The other subjects all produced countable plurals but, of course, shifted the sense of the source term to a greater or lesser extent:

use countable plural
  preserve sense: *peoples*
  shift sense: *country, nation, population*
use mass noun: *people*

Source word: musta'mara

Here *colony* was clearly the unmarked choice, while the marked choices simply involved a shift of sense:

colony	10/16	P3
occupy	4/16	S4
imperial	1/16	S4
undeveloped	1/16	S4
omissions	0/16	

The network of choices is shown here:

preserve sense: *colony*
shift sense: *occupy, imperial, undeveloped*

Source word: injāz

There was a remarkable variation with this word, perhaps less surprising given that *Hans Wehr* gives *execution, implementation, realization, effectuation, accomplishment, achievement, completion, consummation*. While *achieve* was the unmarked choice, the alternatives fell into two categories. One group preserved the sense but used different equivalents such as *gain, get, obtain, accomplish*. Within this group, *get* is stylistically inappropriate for the text type. The other category was where the sense was shifted, thus *regain* and *struggle*:

achieve	8/16
gain	2/16
get	2/16
obtain	1/16
accomplish	1/16
regain	1/16
struggle	1/16
omissions	0/16

This is the network of choices:

preserve sense
    stylistically appropriate: *achieve, gain, obtain, accomplish*
    stylistically inappropriate: *get*
shift sense: *regain, struggle*

Source word: bad'a

The choices here were fairly simple. Most used stylistically neutral equivalents like *start* and *begin*, while one chose *commence*, more characteristic of formal written text:

start	11/16
begin	3/16
commence	1/16
omissions	1/16

A simple choice network appears below:

stylistically neutral: *start, begin*
stylistically more formal: *commence*

Source word: 'amalīya

There were many omissions here and no agreement on an equivalent. Of the four choices, *operation* is the ready translational equivalent, and *task* a close alternative; each foregrounds the assumed actor. The word *process* is close in sense, but places the actor in the background, while *scheme* has the different sense of *systematic* and *plan*:

scheme	1/16
process	1/16
task	1/16
operation	1/16
omissions	12/16

The choices can be illustrated as follows:

preserve sense
    actor foregrounded: *operation, task*
    actor backgrounded: *process*
shift sense: *scheme*

Source word: binā'

The unmarked choice is *building*, while three subjects chose the stylistically more formal *construction*, and two subjects shifted the sense with *growth* and *erection*:

building	11/16
construction	3/16
erection	1/16
growth	1/16
omissions	0/16

The choices appear here:

preserve sense
   stylistically neutral: *building*
   stylistically more formal: *construction*
shift sense: *growth, erection*

Source word: naṣāṭ

The translational equivalent *active* was commonly used, but did not meet the definition of an unmarked choice. Two alternatives – *energy* and *vigour* – involved a slight shift of sense; *vitality* shifts the sense more substantially:

active	6/16
energy	3/16
vigour	1/16
vitality	1/16
omissions	5/16

The choice network is:

preserve sense: *active*
shift sense slightly: *energy, vigour*
shift sense substantially: *vitality*

Source word: burūz

This word demonstrated great variation in its equivalents. The difficulty seems to be its character as a dead metaphor. While it has the primary sense of *prominence, protrusion*, it is used here in the very general sense of *appear*. Some subjects tried to reduce it to sense, hence *start, appear, emerge, begin, obvious*. Others created a new metaphor with *highlight, surface, rise*. One tried to retain the primary sense with *project*:

start	2/16
appear	2/16
emerge	2/16
begin	1/16
highlight	1/16
obvious	1/16
surface	1/16
project	1/16
rise	1/16
omissions	4/16

A possible network of choices appears here:

preserve sense with loss of metaphor: *project*
shift sense
   reduce to sense
      APPEAR: *appear, emerge, obvious*
      START: *start, begin*
   new metaphor: *highlight, rise, surface*

Source word: azma

Most subjects found the translational equivalent *crisis*, while a minority were presumably lost for words and chose *problem*. This could be considered a superordinate for *crisis*, although no co-hyponyms of *crisis* were offered, such as *dilemma*:

crisis	11/16
problem	5/16
omissions	0/16

Here are the choices:

preserve sense: *crisis*
shift sense with more general equivalent: *problem*

Lexical transfer strategies and textual competence

Although the preceding section may seem unnecessarily detailed, it can be defended on two grounds. First, there is the general point that translation studies suffers from a dearth of data-based research, and it is a worthwhile aim to give some real data an airing. I would argue that general theorizing has not taken translation studies very far, and new insights must be based on studies of what actually happens in the translation process.

The second point is that a detailed analysis was necessary to show the many strategies used by subjects to produce equivalents for source text words in environments where the variable of syntax is fairly insignificant. What is interesting is the extent to which these strategies reflect the ability of subjects to construct (to a greater or lesser degree) well-formed texts, rather than well-formed sentences without reference to context. The fine detail of the preceding section now allows us to construct a consolidated network of all the strategies observed:

preserve sense
- (P1) choose appropriately from paradigm on general stylistic judgements
- (P2) give connotation that reflects textual concerns
- (P3) make non-textually motivated choice
- (P4) choose inappropriately from paradigm on general stylistic judgements

shift sense
- (S1) choose new sense that reflects textual motivation
- (S2) reduce metaphor to sense appropriately
- (S3) transfer metaphor appropriately
- (S4) choose inappropriate sense

The network can be interpreted in this way: entering at the source word, the translator may choose to preserve or shift the sense. If they preserve the sense, they may:

- (P1) Choose appropriately from a paradigm on the basis of general stylistic judgements, e.g. *achieve* versus *get*.
- (P2) Choose an equivalent that has a connotation that reflects concerns mentioned in the text, e.g. *affluent* to contrast with the lifestyle of Africa.
- (P3) Choose an equivalent uninfluenced by textual factors. This could include transferring a metaphor.
- (P4) Choose inappropriately from a paradigm on the basis of general stylistic judgements, e.g. *achieve* versus *get*.

If they shift the sense, they may:

- (S1) Choose an equivalent that reflects textual judgement, e.g. by incorporating additional meaning that can be predicted from elsewhere in the text, e.g. *silos* for *makāzin*.
- (S2) Reduce a metaphor to sense appropriately, e.g. *appear* for *burūz*.
- (S3) Create an appropriate new metaphor, e.g. *invasion* for *zahf*.
- (S4) Choose an inappropriate metaphorical or non-metaphorical equivalent, eg. *suffer* for *taknīq*.

Of these strategies, P1, P2 and S1 reflect textual competence.

If one eliminates the doubtful *rich* from the category of P2, since it may belong to either P2 or P3, three subjects in our case study used more than two textual competence strategies. Their text samples are shown below, with the examples of textual competence strategies underlined:

Subject 37
In the fifties and sixties, the colonized nations were able to <u>achieve</u> their political independence. The task of building the national economies <u>commenced</u> with energy and enthusiasm. Meanwhile, the socio-economic crisis was surfacing in the developed countries.

While life in Africa is suffocating under the pressure of famine, locusts, poisons of volcanic gases and the flames of civil wars (Sudan – Angola), the <u>siloes</u> of wealthy nations are overflowing with huge grain surpluses.

Subject 45
During the fifties and the sixties occupied countries <u>gained</u> their independence and started their economic and national growth with great enthusiasm and activity, accompanied with the projection of the socio-economic crisis in the capitalistic countries.

Whilst life is choking in the African continent under the pressures of hunger, locusts, poisonous gases and the civil wars (Sudan – Angola), the <u>sylos</u> of the <u>affluent</u> countries are overflowing with surplus grains.

Subject 37 was previously judged to be persistent and risk-taking in disposition, and the text sample confirms this; the translation omits nothing from the source text meaning, is grammatically accurate and is lexically sophisticated. Subject 45 was also judged to be persistent and risk-taking. His/her text is similarly full, although with some slips of detail, for example, *the* civil wars, *capitalistic*, *sylos*.

Subject 43 was the only subject to use two textual competence strategies. However, the subject also demonstrated poor target language grammar and massive introductions of extraneous meaning. One might tentatively suggest that the subject has relatively good textual competence but poor lexico-grammatical competence. This subject was judged to be capitulating and prudent:

Subject 43
In the fifties & the sixties the undeveloped countries <u>achived</u> there political independence, and [. . .] building there national economy with great enthusiasm. Unfortunately they could not solve there economic problems.

While live is very harsh in Africa because of famine due to invasion of loctus, poisonous volcanic gases and national wars. In other parts of the world <u>silos</u> have excess of grain for human consumption.

Concluding remarks

The study reported in this chapter has led to two significant insights about translation competence. The first is that the pattern of omissions and closeness to normative lexical choices allows one to postulate two dimensions of *disposition*: translators can be located on two dimensions of *risk-taking* versus *prudent* and *persistent* versus *capitulating*. The second is that lexical transfers can be used to make judgements about the textual competence of translators, that is the extent to which translators make choices informed by textual concerns. We found that there is a system of choices open to the translator, and that some of these choices reflect the ability to operate beyond the sentence.

To conclude this chapter, let me do a little summing up. I began to model translation competence in Chapter 4, where we saw that second language translators could be roughly categorized according to their ability to produce a formal written style in their translations. I went on to show that the deployment of target language grammar varies in a systematic way, such that the more textually competent second language translators are able to break away from writing that reflects the stylistic patterns of informal speech. Next I focused on lexis and, with the notion of disposition, showed how translators can be described in terms of their attitude to the task. And I returned to the matter of style by showing what word-choice strategies are open to translators, and how they reflect textual competence. At this point, then, we have the foundations of a much more comprehensive understanding of what it means to be able to translate into a second language. In the next chapter, I will move away from examining linguistic structure *per se*, and focus on how much translators know about their own competence, and how they monitor their output.

7 Monitoring translation output

Aims

In previous Chapters I attempted to characterize translation competence in a second language acquisition framework. The impetus behind the work was the lack of a general model to underpin the teaching and learning of translation. The work reported in this chapter arose from a different kind of need – the need to find answers to a pressing practical difficulty. My difficulty was that when my students failed translation subjects or assignments, they often expressed inordinate surprise; some students seemed to think they were much better translators than they really were. In investigating the problem, I was led to the conclusion that here was another facet of translation competence.

Issues in monitoring translation output

There seem to be two dimensions to the problem. First, there is the matter of students' general assessment of their own ability and whether this assessment could be related to any other factors. In fact, as I will show later, among translation students at the University of Western Sydney Macarthur the self-assessment of translation ability was related to whether they were translating into the first language or second language (L2), as well as their migration generation (that is, first versus second generation). Given this, it is reasonable to propose that the capacity to judge one's own translation output should be considered a facet of translation competence; the better a translator's awareness of his/her output quality, the more competent he/she is likely to be.

The second matter is this: translation is a language task that requires intensive 'real–time editing', that is the additions, amendments and deletions that take place as the translators proceed through the text. This real-time editing can be thought of as the translators' opportunity to intervene to improve their output. Now if it is accepted that awareness of output quality varies among translators, then at least part of that variation could be due to the quality of the translators' own intervention, that is the effectiveness of their real-time editing. In fact, I will show later that there is systematic variation in the way that student translators working into L2 make deletions, insertions and amendments as they work.[1] Again, it seems reasonable to include self-editing as a facet of translation competence. I will borrow the term 'monitoring' to include these two facets, with the observation that the term has special uses elsewhere (for example, Krashen, 1977).

Despite the atheoretical impetus for the work reported in this chapter, it can be set in the broad context of language production models and theories. Indeed, my practical classroom dilemma immediately begs questions that have to do with mental processes. Do some translators perform their real-time editing internally, that is, before output is realized as writing? Do some perform at least part of this operation during the act of writing, rather than before? Are there some kinds of editing operation that occur internally and others that typically occur 'externally'? Although I do not attempt to answer these questions by developing a cognitive model, a brief review of some relevant research will help to locate my discussion.

O'Malley and Chamot (1990: 37–42) discuss three-stage models of language production based on Anderson (1985). Such models have a construction stage, which deals with planning, a transformation stage and an execution stage, where a message is rendered into speech or writing. The kind of real-time editing that is done by translators could be thought of as occurring in the transformation stage, where 'language rules are applied to transfer intended meanings into the form of a message. In writing both composition and revision take place at this stage' (O'Malley and Chamot, 1990: 38). However, there is a difficulty here: the revision that takes place in the transformation stage of writing is presumably 'internal' and only accessible through think–aloud verbalizations. The revision that takes place while writing is going on (that is the kind that is observed in deletions and amendments) would appear to belong to the execution stage. This raises the possibility, then, of revision as a process that can take place at various points in the language production process.

The term revision is also used in the sense of working over written texts (not necessarily one's own and not translations) after they have been written rather than during their production. There is a smallish literature on this variety of revision summarized in Hayes et al. (1987: 176–80), which goes on to propose a cognitive model of revision based on think–aloud protocols; some parallels between my study and these revision studies are briefly raised later, especially with regard to the distinction in strategies used by experienced and inexperienced writers.

A related variety of revision is discussed in the literature of translation studies in the sense of a translation bureau quality-control procedure.

This field is served by its own small prescriptive literature. Although Mossop (1982) does discuss self-revision, this is not quite the same thing as the virtually instantaneous output repair we see when we observed translation being done in real time.

The issue of monitoring has also been a concern among researchers in the second language acquisition field. Krashen's Monitor Model is well known, with its checking facility that monitors spontaneous language output for its agreement with learned rules (Krashen, 1977). The model has been heavily criticized because, among other things, 'it is not expressed in terms of testable propositions about mental structures' (Pienemann and Johnston, 1987: 66). For my purposes, the problem with the model is its provenance; the Monitor is proposed to support a theoretical view of language learning which tries to distinguish learning from acquisition, whereas the monitoring that I discuss is inferred from empirical data.

The idea of monitoring is used less theoretically elsewhere in second language acquisition research. For example, self-monitoring is discussed as a second language learning strategy in O'Malley and Chamot (1990), and here there are some important parallels with the framework for self-editing that I propose later in this chapter. On the basis of think-aloud data, it is claimed that 'In language production, students monitored at different levels, as in monitoring at the word, phrase, or sentence level, and also monitored for style, for their writing plans, and for the effectiveness of their choice or strategy' (O'Malley and Chamot, 1990: 136–8). I will show that translation students similarly monitor at different levels.

Monitoring is also discussed in translation studies. The model proposed in Krings (1986), based on think-aloud data, contains a set of monitoring strategies that include 'L2–intuitions, spot-the-difference, monitoring-by-rules, special strategies for using reference books' (p. 269). Kalina (1992), proposes monitoring strategies in interpreting, which are intended 'also to check whether the interpreter's own production is in line with his/her planning'. They are said to 'extend over practically all stages of the process', although one wonders how this can be known when 'they become identifiable only when monitoring leads to the conclusion that a correction is necessary and possible' (Kalina, 1992: 254). Bell (1991) avoids inventing a monitor at all in his model of the translation process, despite its heavy reliance on notions from psychology and cognitive science.

Let me now return to the task at hand. In this chapter I investigate two questions:

1. The extent to which student translators are aware of the quality of their output.

2. Students' ability to repair output during the course of their work into the second language (real-time editing).

Quality of output is discussed in relation to a data set called ASSESS-MENT, and real-time editing in relation to a data set called CLASS-WORK. I will conclude that the varying awareness of translation quality output in a group of translation students appears to be a function of their types of bilingualism, but that in general, awareness of quality is lower for translation into the second language. In the examination of the ability to edit output, I will show that this ability differs systematically from student to student. I propose a framework for analysing this kind of editing and show how editing ability can be profiled.

Quality of output: the assessment study

This data set arose from an attempt to understand university students' perceptions of their ability to translate in and out of the first language. The students were in their first year of a Bachelor degree in interpreting and translation, and they had taken a selection test about four months previously. It was reasoned that their translation tutors' assessment would be close to an objective measure of their ability, and in addition that the results of the entrance test would also be likely to reflect at least some facet of their ability to translate. This last point provided a measure independent of the tutors' assessments.

The method was as follows. Students attending a mass lecture in translation theory were alerted in mid-semester that they would be asked to assess their ability towards the end of semester, and that their participation was optional and part of an experiment. Guarantees were given verbally and in writing that the results were unconnected with their regular assessment procedures. Of the 44 students, 16 were taking classes in Spanish–English translation, 12 in Italian–English, 12 in Arabic–English, one in German–English and three in Vietnamese–English. All students were taking translation in both directions, prior to specializing in the middle of their second year. At the same time their language-specific tutors were warned that they would be asked to assess each student independently at the end of semester. Of the 44 students, 26 were eventually included in the study.

At the final lecture a form was given to students to make their self-assessment and a similar form given to the tutors. Assessments were to be made on a scale of 0 to 10, with each assessment to be made relative to the

TABLE 7.1   Tutors' ranking: English to Spanish translation

Rank	n
0	0
1	2
2	0
3	1
4	5
5	2
6	0
7	1
8	1
9	3
10	1
Total	16

TABLE 7.2   Tutors' ranking: translation from all languages into English

Rank	n
0	0
1	0
2	2
3	2
4	1
5	9
6	2
7	4
8	3
9	3
10	0
Total	26

other students in the group concerned. A score of 0 was to represent the poorest student and 10 the best. Although this is strictly a ranking procedure, it was hoped that it would be closer in nature to an interval scale with a normal distribution so that the Pearson product–moment procedure could be used. Indeed, this seems to have happened, as Tables 7.1 and 7.2 show. Here the tutor's assessment of the largest group – Spanish – is compared with the self-assessments of the 26 students across a number of languages, whose scores were included in the study.

The students' entrance test scores were retrieved and converted to standardized scores (T-scores), the English test scores on the basis of the whole candidature for the previous four years and the other language test scores on the basis of the candidature for each language for the same period. For the analysis, the T-scores of the C-test and the dictation test were totalled to give a single figure. The number of complete sets of data for each student was reduced by certain factors, one of which was the untimely death of the Vietnamese tutor. Otherwise, 27 of 44 students volunteered self-assessments, and the number of entrance test scores was reduced by the discovery that three of the 44 had not taken the test. A tutor's assessment of the single German student was not asked for.

In summary, 26 students had entrance test scores and self-assessments, 37 had entrance test scores and tutor's assessments, and 22 had tutor's assessments and self-assessments[2]. The summary results appear in Table 7.3 (overleaf).

Pearson product-moment correlation matrices are shown in Tables 7.4–7.6. The correlation matrices are consolidated and reproduced in Table 7.7, but for ease of interpretation the correlation coefficients are replaced with the notations *lo* (.1–.5), *hi* (<.01), *vhi* (<.001).

The correlations give us some important clues about students' views of their own ability. Let us first dispense with the cells in the matrix that are unlikely to produce a significant correlation. For example, there is no obvious common factor to cause a student's entrance test in Spanish to correlate with his/her self-assessment of translation into English. The combinations in question are: other test/self into English, other test/ tutor into English, English test/self into language other than English, English test/tutor into English, self into English/tutor into language other than English, self into language other than English/tutor into English. In each case the correlation is lo or non-existent.

Of the remaining group, there are two lo correlations and four hi or vhi. The lo correlations each involve skills into English; students' self-assessment into English correlates poorly with their English test scores and with their tutors' assessments into English. In case one suspects that it is the tutors who are assessing poorly, their assessments into English correlate very highly with the English test results. This begs the question of what the tutors were really assessing; it is quite possible that their judgements were a complex of views on students' ability in English and ability to translate. The experiment provides no way of untangling this conundrum.

The highly correlating cells are all to do with skills into the (usually) first language. Students' self-assessments into the language other than English correlate highly with their tutors' assessments and very highly with the language other than English test scores. As a final check, tutors' assessments and language tests correlate well.

TABLE 7.3   Summary results of assessment experiment

A	B	C	D	E	F	G	H	I	J	K
Arabic	59	52	111	7	37	41	78	4	2	5
Arabic	59	52	111	6	41	47	88	7	4	4
Arabic	57	43	100	7	46	46	92	5	8	2
Arabic	37	51	88	—	47	50	97	—	1	1
Arabic	53	48	101	7	44	53	97	7	7	8
Arabic	50	49	99	7	45	55	100	6	10	10
Arabic	50	50	100	—	45	55	100	—	6	3
Arabic	64	51	115	—	47	55	102	—	5	5
Arabic	46	54	100	—	56	51	107	—	9	8
Arabic	53	49	102	—	60	51	111	—	3	6
Arabic	75	44	119	—	63	52	115	—	5	9
Arabic	43	39	82	—	74	52	126	—	4	7
German	66	58	124	8	46	51	97	5	—	—
Ital.	—	—	—	—	—	—	—	—	9	8
Ital.	—	—	—	—	—	—	—	—	7	6
Ital.	—	—	—	—	—	—	—	—	7	6
Ital.	63	54	117	3	39	29	68	2	6	4
Ital.	55	57	112	3	39	40	79	2	5	4
Ital.	51	47	98	6.5	46	34	80	5	5	3
Ital.	50	57	107	8	45	42	87	7	7	6
Ital.	55	55	110	5	48	44	92	5	6	4
Ital.	61	57	118	8	50	57	107	5	7	6
Ital.	58	55	113	6	63	46	109	5	6	5
Ital.	63	58	121	8	67	62	129	7	8.5	8
Ital.	73	59	132	9	81	62	143	9	10	9.5
Span.	57	56	113	—	33	47	80	—	6	4
Span.	53	55	108	—	32	54	86	—	6	4
Span.	45	53	98	—	42	45	87	—	2	1
Span.	62	58	120	10	48	46	94	6	7	5
Span.	47	55	102	7	47	51	98	5	5	4
Span.	43	46	89	3	46	53	99	3	1	1
Span.	30	43	73	—	44	56	100	—	3	4
Span.	61	57	118	—	47	53	100	—	8	8
Span.	42	48	90	—	55	48	103	—	6	9
Span.	42	47	89	8	56	48	104	9	5	4
Span.	59	57	116	7	51	54	105	5	5	3
Span.	64	56	120	7	49	58	107	5	9	5
Span.	54	56	110	—	54	57	111	—	5	7
Span.	65	57	122	—	58	55	113	—	10	10
Span.	53	53	106	5	60	58	118	8	5	9
Span.	46	53	99	8	67	63	130	9	6	9
Viet.	38	47	85	3	34	48	82	3	—	—
Viet.	41	36	77	6.5	50	51	101	8	—	—
Viet.	44	35	79	5	52	52	104	8	—	—

Key:
Column A = Language; Column B = English C-test T-score; Column C = English dictation T-score; Column D = Totalled English test score; Column E = Self-assessment into English; Column F = Other language C-test T-score; Column G = Other language dictation T-score; Column H = Totalled other language test score; Column I = Self-assessment from English; Column J = Tutor's assessment into English; Column K = Tutor's assessment from English

TABLE 7.4 Correlation of language test and self-assessment

	Self into English	Self from English
English test	.38 (p = <.05))	−.14 (p = >.1)
LOTE test	.48 (p = <.02)	.69 (p = <.001)
n = 26, df = 24		

TABLE 7.5 Correlation of language test and tutors' assessment

	Tutor into English	Tutor from English
English test	.52 (p = <.001)	.29 (p = <.1)
LOTE test	.30 (p = <.1)	.60 (p = <.001)
n = 37, df = 35		

TABLE 7.6 Correlation of tutors' assessment and self-assessment

	Tutor into English	Tutor from English
Self into English	.50 (p = <.02)	.41 (p = <.1)
Self from English	.36 (p = .1)	.62 (p = <.01)
n = 22, df = 20		

TABLE 7.7 Consolidated correlations matrix

	Self into English	Self from English	Tutor into English	Tutor from English
English test	lo		vhi	lo
LOTE test	lo	vhi	lo	vhi
Self into English			lo	lo
Self from English				hi

Under- and overestimation of translation competence

Bearing in mind that the calculations made so far are based on a multilingual group with a range of abilities, it would be interesting to delve into language-specific questions, and I now discuss the extent of under- and overestimating and whether this differs between language groups and ability levels.

To investigate mis-estimation, the following procedure was developed. The language test scores were ranked from 1 to 10 by intervals so that the normal distribution of the T-score was preserved in the ranking. Each ranking was deducted from the relevant self-assessment, as was the relevant tutor assessment. The two results were averaged to give a positive or negative figure, so that a positive figure indicated an overestimate on the student's part and a negative figure an underestimate. Two examples are shown below.

Overestimate

self-assessment:	7
ranked language test:	3
tutor's assessment:	5

self-assessment – ranked language test = 4
self-assessment – tutor's assessment   = 2
average difference (overestimate)   = 3

Underestimate

self-assessment:	2
ranked language test:	6
tutor's assessment:	5

self-assessment – ranked language test = −4
self-assessment – tutor's assessment   = −3
average difference (underestimate)   = −3.5

The results are shown in Table 7.8.

Finally, each of the English rankings and tutor assessments into English were totalled to give a single figure. These were then ranked and divided into three groups of roughly equal size. For these lower, middle and upper groups the proportion of over- and underestimates was calculated. The same procedure was carried out for the data into the language other than English. Results are as shown in Table 7.9.

The consolidated correlation matrix in Table 7.7 shows that for all students self-assessments into English correlate poorly with other measures, and that their self-assessments into the language other than English correlate well with other measures. On the face of things, it appears that

TABLE 7.8   Overestimates and underestimates of translation competence

	Arabic		Italian		Spanish		All	
	n	%	n	%	n	%	n	%
Overestimated into English	4	40	2	11	6	38	12	27
Overestimated from English	4	40	3	17	5	31	12	27
Underestimated into English	1	10	7	39	2	13	10	23
Underestimated from English	1	10	6	33	3	19	10	23
Totals	10	100	18	100	16	101*	44	100

* *Total of 101 due to rounding*

TABLE 7.9   Estimates into English and language other than English

	Lower group		Middle group		Upper group	
	n	%	n	%	n	%
Into English						
Overestimates	7	88	3	43	2	29
Underestimates	1	12	4	57	5	71
Totals	8	100	7	100	7	100
From English						
Overestimates	5	71	6	75	1	14
Underestimates	2	29	2	25	6	86
Totals	7	100	8	100	7	100

students have a good awareness of their ability to translate into their language other than English and a poor awareness into English. The result does, however, allow another interpretation as far as the language other than English is concerned, namely that students may have been consistently overestimating or underestimating.

Differences in estimation among language groups

For the group as a whole, over- and underestimates in each language direction are fairly evenly distributed. When broken into language groups, however, the picture changes. The Arabic students greatly overestimate their ability into their first language and into English. The Spanish students follow almost the same pattern, overestimating into Spanish and into English. But the Italians reverse the pattern, underestimating into English and Italian. Given that the Arabic and Spanish students are in the majority in the sample, the high correlation into the language other than English for the group as a whole is satisfactorily explained; the majority of the students are Arabic or Spanish speakers.

When the students are stratified into three ability groups the picture is further clarified. Both the lower and middle groups into the language other than English overestimate their ability, while the upper group underestimates; again this confirms the interpretation of the original correlation matrix, that students tend to overestimate into the language other than English. The three ability groups into English show a regular cline such that the lower group overestimates, the middle group is fairly evenly split, and the upper group underestimates. This is consistent with the original poor correlation since the overestimates would tend to neutralize the underestimates.

To interpret this conclusion one first needs to recall the questionnaire data which was discussed in outline in Chapter 3. Why do the Spanish and Arabic speakers tend to overestimate their ability and the Italian speakers tend to underestimate? There is the question of identification; the Arabic speakers virtually always cited Arabic as their first language, whatever their generation (in migration terms). The Spanish speakers similarly cited the language other than English, even though in migration terms they were a maturer group with an emerging second generation. In contrast, the Italian speakers tended to cite English, even though they were mostly home language speakers of Italian. Could the Italian speakers' overall lack of confidence in their ability reflect a lack of strong identification with either the migrant culture or the host culture?

Experience of language education might provide another clue. Many of the Arabic and Spanish speakers had had formal education in the language other than English and had studied languages as academic subjects at school. Most of the Italian speakers had had their formal education in English after beginning life as Italian dialect speakers; if they had studied Italian, it had been the standard variety picked up as a high school subject. What this comparison suggests is that the Italian speakers are reticent about their ability, while the other 'old hands' at language learning are more self-assured.

One ventures to think that the odd correlations observed between the test components discussed in Chapter 3 have some relation to this. In the Italian candidates there was a significant correlation between the English

C-test and both the Italian C-test and Italian dictation, but no such correlation in the Arabic and Spanish groups. It was suggested that this might reflect a benefit of language maintenance; the better the Italian, the better the English. What this could also reflect is a qualitative difference in the bilingual competence of first- and second-generation speakers. For the former group, who have acquired the second language later in life, the two competences are separate, while for the latter group of childhood acquirers of the second language the two competences are intertwined. The terms 'coordinate' and 'compound' bilingualism respectively provide a handy, if oversimplified, dichotomy. While many researchers have reported that bilingualism promotes metalinguistic ability (for example, Ben Zeev, 1977 and Mohanty, 1983), Galambos and Goldin-Meadow (1983) report that while child bilingualism promotes a syntactic orientation, the effect was observed to disappear by kindergarten in a data-based study. Is this a key difference between the Italian speakers and the others – an intertwined bilingual competence, poorer metalinguistic ability, less confidence in their capacity to judge their language ability, a tendency to underestimate?

The second conclusion concerns the difference in estimations between the upper and lower ability groups. Working into English, it will be recalled that the lower group overestimated and the upper group underestimated. This can be accounted for by the loading of characteristically overestimating Arabic speakers in the lower groups (three in the lower group, two in the middle group) and underestimating Italian speakers in the upper groups (one in the lower group and four each in the middle and upper groups).

The overestimation by the lower and middle groups into the language other than English must be, then, a quite separate phenomenon since the three language other than English groups' data had similar distributions. What is observed here is a more general characteristic to the effect that the poorer the target language ability, the less likely is the speaker able to assess that ability. The contrary case is that with knowledge comes modesty.

Summary of the assessment study

To conclude this section, it appears that the ability to estimate translation ability differs between language groups but more fundamentally between types of bilingualism, and that poor language competence is linked to overestimation and good language competence to underestimation. I move now to the second major topic in the areas of monitoring – real-time editing.

Monitoring ability: the editing study

In this section I develop a framework for the analysis of real-time editing. The framework is used to make qualitative descriptions of the monitoring ability of student translators. These descriptions lead me to claim that monitoring ability differs systematically among student translators, and that this is a describable facet of translation competence.

Dimensions of editing

In the course of teaching a third-year undergraduate class in Arabic to English translation, I collected a number of handwritten student translations carried out in class. These handwritten texts included valuable data on editing – the deletions and insertions – that were lost in the word-processed text that the students normally produced. The source texts I have called *Unemployment* and *Lady Di*. The texts differ considerably in style: *Unemployment* is a dour editorial piece with much subordination and transparent lexis; *Lady Di* is magazine gossip characterized by jokey vocabulary, metaphors and simple sentences. The data I collected suggest that there are at least six dimensions of editing that can be described. These are strategy, purpose, level, frequency, economy and effectiveness.

In the dimension of strategy, five such strategies are apparent: I have called these False Start, Bracketed Alternative, Deletion, Insertion and Partial Switch.

In False Start the translator begins a string, deletes what has been written, then resumes. Occasionally, the deleted material may be repeated on resumption, for example, The ~~subject~~ matter is not. . . .

With Bracketed Alternative the translator writes an alternative in brackets after a word or phrase, for example, from (psychological doctor) psychiatrists.

With the Deletion strategy, the translator deletes material from within a previously completed string, for example, She love~~d~~.

The Insertion strategy works by material being inserted in a previously completed string with a caret, indicated by chevrons in this example: and <the> time has come.

In Partial Switch the translator uses deletion and insertion to switch the position of some material, although in the new position less or more of the original appears: The subject is not only a <a matter of popularity> ~~subject of popularity subject~~.

Editing appears to have the two main purposes of correction and revision. In editing for correction, the translator attempts to correct some structural target language error, for instance, by inserting a definite article, rearranging the order of a noun phrase or deleting letters from a wrongly spelt word, for example, number one in all ~~Europpe~~ Europe. In editing for revision, the translator makes a revision to the translation itself, regardless of its structural well-formedness or otherwise, for example, by changing the choice of a word or rearranging the order of a clause: the <wife of> <~~Prince's wife still~~> Prince Charle's ~~wife~~. In fact, this example contains three revisions, all aimed at setting up an *of* possessive. It is quite easy to follow the process step by step:

First attempt: the Prince Charle's wife

In the first revision, the subject appears to be unhappy with the possessive *'s* not being attached to the head word, and an insertion is made which sacrifices the prince's name:

Revision 1:   the <Princes's wife still>˙ Prince Charle's wife

The subject rejects this strategy in Revision 2:

Revision 2:   the <~~Princes's wife still~~> Prince Charle's wife

In Revision 3 the subject tries out the *of* possessive:

Revision 3:   the <wife of> <~~Prince's wife still~~> Prince Charle's ~~wife~~

The distinction between correction and revision cannot be a rigid one. Editing purpose can only be inferred from the written data, and it is difficult to disentangle the intentions of the translator from the opinion of the analyst. While there will be clear examples of correction and of revision, there will be contentious examples. Correction is firmly anchored in lexico-grammar; it deals with breaches of spelling, morphology and syntax, where the translator's thoughts are 'Look out, that's not written properly'. Revision is anchored at two points. It has to do with semantic equivalence – the intention behind a revision might be 'That's not what the original really means – let's try another word', and it has to do with creating texts appropriately – 'That's not the right way to say it in this kind of text', or 'The text doesn't flow properly like that'. These verbalizations are of course imagined, and have nothing to do with the verbal protocol method. In fact, there are parallels between my correction/revision distinction and the self-monitoring strategies discussed in O'Malley and Chamot (1990). My notion of correction is very much like 'Production monitoring: checking, verifying or correcting one's language production' (p. 137). My notion of revision may be somewhat equivalent to:

Style monitoring: checking verifying or correcting based upon an internal stylistic register.

Strategy monitoring: tracking use [sic] of how well a strategy is working.

Plan monitoring: tracking how well a plan is working. (O'Malley and Chamot, 1990: 137)

Editing evidently occurs at a number of structural levels (see O'Malley and Chamot, 1990: 136–8); correcting the spelling of a single word is clearly quite different from recasting a clause. Three levels are proposed here: clause, phrase and word. There is no reason why editing should not also occur at sentence and text level. The level is often hard to determine, especially where it involves, say, recasting a word (for example, a time adverb) as a phrase (for example, a prepositional phrase). In fact, the difficulty lies in the attempt to achieve analytical economy by describing a dynamic process with static levels. The assignation of levels is, then, rather *ad hoc*. Some examples are:

Word level: Insertion of additional letters in a misspelled word.
              Replacement of a word by another word or a phrase.
Phrase level: Correcting definite articles.
              Replacing an *of* possessive with a *'s* possessive.
Clause level: Switching the position of an adverb phrase in a clause.
              Changing the choice of subject in a clause.

A clear difference in students' frequency of editing was observed. This can be measured very easily by counting and comparing the number of edits by each subject. A handy, if rather arbitrary, unit of measurement is edits per 100 words of source text.

Some students appear to be more economical in their editing than others. This can be easily measured by calculating the mean number of words per edit by each subject.

I have already proposed that editing may be for correction or revision. It seems that it should be much more straightforward to evaluate the effectiveness of correction than of revision since correction is to do with violations of structural rules but revision is more subtly judged. In the light of this, I propose a rough and ready measure of editing effectiveness that is heavily biased towards correction. The measure uses the segment as its basic unit and is based on a calculation of the percentage of segments in each text with uncorrected errors and no edits, uncorrected errors and edits, edits and no uncorrected errors, and no edits and no uncorrected errors. The measure allows a picture of the quality of output and the effectiveness of editing. A handy graphical representation can be

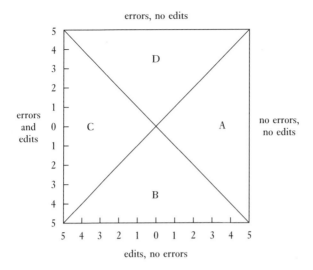

errors, no edits

FIGURE 7.1 Editing effectiveness grid

built in the following way. Each percentage score is divided by ten and then squared to give an easily manipulable logarithmic score. These scores are then plotted on a grid, the central point of the area plotted by the four scores is found geometrically, and the scale is adjusted. The resulting grid gives four quadrants, as we see in Figure 7.1.

The interpretation of the quadrants is as follows:

Quadrant A: The subject's output is good and little real-time editing is required.
Quadrant B: The subject's output is poor, but it is ameliorated by effective editing.
Quadrant C: The subject's output is poor, and although they edit, it is to little effect.
Quadrant D: The subject's output is poor, and little editing is attempted to ameliorate it.

To summarize this section, the various dimensions of editing are shown in Table 7.10 (overleaf).

Profiling the editing of individual translators

The analytical techniques described above can be used to characterize the editing ability of a translator and thereby provide a rather subtle diagnostic of translation competence. My feeling is that the conclusions to be

TABLE 7.10   Dimensions of editing

Dimension	Features
Strategy	False Start Bracketed Alternative Deletion Insertion Partial Switch
Purpose	Correction Revision
Level	Word Phrase Clause
Frequency	Low to high: Edits per n words
Economy	Low to high: Words per edit
Effectiveness	Interaction of uncorrected errors and no edits, uncorrected errors and edits, edits and no uncorrected errors, and no edits and no uncorrected errors

drawn from these kinds of data are likely to be qualitative and fairly general, but neverthless of great value. The strategy in the following pages will be to examine the data for the students E1, E2 and E3 for the *Unemployment* and *Lady Di* texts, and to work towards a qualitative statement about each student.

The editing strategies, purpose and level for the *Unemployment* and *Lady Di* texts are shown in Tables 7.11 and 7.12, and the data for the two texts are summarized in Table 7.13. Calculations and grids for editing effectiveness appear in Table 7.14 and Figures 7.2–7.4.

The interpretation of editing data

Editing data can be interpreted to give a picture of a translator's ability to monitor output. This picture is not a black and white one, and one would certainly not expect to obtain a simple quantitative measure. Rather, the data allow a qualitative description that may differ in its dimensions and reference points from one translator to another. In the following paragraphs I attempt to construct an evaluative framework within which to make such descriptions. I then examine and describe the monitoring ability of the three students using this framework.

TABLE 7.11 Student editing of *Unemployment* text

Student	Strategy			Purpose			Level		
	E1	E2	E3	E1	E2	E3	E1	E2	E3
Segment									
1	—	FS	—	—	CO	—	—	P	—
2	—	—	—	—	—	—	—	—	—
3	—	—	—	—	—	—	—	—	—
4	BA	FS	FS	R	CO	R	W	P	CL
5	FS	—	—	R	—	—	CL	—	—
6	—	—	—	—	—	—	—	—	—
7	—	—	—	—	—	—	—	—	—
8	FS	FS	—	R	R	—	CL	CL	—
8	FS	—	—	R	—	—	P	—	—
9	—	FS	FS	—	R	R	—	CL	CL
10	FS	—	—	CO	—	—	W	—	—
10	FS	—	—	R	—	—	W	—	—
11	—	—	—	—	—	—	—	—	—
12	—	—	—	—	—	—	—	—	—
13	FS	FS	—	R	R	—	CL	W	—
13	FS	—	—	R	—	—	CL	—	—
14	—	FS	—	—	R	—	—	W	—
15	—	—	—	—	—	—	—	—	—
16	BA	—	—	R	—	—	W	—	—
17	FS	—	—	R	—	—	CL	—	—
17	FS	—	—	R	—	—	W	—	—
18	FS	FS	—	R	CO	—	W	P	—
18	—	FS	—	—	R	—	—	CL	—
19	—	—	—	—	—	—	—	—	—
20	—	—	—	—	—	—	—	—	—
21	—	—	—	—	—	—	—	—	—
22	FS	—	FS	R	—	CO	W	—	P
23	BA	FS	—	R	CO	—	W	P	—
23	—	FS	—	—	R	—	—	W	—
24	FS	—	FS	R	—	CO	CL	—	P
24	FS	—	—	R	—	—	CL	—	—
24	FS	—	—	R	—	—	CL	—	—
24	FS	—	—	R	—	—	CL	—	—
25	DE	—	—	CO	—	—	W	—	—
25	FS	—	—	R	—	—	W	—	—
25	FS	—	—	R	—	—	W	—	—
26	FS	—	—	R	—	—	W	—	—
27	FS	FS	IN	R	R	R	CL	CL	CL
27	FS	FS	IN	R	R	R	CL	W	CL
27	FS	FS	—	R	R	—	CL	W	—
28	FS	FS	IN	R	CO	CO	P	P	P
28	—	FS		—	—	CO	—	—	P
29	DE	—	FS	CO	—	R	W	—	CL

Key for acronyms in Tables 7.11 and 7.12: FS = False Start; BA = Bracketed Alternative; DE = Deletion; R = Revision; CO = Correction; CL = Clause; I = Insertion; W = Word; P = Phrase

TABLE 7.12   Student editing of *Lady Di* text

	Strategy			Purpose			Level		
Student	E1	E2	E3	E1	E2	E3	E1	E2	E3
Segment									
1	IN	—	—	R	—	—	P	—	—
2	—	—	—	—	—	—	—	—	—
3	—	—	—	—	—	—	—	—	—
4	DE	DE	FS	C	C	R	W	W	W
4	IN	FS	—	C	C	—	W	W	—
4	—	IN	—	—	C	—	—	W	—
5	—	IN	DE	—	C	R	—	W	W
5	—	—	IN	—	—	R	—	—	W
6	—	—	—	—	—	—	—	—	—
7	FS	FS	DE	R	C	C	W	W	W
7	FS	—	—	R	—	—	W	—	—
8	FS	FS	IN	R	C	R	W	W	W
9	FS	—	DE	R	—	R	W	—	W
10	—	FS	DE	—	C	R	—	P	P
10	—	PS	PS	—	C	R	—	P	P
11	FS	FS	IN	R	C	R	P	W	W
12	—	FS	—	—	C	—	—	W	—
13	FS	DE	—	R	R	—	C	C	—
13	—	DE	—	—	R	—	—	C	—
13	—	FS	—	—	R	—	—	C	—
13	—	FS	—	—	R	—	—	C	—
13	—	IN	—	—	R	—	—	C	—
13	—	IN	—	—	R	—	—	W	—
14	FS	FS	—	R	C	—	C	W	—
15	FS	DE	IN	C	R	R	P	P	W
15	FS	IN	—	R	R	—	C	P	—
15	FS	—	—	R	—	—	C	—	—
15	IN	—	—	R	—	—	P	—	—
15	FS	—	—	R	—	—	W	—	—
16	—	—	FS	—	—	R	—	—	P
17	FS	—	—	R	—	—	W	—	—
18	FS	—	—	R	—	—	C	—	—
19	—	IN	—	—	R	—	—	W	—
20	FS	FS	—	R	C	—	P	C	—
21	IN	—	—	C	—	—	P	—	—
22	—	—	—	—	—	—	—	—	—
23	—	FS	FS	—	R	R	—	C	C
24	—	—	—	—	—	—	—	—	—
25	—	IN	IN	—	R	R	—	P	W
25	—	DE	—	—	R	—	—	W	—
26	—	FS	—	—	R	—	—	W	—

TABLE 7.13   Summary of student editing: *Unemployment* text in plain type, *Lady Di* text in italics

Dimension	Student E1	E2	E3
Strategy			
False Start	81%	100%	67%
	74%	*48%*	*23%*
Bracketed Alternative	7%	—	—
	—	—	—
Deletion	11%	—	—
	5%	*20%*	*31%*
Insertion	—	—	33%
	21%	*28%*	*38%*
Partial Switch	—	—	—
	—	*4%*	*8%*
Purpose			
Correction	11%	36%	44%
	21%	*48%*	*8%*
Revision	89%	64%	56%
	79%	*52%*	*92%*
Level			
Clause	44%	29%	56%
	26%	*28%*	*15%*
Phrase	7%	36%	44%
	32%	*20%*	*23%*
Word	48%	36%	—
	42%	*52%*	*61%*
Frequency			
Number of edits	27	14	9
	19	*25*	*13*
Edits/100 words	22%	12%	7%
	19%	*25%*	*13%*
Economy			
Number of words per edit	1.81	1.14	1.44
	1.42	*1.60*	*1.38*

In editing strategy, one would generally expect to find a narrow range of strategies in poorer translators and a wider range in better translators. A variety of strategies ought to reflect editing at various structural levels. For example, deletions and insertions ought to be more characteristic of word- and phrase-level edits, while false starts ought to be more characteristic of phrase- and clause-level edits where a long segment requires complete recasting.

TABLE 7.14   Summary of students' editing effectiveness

Students	E1	E2	E3
Segments with:			
Errors, no edits	19%	19%	34%
	33%	*15%*	*15%*
Errors, edits	31%	13%	17%
	25%	*8%*	*19%*
Edits, no errors	25%	16%	6%
	25%	*50%*	*35%*
No edits, no errors	25%	53%	47%
	17%	*27%*	*31%*

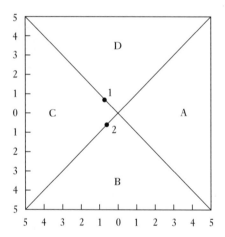

FIGURE 7.2   Editing effectiveness grid for student E1: 1 = *Unemployment*,
2 = *Lady Di*

The interpretation of editing purpose data will depend on output quality. While one would generally regard revision positively as a reflection of the translator's ability to test hypotheses about translation, one would interpret correction favourably in translators with linguistically poor output. Where a translator did little correction, this would be regarded negatively where output was poor and neutrally where output was good.

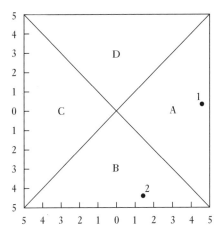

FIGURE 7.3 Editing effectiveness grid for student E1: 2 = *Unemployment*, 2 = *Lady Di*

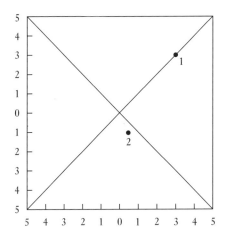

FIGURE 7.4 Editing effectiveness grid for student E1: 3 = *Unemployment*, 2 = *Lady Di*

The interpretation of editing level will be related to the structural challenges of particular texts. Where a text presents syntactic challenges (for example, because of many complex clauses) one would expect good translators to use more phrase- and clause-level edits. Where the challenge is lexical (simple syntax but varied or obscure vocabulary) word- and phrase-level edits will be favoured. A poor translator will be predicted to focus on one level regardless of the differences in structural challenge.

Editing frequency demands subtle interpretation. It will, on the one hand, be related to output quality so that one would expect it to favour translators with poor output and frequent edits over those with poor output and few edits. On the other hand, it will also be related to structural challenge. Because of the larger segment size of phrase- and clause-level edits, less frequent editing will be predicted with syntactically challenging texts and more with lexically challenging texts. Editing economy works similarly. Generally, one would interpret economical editing favourably, simply because it would reduce the amount of physical effort and time taken by the translator. But it would also be related to structural challenge; in general, phrase- and clause-level edits are likely to be less economical than word-level edits because of the need to rewrite long segments. Finally, editing effectiveness has the clearest interpretation and can be used as a confirmatory measure in a description of monitoring ability.

There is some commonality between these findings and those of Hayes et al. (1987), although that work appears to focus on what I call revision, rather than correction, and is of course restricted to a monolingual context. One important observation is that novices and experts differ in their approach to editing in that 'experts see revision as a whole-text task' (Hayes et al., 1987: 233). There is clearly common ground here with the notion of editing level, and my suggestion that higher-level editing reflects textual competence. Similarly, 'novices persistently fail to perceive text problems that experts detect easily' (p. 233) – a clear parallel to editing effectiveness, and a possible parallel to my earlier finding that translators into the second language have poorer judgements about output quality than into the first language. This parallel would involve equating second language writing with the notion of 'novice' and first language writing with 'expert'. The evaluative framework is summarized in Table 7.15.

Individual translator profiles

Student E1 displays a narrow range of strategies, using false starts extensively. While she makes many revision edits, this is not offset by good output. Indeed, her output is rather poor, as her location on the editing effectiveness grid shows; she is located on the cusps of quadrants C–B and C–D, and clearly neglects to make necessary correction edits. She does appear to respond to an extent to the different structural challenges of the two texts, increasing the number of phrase-level edits in *Lady Di*. But her focus seems to be at the phrase and clause level in both texts –

TABLE 7.15   Evaluative framework for monitoring translation output

Poorer translators	Better translators
Narrow range of strategies	Wide range of strategies
No use of revision	Use of revision
No use of correction to ameliorate poor output	Use of correction to ameliorate poor output
Levels inappropriate to structural challenge of text	Levels appropriate to structural challenge of text
Focus on one level	Focus on a variety of levels
Little editing to ameliorate poor output	Frequent editing to ameliorate poor output
Frequency inappropriate to structural challenge	Frequency appropriate to structural challenge
Uneconomical editing	Economical editing
Economy inappropriate to structural challenge	Economy appropriate to structural challenge
Ineffective editing	Effective editing

there is not the increase in word-level edits that one would expect in *Lady Di*. Editing frequency is reasonably high, although the focus on revision means that these frequent edits do not address the problem of linguistically poor output. There is also not the relatively higher frequency that one might expect in *Lady Di* to account for the word-level problems. Editing in *Unemployment* is very uneconomical because of the tendency to carry out large false start revisions. As seen previously, editing effectiveness is rather poor. To summarize, E1's monitoring tends to focus on revision at the expense of much needed correction and her adaptability to the different structural challenges of the two texts is unimpressive.

Student E2 uses more varied strategies, and her switch from exclusively false starts in *Unemployment* to a mix of false starts, insertions and deletions in *Lady Di* points to an ability to respond to differing structural challenge. She balances revision and correction, appropriately using less correction in *Unemployment*, where her output is better, and more in *Lady Di*, where her output is poorer; in her editing-effectiveness grid she is placed in quadrants A and D respectively. She edits at an almost equal mix of levels in *Unemployment* and appropriately increases the proportion of word-level edits in *Lady Di*. Again, in response to the structural challenges of the texts, editing is much more frequent in *Lady Di*, although the edits for this text are less economical. To summarize, E2's monitoring is characterized by a good awareness of the need for correction and the ability to tailor editing strategies to the structural demands of different texts.

If student E1 is systematically poor in her monitoring and E2 is systematically good, then student E3 appears to be more haphazard, although it must be said that E3 makes fewer edits than the other two, so that any conclusions must be more tentative. Like E2, he uses a wider range of strategies in *Lady Di*, which augurs well. But while revision and correction are well balanced in *Unemployment*, there is virtually no correction in *Lady Di*; this is despite the fact that output is mediocre in both texts. His use of levels appropriately meets the structural challenges of the texts, with clause- and word-level edits in virtually complementary distribution. His editing frequency is low, as pointed out earlier, and at a level where comparisons between the two texts may be invalid. The values for editing economy are perhaps also invalid given the low editing frequency. E3's editing effectiveness does, however, give some stronger clues. His position on the cusp of quadrants D and A for *Unemployment* and the cusp of A and B for *Lady Di* suggests mediocre output; in both cases little editing is done. My summary of E3 is more tentative: his monitoring does suggest an ability to address different structural challenges, while he has a tendency towards revision at the expense of correction of linguistically mediocre output.

Concluding remarks

In the first part of this chapter it was demonstrated that a group of student translators working into the second language have a poorer idea of the quality of their output than when they work into their first language, and it was claimed that the ability to monitor output is a facet of translation competence. From this general premise I set out to discover how the monitoring of output can be assessed through real-time editing data from handwritten translations. In the second part of the chapter a framework for collecting and analysing these data was developed and the framework used to make qualitative statements about the monitoring ability of three student translators. It was found that this ability did differ systematically from student to student and it was concluded that the abilty to monitor output is indeed a describable facet of translation competence.

Notes

1. My students were writing by hand. Tommola (1986) describes a method for monitoring translation by recording key strokes.
2. It would have been preferable to collapse the test results and tutors' assessments so that self-assessment simply contrasted with other assessment. However, adding T-scores to ranks would have produced a mathematical nonsense. I have resorted to collapsing the data later, but only as a basis for dividing subjects into three groups.

8 Towards a model of translation competence

Aims

This chapter brings together and summarizes the research described in Chapters 3–7. I begin by discussing the extent to which the findings satisfy the three requirements of a model of translation competence that I set out in Chapter 1. Next I set the findings in the wider context of translation research, noting that the fact that they are data-based sets them apart from much other research. The limitations of the research are dealt with next, and a considerable list of omissions from the model is listed and discussed. Finally, I discuss the wider applicability of the research to different language pairs, to different subjects, to different genres and to translation into the first language. The chapter concludes with a discussion of the practical implications of modelling translation competence for pedagogy and assessment.

Components of the model and their implications

In Chapter 1, I claimed that a model of translation competence ought to do at least the following:

(a) It should show whether translation competence is divisible into components, and if so describe those components and their inter-relationships.

(b) It should be able to describe the developmental pathway taken in learning how to translate.

(c) It should include means for describing the differences between the performance of different translators.

At the same time I made clear my intentions to focus on the language development aspects of translation competence at the expense of psycholinguistic aspects.

With regard to requirement (a), I have identified three components of a model of translation competence: target language textual competence, disposition, and monitoring competence. The genesis of these components lay in the preliminary study in Chapter 3. There I proposed that a key element in translation competence into the second· language was textual competence, or the ability to manipulate the genre potential of the target language by deploying grammar and lexis above the level of the sentence. The preliminary study gave some empirical confirmation that the proposal was worth pursuing.

I went on to test the notion of textual competence through analysing the distribution of a set of linguistic features in translations. These features had known distributional norms across authentic English texts. It was found that among the translators there was systematic stylistic variation ranging from language more typical of informal spoken English to language more typical of formal written English. In this process, however, it began to appear that some variation was due to a more general, individual factor which I called *disposition*.

The next step was to test the notion of textual competence through analysing lexis in a way that attempted to control for a syntactic variable as far as possible. Subjects with superior textual competence could be identified in this way, and the judgements made here confirmed to an extent the judgements made through examining structural features. However, lexis yielded a much less delicate gradation than structural features. What the examination of lexis did do was to illuminate the notion of disposition in much more detail, so that it was possible to profile this aspect in a systematic way.

The two components of the model so far had their origins in theory: target language textual competence was grounded firmly in theory, that is the idea that translation competence into the second language is a function of second language textual competence; disposition emerged as a result of falsifying part of that theory, that is by showing that some variation in translation competence was due to factors other than second language textual competence.

The third component – monitoring competence – is not theoretically underpinned, despite various attempts to propose monitoring devices in some branches of language acquisition and cognitive processing studies, as I was at pains to point out in Chapter 7. This component owes nothing to these attempts and is based purely on the empirical study of a practical problem. It is, then, somewhat removed from the other two components in provenance. The three components are summarized diagrammatically in Figure 8.1.

Let me now turn to some implications of this. The very act of proposing that a competence can be divided into separate, underlying components implies the relative independence of those components. With regard

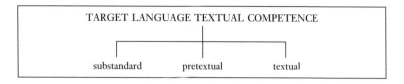

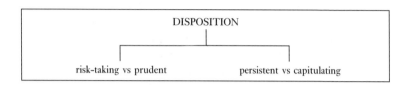

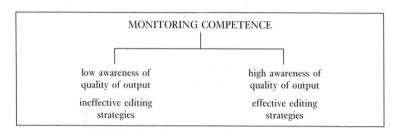

FIGURE 8.1   The three components of the model

to requirement (b), it also implies the potential for the development of the components through time. For example, the ability to ride a bicycle might comprise a number of components such as balance, stamina, mental agility, and others. In an average group of cyclists in a park on a Sunday morning one is likely to find all kinds of combinations of those components, including some with little stamina and good balance, some with little mental agility but plenty of stamina, and so on. The interrelationship among the components will be a function of the different kinds of competence: the pattern for a sprint racer will be different from that for a long-distance tourer. The development of the components will be reflected in the increasing skill with which a child rides his/her first bicycle.

Relative independence of the components

There is no reason why a model of translation competence should not reflect the same relative independence among its components. And in the case of the model presented here, there are good reasons why the components should be independent, since each component has to do with a different facet of the translation process. The textual competence component is a facet of target language competence – in fact, the ability to deploy the resources of the target language in a highly specialized way. The disposition component reflects individual characteristics of the translator unrelated to language competence, and the way in which these characteristics impact on the job of translating. The monitoring component has to do with both target language competence and individual approach. Indeed, these three components could be rephrased as three everyday questions that one might ask about a potential translator (especially a potential translator into the second language): (a) Can they produce translations in stylistically good English? (b) Do they have the right personality for translating? (c) Can they turn out text that needs the minimum of revising?

While the components are relatively independent, there is, however, the question of optimum combinations. In Table 8.1, for example, it can be seen that Subjects 45 and 37, who were ranked highest in textual competence (being the only subjects with textual competence confirmed by lexis), were also rated as risk-taking. However, subjects rated as

TABLE 8.1   Consolidated ratings of textual competence and disposition

Subject	Textual competence demonstrated in structure? (mean rank)	Textual competence demonstrated in lexis?	Risk-taking disposition?	Persistent disposition?
45	15.5	yes	yes	yes
37	15.5	yes	yes	yes
28	14	no	no	no
19	13	no	no	yes
21	11.5	no	yes	yes
49	11.5	no	no	yes
47	10	no	no	no
11	9	no	no	no
31	8	no	yes	no
50	7	no	no	yes
12	6	no	yes	no
38	5	no	yes	no
8	4	no	yes	yes
43	3	yes?	no	no
9	2	no	yes	no
36	1	no	—	—

risk-taking were to be found at all levels of ability. The difference is, of course, that a subject with high textual competence calculates the risks, while a subject with poor textual competence just makes a bet with long odds. On the other hand, persistent disposition is more likely to be found among subjects with good textual competence; note that Subject 28 in Table 8.1 scored artificially high on structural aspects of textual competence because of a substandard, telegraphic text. With 28 removed, the top five subjects in textual competence are rated as persistent. Bear in mind that as persistent disposition gives way to capitulation, target language deficits may be responsible so that disposition shades into lack of language competence.

The optimum combination, then, appears to be high textual competence and a risk-taking but persistent disposition.

The developmental dimension

The second implication of a model of competence is that of a developmental dimension. I believe that only the textual competence component can be considered developmentally, and that it should be properly considered an aspect of second language acquisition. This, however, raises some difficulties. The present state of knowledge of the structural aspects of second language acquisition theory is the result of intensive research at the level of the sentence and below. The line of research beginning with morpheme studies such as Dulay and Burt (1974) and refined into the learnability hypothesis of Pienemann (1983) is largely irrelevant to the level of language dealt with here. While Pienemann and others claim that a universal order of acquisition of grammatical structures can be shown, my work assumes that these structures have been acquired, and focuses on their deployment at text level. In Chapter 4, I made the first halting steps towards an order of acquisition of textual competence in translation into the second language, which were partly confirmed in Chapter 5 (although it must be remembered that the data are cross-sectional): I proposed that there was a substandard level of competence (the top end, perhaps of Pienemann's spectrum of interest); then at the pretextual level, it appeared that subjects could generally construct well-formed English, but in a way that resembled informal spoken genres; at the textual level, subjects were able to deploy English sentences in a way that resembled the formal written genre required by the source text. With the strong caveat that the data are cross-sectional, I am prepared to say that there is a developmental dimension to the textual component, and that the model has the potential to meet requirement (b).

Describing the differences between the performance of
different translators

Dealing with requirement (c) requires a little discussion. It would be
circular to simply answer 'yes' to the question 'Does the model include
the means to describe the differences between the performance of different translators?'. What I have done here is observe differences in
performance and suggest reasons for them – the differences could have
been demonstrated without any model at all. The proper way to deal
with requirement (c) is to argue that the model will describe differences between translators better than existing models do. In other words,
I must be able to claim that the use of the model will improve on existing methods of translation competence assessment such as translation
tests.

Translation testing is normally based on the error model of marking,
that is the marking of errors in relation to some not necessarily explicit or
fixed 'ideal' version to which the student version is expected to approximate (see Hosington and Horguelin, 1980 and NAATI, 1993 for
Canadian and Australian examples respectively). Such a model refers to
underlying competences only incidentally and negatively by tagging an
error and, according to the comprehensiveness of the accompanying comments, by indicating the error type.

The problem with error-deduction translation testing is that there
appears to be no explicit learning theory on which it is based. Implicitly,
there seems to be an idea that a global competence can be assessed
but no real consideration is given to any notion of learning or underlying competence. The aspects of a model of translation competence
presented in this work have the potential to improve the validity of
translation tests and in turn the kind of information that they can generate. There is no reason why the marking of a translation test should not
include an analysis of textual competence, disposition and monitoring
competence. Incidentally, this would entail the accumulation of norms
for particular test texts, with the added bonus of an increase in test
reliability.

Another possibility is that a quite different approach to assessment
could be taken, parallel to the acquisition-based procedure proposed in
Pienemann and Johnston (1986). If one accepts that developmental path-
ways can be discovered for translation into the second language, then it
follows that the outcome of assessment could be to locate the learner at a
point on the pathway. In conclusion, I believe the model does include the
means to describe differences between the performance of translators in
much more insightful ways than existing methods.

Relationship of the model to other trends in translation research

Research in translation studies often lacks the element of empirical validation. Typically, a theoretical standpoint is used to kick-start the discussion. For example, it might be claimed that a discourse approach is the best one for teaching translation; examples of good practice are then given to validate the approach. The model developed here could be accused of being kick-started in the same way in that I have hypothesized that textual competence is a key element in translation competence. What I have done, however, is to provide the empirical validation that is lacking in many other studies: I have shown systematically the relevance of textual competence and have begun to describe its manifestations.

There is a dichotomy of standpoints in the linguistic theories from which models of translation may be derived – the functional standpoint that concerns the relationship among the writer, the text and the real world – and the neo-Cartesian standpoint that is concerned with mental processes. This work nods in both directions. On the one hand, the notion of textual competence owes something to a functional standpoint by examining the details of how translators can deploy language to meet the expectations of a particular readership. On the other hand, the notions of disposition and monitoring competence belong more in the psycholinguistic or psychological domain: disposition concerns how individuals' translation performance is mediated by their overall individual approach (I hesitate to use the term *personality*); monitoring concerns how and to what extent translation output is checked.

The eclecticism of the model does, in fact, say something about the difference between a model of the translation *process* and a model of translation *competence*. A model of the process ought to provide a coherent set of explanations for observed data, and, given the rift between the functional and the neo-Cartesian views of language, should be grounded in one or the other in order to be coherent. A model of translation competence need not meet this rigorous criterion because its aims are more modest; in the end it asks why and how the abilities of translators differ and develop.

It may draw on models of or theories about the translation process and it may contribute to the falsification of these models or theories. A pertinent example here is Krings's model of the translation process (Krings, 1986). While the model will account for monitoring strategies, it can be criticized because it does not account for disposition.

If a model of translation competence is permitted to be eclectic, then I should mention some aspects that suggested themselves during the work but were not included. First, I did not consider target language competence at the level of the sentence and below, except to speak in general terms about substandard competence and errors. The details of the substandard competence of subjects are not of central importance to the question of textual competence, but could be of interest in second language acquisition research that examined the boundary between sentence level and text level.

Another facet not discussed here is real-world knowledge, the lack of which may contribute to poor translation. I chose not to deal with this because the source texts used were not specialized in content, although the unused *Einstein* text did seem to reveal knowledge gaps about the theory of relativity. Real-world knowledge could be a fruitful line of enquiry; it would be very interesting to know what kinds of strategies individual translators might use to plug knowledge gaps, and whether the notion of disposition could be independently tested – do some translators give up, and some create artificial meaning?

A notable omission in my work is a study of *cohesion*, claimed by some writers to be a key element in the ability to translate (see, for example, Kachroo, 1984). My feeling is that cohesion in translation into the second language deserves a large study of its own. Such a study might proceed by establishing norms for the use of cohesive devices in specific target language genres, and then comparing these with the ways in which translators into the second language use the same devices.

Yet another facet that I have not explored is a *matching* component. This was hinted at in Chapter 5 in the discussion of the choices of verb forms that the subjects made in translating English agentless passives, while Campbell (1983) establishes a set of possible choices for translating Form V Arabic verbs into English. A matching component of translation competence would be concerned with the extent to which these choices are known to the translator. A good example is the Arabic particle *qad*. A high degree of matching competence would be reflected in the translator who knows that the two immediate choices in English are (a) a possibility modal, or (b) a past perfect verb.

The facet of *stamina* was also not examined. By stamina I mean the capacity a translator into the second language has to keep producing well-formed language. Informal classroom observations have suggested to me that in some students, target language control breaks down more quickly than in others; and that the aspects of the target language system to break down under pressure differ from one subject to another. Spelling and the use of articles are examples; at least one student has been seen to revert to French spellings (French having been acquired as a second language before English). The monitoring component might be extended to examine this. In this study, stamina was not examined because I felt that the texts were not long enough for reliable conclusions to be made.

The contribution of *first language interference* to translation competence was also not looked at here. Principally, there was a theoretical objection. I have already signalled a heavy debt to second language acquisition theory, and in that spirit I suggest that interference is a somewhat redundant concept. If translations into the second language represent points on the interlanguage continuum, then one should reject as simplistic the idea of one system (the first language) impacting in a predictable way on another (the second language). But this does not mean that interference cannot play a role at all, just that the role needs to be more subtly understood. One useful line of enquiry would be to examine how translators differ in their ability to modify or recast rhetorical devices in the source language that are less acceptable in the target language; the often-claimed tendency of Arabic prose to parallelism is an example. This kind of work requires, once again, reliable norms for both languages – does Arabic prose really favour parallelism? Again, what are the rhetorical devices used to express irony in Arabic, and how do they differ from those used in English? How do individual translators vary in their ability to tailor a target text to the devices characteristic of the target language?

Finally, I have not looked at the range of ability in conscious strategies such as the use of references, dictionaries, computer aids, and so on. In fact Krings (1986: 269) includes the use of reference books as one element of his comprehension strategies.

Wider applicability of the model

The model, or fragment of a model, as it stands is based on a narrow set of data. The possibility of its wider applicability would require replication across different data sets. I suggest that it could be tested further in this way by examining (a) different language pairs, (b) different subjects, (c) different genres, and (d) translation into the first language.

Different language pairs

Replicating the model with different language pairs ought not to compromise the central point that textual competence is a key facet of translation competence. It ought, however, to reveal differences of emphasis from one language to another that could be useful for the *implementation* of the model. For example, speakers of a language that has not borrowed heavily from the stock of European metaphors may differ in their ability to deploy English metaphors in a textually competent way[1].

Different subjects

The subjects of this work are all drawn from an immigrant minority in Australia; Arabic has only quasi-official status and is taught principally in the context of language maintenance as a result of community pressure (see Campbell et al., 1993 for an extended analysis of Arabic in Australia). There are no mechanisms through which Australian society recognizes or discusses equivalent genres between the two languages. In a different context of bilingualism, for example Canada, where a massive government-sponsored translation movement makes texts in equivalent genres accessible, a replica of the study might reveal more subtle differences in textual competence.

Different genres

Genre is not socially neutral. As Halliday points out, the 'language of "events into things"' . . . was a semiotic for capitalism, maintaining a clear distinction between "those in the know" and the rest' (Halliday, 1993: 76). The nominalized language of technical discourse, says Halliday 'leached into the discourse of administration and commerce'. It eventually became and 'remained, by and large, a middle class prerogative and preserve' (p. 76).

It is no accident that most of the source language texts used as data here are of this nominalized and abstract type. The subjects in this study were all trying to enter 'the gateway into knowledge and power' (p. 76). One of the gateways for immigrants is to use the asset of language to become an accredited translator, and the key to the gate is the ability to write in the language of power. This, then, is why the genres studied here are significant; in the light of Halliday's claims, to assess textual competence is no more than to judge whether an immigrant translator 'writes like us' (that is the formal written language of the powerful) or 'just picked the language up' (that is the informal spoken language of the powerless). That is why accreditation examinations and university examinations in translation in Australia (at least in languages like Arabic) use the texts they do, and why textual competence is a key issue. Certainly other genres could be studied, but it is the language of power that really matters to immigrants trying to become translators.

Translation into the first language

There is no reason why the three components in the model should not be applicable to translation into the first language; replicated studies ought to reveal some similarities and some differences. Let me deal with the likely similarities first.

Disposition, I have claimed, reflects the individual's approach to the task. If disposition is a non-linguistic phenomenon, then it ought to be more or less common whether one is translating into the first language or the second language. However, disposition may manifest itself slightly differently between the first language and the second language. I mentioned earlier in this chapter that *capitulation* shades into target language competence; in other words, translators into the second language may behave in this way as the result of their overall approach to the task, or because they have deficient target language competence. In translation into the first language, capitulation may be because of both overall approach and poor source language comprehension.

Monitoring is quite a different matter. I claimed in Chapter 7 that translators are generally much less aware of their competence into the second language than into the first language; a replicated study would be expected to confirm this. I also claimed that subjects edit for two reasons: revision and correction. In translation into the first language, one would expect to encounter mainly revision; correction would be of a quite different nature, and the making of errors and the inability to correct them would be a matter of carelessness rather than a function of language ability.

In translation into the first language, textual competence must be highly relevant, but of a different nature. While I am concerned in this study with a fairly crude division between a formal written genre and an informal spoken genre, textual competence into the first language ought to concern itself with much more subtle distinctions; can the subject translate into a number of genres, for example the language of insurance policies, committee reports, patent applications, etc.? The power of language is still an issue, but at a far higher level of operation than that of the immigrant translator trying to break through the genre barrier. The potential textual competence demanded of the translator into the first language is staggering: it is the ability to possess the linguistic power of the lawyer, the doctor, the engineer, the politician, the public servant.

Translation competence, pedagogy and assessment

The impetus for this book, as I have mentioned elsewhere, has been my experience in teaching translation to non-native speakers of English, and at this point it is time that we went back to the arena of pedagogy to discuss the practical consequences of having a model of translation competence that deals with translation into the second language. First, we present a kind of pedagogical manifesto, which will act as a set of guiding principles for the ensuing discussion where I will examine translation pedagogy and assessment from the points of view of the various stakeholders in the enterprise.

There are four fundamental principles that follow from the idea of modelling translation competence:

1. Translation competence can be separated into relatively independent components, and those components can be used as building blocks in curriculum design.
2. Translation education is a matter of intervention in the development of the various components of translation competence.
3. Students are likely to attain different levels of achievement in the various components of translation competence given the imbalance in their bilingual skills.
4. The assessment of translation quality is best seen as a matter or profiling the competence of learners, rather than simply measuring the quality of their output.

Like any educational enterprise, translation pegagogy and assessment revolves around the complementary interests of its stakeholders. In the following sections, the positions of the main stakeholders are discussed in the light of what we have learned of translation competence. These stakeholders include students, teachers, course designers and accrediting bodies.

Students and translation competence

For the student, a model of translation competence can be used to provide a source of knowledge about their level of achievement. This is in contrast to conventional methods of feedback, which provide relatively unhelpful and unsystematic information. Without a model of translation competence student feedback is conventionally obtained through:

(a) ephemeral reactions of teachers during discussion of translations generated around the class.
(b) marked translations done as homework or individual class assignments.
(c) ordinary academic grading of work done in supporting subjects such as language improvement work and contextual studies.

Feedback of type (a) is self-evidently poor, if only because of its inability to sample student achievement. Translation teachers are all too aware of the tiny amount of work that can be done in 'around the class' exercises, and of the rather artificial nature of the common practice of the teacher writing on the board the best preferred oral translation. And while class discussions of textual analysis are no doubt extremely valuable, their ability to reveal student achievement is virtually non-existent. Feedback of type (c) is similarly limited since it impinges only very indirectly on the business of actual translation. Our most serious criticism is of type (b), the marked translation, which fails to inform students for several important reasons. These are:

- Failure to sample.
- Failure to quantify.
- Failure to refer systematically to underlying competence.

To take the first criticism, let us consider the translation text as a sampling instrument. A characteristic of texts is that they present a random sample of items or problem types and that these items are drawn from an infinitely large stock of lexical items and lexical-syntactic combinations. Disregarding our model and focusing just on structural problems for the time being, the optimum demand would be for a text to sample a statistically significant number of lexical and grammatical problems. The characteristics of texts that we have mentioned preclude this possibility unless they are extremely large. The *Unemployment* text, for example, contains eight sentences, of which seven (87%) are heavily nested complex sentences, while *Lady Di* has 19 sentences of which 16 (84%) are simple sentences. *Lady Di* clearly does not sample subordination, but the number of subordinations in *Unemployment* is still worryingly small. In vocabulary, the two passages vary, with a lexical variety ratio (types/tokens) of 0.62 for *Unemployment*, and 0.75 for *Lady Di*. Even granted that around 90 types in each passage is a respectable number for us to base statistics on, there remains the problem that it is an infinitesimally small sample of the possible range of vocabulary that a translator should be able to handle. Redundancy also decreases the power of the text to inform the student; easy or repeated chunks are redundant, while difficult unique chunks occur in insignificant numbers. The term *baṭāla* gave virtually no candidate a problem – most translated it as *unemployment* – and may just as well have been ignored by the marker. The three possible strategies to improve the sampling ability of marked texts are to create specially written texts (whose textuality is compromised), to use extremely long texts (with the disadvantage of being unwieldy as teaching resources), or to identify and ignore redundancies (and hope that the remaining items constitute critical cases).

The second criticism is the failure to quantify achievement. The marking of student translations tends to be qualitative; typically the marker uses deletions, carets, comments and rewritings to approximate the student version to an 'ideal' version. Quantitative feedback is most often in the form of a *post-hoc* norm-referenced grade to satisfy institutional requirements. It is only by a feat of extraordinary analytical ability that a series of marked and graded translations can be pieced together to form a longitudinal quantitative record.

The third criticism – the failure to address underlying competences – is based on the 'error' model of marking usually adopted, that is the marking of errors in relation to some not necessarily explicit or fixed 'ideal' version to which the student version is expected to approximate. Such a model refers to underlying competences only incidentally and negatively by tagging an error and, according to the comprehensiveness of the accompanying comments, by indicating the error type.

Given these criticisms of marked translations as a means of student feedback, we might be tempted to discard the notion altogether. The extreme alternative is for student feedback to come solely from a period- ically reviewed translation competence profile. However, this raises the question of face validity: as stakeholders in translation education at the very coalface, neither student nor teacher is well served by a system of feedback that looks quite different from the task at hand.

What needs to be grasped is that feedback through marked translations and a translation competence profile have different though valid purposes and characteristics. A marked translation is characterized by:

Rapid feedback: A translation can be marked and returned within hours.

Feedback into teaching: The results of marking can be used as the basis of a following class.

Focus on specific teaching points: Where there are common errors in a batch of marked translations, the teacher can focus on these in a fol- lowing class.

Low reliability: The inability of the test to sample widely gives an in- built low reliability.

Face validity: The test has face validity in that it has the appearance of testing the skill that is being taught.

A translation competence profile, on the other hand, has these char- acteristics:

Slow feedback: Profiling competence is slow and incremental.

Feedback into learning: The information given in a translation compe- tence profile is likely to shape the way the student learns, rather than the way the teacher teaches.

Focus on underlying competences: The profile addresses individual components of competence.

Potentially high reliability: The profile is likely to be more reliable in the sense that it is obtained systematically over time.

Construct validity: The fact that it is based on a theory of learning means that the profile will have a high construct validity.

In conclusion, the complementarity of the marked translation and the translation competence profile means that the student is best served by both kinds of feedback: marked translations shape teaching, a profile shapes learning.

Teachers and translation competence

Our model of translation competence impinges on the teacher in at least four ways:

1. In the diagnosis of student problems.
2. In the design of individualized teaching and learning strategies.
3. In the evaluation of teaching.
4. In student assessment.

Diagnosis of student problems

Diagnosis of student problems in translation can only be effective if based on the idea of separable underlying competences. Some examples will illustrate the point.

In the study described in Chapter 4, many candidates switched the actor and patient in their translations of *yuwājihuhā al'ālam*, producing *which face the world* or suchlike instead of *which the world faces*. The underlying reasons for the switch might be found in at least two of our components:

Disposition: The translator is a risk-taker who is prepared to sacrifice the source language (SL) structure for a (to them) more satisfying target language (TL) version.
Monitoring: The translator automatically reproduced the approximate SL word order and failed to monitor the misassigned syntactic relation in the TL.

The bald product data represented by the TL versions cannot tell us what motivated the switch, and if the texts had been homework assignments, the teacher's annotation (presumably a comment to the effect that there had been a switch) would not be diagnostic but prescriptive; not 'the real problem is . . .' but 'you should have written . . .'.

Another example comes from a piece of work not mentioned in the case studies where one of my students offered *alife and dead* for *ḥayyan wa mayyitan*. The oddity is simply in *alife* for *alive*. The rationale could be found in several components:

Level of textual competence: The incorrect morphophonemic form derives from the fact that the student is at the substandard level of competence; he/she does not have that part of the target language system at his/her command.

Monitoring: The student made a processing error under pressure of time, and failed to spot it.

In both cases a periodically reviewed profile of the student's underlying competences gives the teacher a much better clue as to the reasons for the errors, the significance that should be attached to them, and the best course of pedagogical action.

Design of individualized teaching and learning strategies

While actual translation will be a central teaching and learning strategy in any programme of translator education, the notion of separable translation competences allows for the design of other strategies which may not involve actual translation. The principle that individual translators will develop in the various competences at different rates strongly suggests that individualized strategies are the most appropriate. I do not suggest any radical teaching and learning techniques here, rather the selection of well-tried techniques to intervene in the development of specific components of translation competence. A student with poor monitoring ability, for example, might be given proof-reading exercises, or exercises in close analysis of their free composition in the target language to recognize and classify errors.

The most significant aspect of this is that it provides a means of individualizing translator education programmes to some extent. A difficulty is that translation education traditionally favours a teacher-centred approach because of the common belief that the purpose of student translation work is to approximate an ideal version. As long as the translation text is the focus of translator education, then a shift to a student-centred approach is unlikely. Using translation competence as the focus allows much of the responsibility to shift to the student through accurately focused individualized work.

The evaluation of teaching

The sources of data on the evaluation of teaching are typically:

- Teachers' self-assessments.
- Peer assessment.
- Student opinions by way of questionnaires, etc.
- Student grade averages.

While I do not wish to venture too far into an area with its own specializations, I am prepared to claim that the use of a translation competence profile is likely to provide information that will contribute to the evaluation of teaching. The key to the process is that the profile will provide comparative data more effectively than other methods. Student grades, for instance, are often anchored to a normal distribution so that objective differences from year to year are masked. In the absence of a convincing criterion-referenced scheme for marking translation work (although see Hosington and Horguelin (1980) for a Canadian solution) it is hard to imagine a way to compare one student group to another and therefore make some quantitative judgement about teaching effectiveness. Moreover, it is a maxim in this book that underlying competences can be described and intervention effected at the level of the competence; in that case the evaluation of teaching ought to be made, in part at least, on the basis of progress in the development of the competences. The question that a longitudinal translation competence profile can ask on the teacher's behalf is, then, 'To what extent did my teaching cause progress in class X this year as opposed to last year?'

Student assessment

Finally, the profiling of translation competence provides an extra source of data for use in student assessment, which has already been discussed from the student's standpoint. Looked at from the teacher's assessment perspective, the use of these two sources of data – marked translations and a competence profile – fits comfortably with the dictum that assessment is based on, but not slavishly beholden to, measurement. Assessment can, then, be based on 'objective' data from the translation competence profile, and more 'subjective' professional judgement applied to tests and examinations.

Accrediting authorities and translation competence

Accrediting authorities are major stakeholders in the enterprise of translation; their requirement is for methods of assessing translation performance that will provide a guarantee that the accredited translator will perform consistently well at a defined level. Our discussion here centres on the difficulties associated with translation tests, and suggests that accrediting authorities could benefit from combining such tests with the profiling of competence. We begin with a brief survey of translation marking scales and then go on to discuss accreditation testing in the context reliability and validity.

Marking scales

All accrediting authorities use marking scales of some kind. For example, the marking scale of the National Accreditation Authority for Translators and Interpreters (NAATI) in Australia is a quantitative procedure that serves to give some weight to a qualitative judgement. Indeed, this is made quite explicit in the guide to markers, which advises them to make a general assessment of the script and then to do a quantitative marking by deducting errors. My experience as an examiner for the Authority is that the quantitative aspect is mainly of importance in documenting borderline failures; passing or failing candidates are generally identifiable on a first reading. There is flexibility in the weighting of errors; if there were not, the system would be grossly unfair since it has no means of moderation on the grounds of the difficulty of the source text, or even the language pair: in Chinese to English, in French to English, from one year to the next, the candidate begins with a bank of 50 points per text and loses them according to the same scheme.

Canadian marking scales are described in Hosington and Horguelin (1980). The marking scale of the Canadian Translators and Interpreters Council (described on page 14) is a deductive system with the error points graded according to the nature of the error. Points are deducted thus:

Nonsense	−20
'Contresens'	−10 to −15
Omission	−5 to −15
'Faux sens'	−5 to −15
Excessive borrowing	−5 to −10
Syntax and grammar	−5 to −10
Spelling	−2 to −5
Overall quality (composition)	+ or −20

An elegant piece of arithmetic allows a coefficient to be built in to account for the level of competence being tested, so that raw marks may be adjusted to meet the requirements of the test; a stiff test will demand a higher pass mark. Other than this coefficient, the procedure seems to differ little from that of NAATI. The Canadian Language Quality Measurement System (CLQMS) works quite differently. Here the SL text is broken into translation units (although the theoretical rationale for the breakdown is not discussed) and a grid of 15 criteria is built (Hosington and Horguelin, 1980: 15–16). There are three groups of criteria: under 'translation process' are meaning, terminology, structure, effect, shifts; 'composition' includes 'editing, syntax, usage, style, logic, tone'; criteria affecting both the 'SL text and TL text' are 'nuance, additions, omissions, approach'. The grid allows for an assessment of the quality of the translation, a quantification of its strengths and weaknesses, and a guide to the complexity of the SL text. The capacity to account for different SL texts puts this method far in front of simple deductive schemes, as does the final output of the procedure – a file containing all the data acquired so that employers can make their own judgement.

So much for marking scales in everyday use. The procedure described by Fau (1990) is admittedly experimental. Here, the theory of fuzzy logic is employed to make sense of judgements like rather good, very bad, etc., since, as Fau rightly claims, translation assessment is traditionally qualitative rather than quantitative. A hierarchy is then set up, beginning with a linguistic variable (in the special sense of a piece of natural language that can be computed) of quality. The next level is a binary split into good and bad, followed by a level of fuzzy-restricted values such as very good, rather bad, etc. Finally, the fuzzy-restricted values are tied to a set of base values from 10 to 100. All of this is fine, as it goes, until we come to what we might call the expert system behind the fuzzy logic. In a thinly disguised Hallidayan functional classification, judgements on factual, affective and structural information transformation are reinterpreted as judgements on the central, accompanying and structural messages. The degree of gain or loss in each of the three messages is determined in a random sample of sentences, and some fuzzy mathematics follows. Now is established a level set (presumably a criterion of acceptability) and 'we will give our verdict on the quality of a certain work of translation with such fuzzy labels as Good or Bad translation, but this time such labelling is felt to be less fuzzy, as we are aware of its actual grade of membership' (Fau, 1990: 53). This less than impressive result has a lot to do with fuzzy logic and not much to do with translation. At least two faulty assumptions leap from the text. First, the expert system is based on no more than 'A brief survey of the views of some of the most influential writers in various periods and cultures (Fau, 1990: 45), and the random selection of sentences completely ignores the significance of the textuality of the passage chosen for the test.

Accreditation testing and reliability

Test reliability is of crucial importance to accrediting bodies, who are charged with providing a guarantee to the public that a translator's work is to be relied on. Educational measurement and evaluation theory offers a number of ways of assessing test reliability, including equivalent forms, test-retest, split-halves, the Kuder–Richardson formulae and the inter-marker method. In norm-referenced objective testing (for example, multiple-choice tests), reliability coefficients are calculated on any of these bases. Can they be used for translation testing?

The use of equivalent forms in translation testing would seem at first sight to be quite practical; one would find two very similar texts, set each as a separate examination paper for one group of subjects, then correlate the two sets of scores obtained. The difficulties arise in finding two very similar texts. In what should the similarity reside? An obvious way would be to take a single homogeneous text and divide it into parts so that the style, content and complexity of each part were similar. However, Tirkonnen-Condit (1985) warns against the use of extract texts for single tests, let alone retests. Otherwise, one can imagine some procedure whereby an 'equivalent' text was found with similar word and sentence statistics to the original, that is average word and sentence length, proportion of passive sentences, vocabulary variety, etc. Inexpensive computer utilities are able to provide some of this basic information in a few seconds, but they clearly cannot give any clue as to the similarity or otherwise of the texts at discourse level. One can imagine a painstaking process of estab-lishing discourse equivalence that involved identifying the text type, check-ing the similarity of coherence, and then comparing the microlinguistic exponents. Furthermore, there is the practice factor; whichever means were found to ensure the 'equivalence' of the forms, the first text would provide good practice for the second so that the two forms would not be equivalent in reality.

The drawbacks of the test-retest method are common to any discipline, not just translation. The method is flawed because of the problem of memory and the problem of the effect of instruction or practical experi-ence. If too short a time has elapsed between the two test sessions, then a subject may remember the original occasion and use the remembered experience in the second session; if too long has elapsed, then some subjects may have improved their skills through instruction or experi-ence, while others may have remained static or even deteriorated.

The split-halves method is often used in objective testing because it avoids the problems of equivalent forms and test-retest. In this method, a score is obtained for two halves of the test, usually divided into odd and even numbered items. The method depends on the test being divisible into a usable number (say 40 at least) of items of potentially equal weight. Can it be used for translation? In principle, a translation marking scheme that is based on discrete units of translation (for example, the CLQMS system) ought to accommodate the split-halves method if a value can be assigned to each item. However, the approach is likely to founder for a number of reasons: the division into units (that is, items) must be arbitrary since linguistic units function at different levels simultaneously; easy stretches and chunks contribute nothing to the measurement process and make the test highly redundant; and the fact that virtually any string in a source text may have numerous target versions makes the business of assigning a value to each unit extremely difficult. Similar difficulties apply to the Kuder–Richardson formulae, which require correct/incorrect judgements for each test item. Fuzzy logic is seen as one solution to giving computable values to subjective judgements in Fau (1990), but the Kuder–Richardson procedure would need considerable tweaking to accept fuzzy values rather than correct/incorrect values.

To return to the central problem: can we find a way to judge whether a translation test will give a consistent result, so that the clients of accredited translators can have confidence in the test? Given the difficulties outlined above, the only recourse is to judgements of inter-marker reliability. In this case, one marker's set of scores for a group of subjects is correlated with another marker's scores for the same subjects on the same test. If this procedure is repeated over a number of tests and a number of markers, a picture is eventually built up of the reliability of the total testing process (for example, the accreditation authority or professional body). We have, however, come a long way from the translation test itself; even if the testing organization satisfies itself as to its overall reliability, that is no guarantee that any individual test is reliable.

It is virtually inevitable that accreditation tests will have to rely on inter-marker reliability. However, it is reasonable to suggest that the overall process of accrediting translators can be made more reliable through the use of translation competence profiles used in conjunction with orthodox tests. As we have seen in the case studies in this book, translated texts can reveal extremely insightful information about the separate competences that underlie the ability to translate. There is no reason why accreditation tests cannot be analysed to provide the same kind of competence information, which can then be used to supplement the judgements made from orthodox marking, and therefore increase the reliability of the test. I mentioned previously that borderline cases present the main difficulties in translation accreditation tests; if there were supplementary information on a borderline candidate's level of textual competence for example, the decision to pass or fail the candidate would be a better informed one.

Accreditation tests and validity

It is useful here to distinguish several types of validity:

- Concurrent validity.
- Predictive validity.
- Ecological validity.
- Construct validity.
- Face validity.

A test is said to have concurrent validity if there is a good correlation between it and another test intended to measure the same thing. Unfortunately, there is no accepted alternative to translation testing, and concurrent validity cannot easily be judged. A model of translation competence can, however, solve this problem by specifying the separate components of competence, so that they can be tested independently. Using the model proposed in this book, separate tests not involving translation could be designed to test textual competence, disposition and monitoring, which would then provide the yardstick for us to assess the concurrent validity of translation tests. In fact, this rather sophistic discussion could be turned on its head; it might be more effective to accredit translators on the basis of tests of separate competences rather than translation tests. We pick up this slightly uncomfortable idea when we deal with face validity.

Predictive validity concerns whether the results of a test correlate with some behaviour that the test predicts. Here we are concerned with whether a translation test provides the grounds for an accrediting authority to predict confidently that a candidate is fit to practise professionally, and it seems that the matter is tied up with the test conditions and the nature of the texts involved. Stern (1984) in his discussion of the American Translators Association accreditation program suggests that the ATA tests are held in relaxed conditions where the candidate is not subjected to deadlines and interruptions; the gulf between the test and the workplace makes one suspicious of the predictive validity of the test. The NAATI professional level tests in Australia generally use journalistic texts, impose a tight time limit, and only allow limited use of special resources, which at least replicates some aspects of the translator's experience – working to an impossible deadline dictated by the client – but of course it hardly predicts the ability to translate highly specialized texts where extensive research is required. The assumed predictive validity of the professional-level texts seems to lie in the notion that an assessment of global competence can be gleaned from a 'general' text, and that this global competence is a guarantee that the candidate can handle other materials. At the specialist level, texts of specific types (medical, scientific, etc.) are carefully chosen with the view that successful candidates will work on such texts in their professional life; and the use of word processors and lexical aids is permitted. These tests may have a better predictive validity than the professional level tests.

Fried (1983) has proposed that in language testing there should be a notion of ecological validity, suggesting that a valid test is one that includes all the language situations that will be relevant to the candidate. Presumably, an invalid language test would be one that did not include some vital situation such as *apologizing* or *writing a letter of complaint*. A maximally ecologically valid test is, one supposes, an ideal rather than a reality. For translation, ecological validity presents a serious worry unless we are confident that a couple of texts will provide a good enough global view for us to be sure that the candidates can handle anything thrust on them in real life. In Fried's terms, accreditation tests of this type must have a very low ecological validity.

Perhaps it is construct validity that poses the most serious problem for accreditation testing: to what extent do such tests concur with the theory on which they are based? In language testing, low construct validity is easy to exemplify: a test for a functionally based language course would have little construct validity if it followed a structurally based format; the table of specifications for a construct-valid test would need to address functions and notions rather than vocabulary and grammar. The problem with translation tests is that there appears to be no explicit theory on which they are based. Implicitly, there seems to be an idea that a global competence can be assessed, and marking schemes usually require markers to categorize errors. However, given that this error categorization is usually based on comparisons between the source and target texts, no real consideration is given to any notion of learning or underlying competence.

Finally, there is face validity, or the extent to which the test looks like a test of what it professes to test. Here translation tests score both high and low. The high score derives from the fact that the candidate sits, pen in hand, doing something very much like what they hope to do professionally; one can imagine the flood of complaints if accreditation candidates were asked not to translate but to take a computer-based multiple-choice test, however valid the authority believed it to be. Translation accreditation tests score low, however, when they present texts that are unlike those that candidates are likely to meet in real life. The mismatch may be obvious (for example, an unaccredited but experienced insurance translator takes a test based on a political article from the press) or much more subtle because of the use of extract rather than full texts. This practice is criticized by Tirkonnen-Condit (1985), who argues that where the whole text is not available, the text type may be misidentified and there is no opportunity for the examinee to 'gradually evolve the macropropositions of the text in the course of proceeding from one minitext to another, and to absorb elements into the knowledge frames stored in her memory' (1985: 198). This results in the 'frame incompatibility' of microlinguistic exponents. Cited is a Finnish example, where the examinee rendered *good and bad* as *hyvä ja paha*, in the 'moral judgement frame' rather than *hyvä ja huono* in the 'amenity frame'. One way to avoid this problem (and increase the face validity of the tests) is by including long sections of texts before and after the section to be translated.

It seems to me that while in one sense translation tests do have high face validity – because the candidate actually translates – the face validity is in essence low because of the tiny sample of possible texts that can be presented. Admittedly, the use of a translation competence profile can never increase the face validity of a test, but it can generally improve the effectiveness of the test procedure along a wide range of criteria.

Concluding remarks

In concluding this book, I return to the four key issues in applied linguistics that I set up as the landmarks we would keep in sight. In considering translation in the context of *second language acquisition*, a cogent case has been put for learning to translate into the second language to be considered as a special type of second language acquisition that is highly constrained by the task at hand. We can make much more fruitful insights into the performance of our translation students if we switch from a focus on product to a focus on process. This view is of course closely related to thinking about translation in an *interlanguage* framework, which gives us the possibility of seeing second language translation output as a developing system rather than a substandard version of some ideal target. Of special importance was the notion that textual skills could be considered in this way; I would venture to say that studies of translation will, in the future, yield very significant understandings about the way textual competence develops in language learners. This is, of course, the essence of how translation relates to the *organization of language above the level of the sentence*. The final landmark was *levels of language competence*. Here we made considerable inroads into profiling the separate elements of translation competence, again especially with regard to textual phenomena.

I look forward to a situation where the phenomenon of translation into the second language is acknowledged not as a problem, but as a normal human activity supported by the assistance and insights that can be gained from the methodical application of linguistic theory.

Note

1. See Blau (1981) for an extensive discussion of how Modern Standard Arabic and Modern Hebrew have absorbed the same set of Standard Average European metaphors through the European language-medium education of their most significant thinkers at the time of the revival of these languages.

APPENDIX 1: Examples of target texts with varying combinations of textual competence, risk-taking and persistence

Seven pairs of texts are listed, selected according to the criteria below.

Subject 45:   High textual competence, risk-taking, persistent
Subject 19:   High textual competence, prudent, persistent
Subject 28:   High textual competence, prudent, capitulating
Subject 8:   Low textual competence, risk-taking, persistent
Subject 9:   Low textual competence, risk-taking, capitulating
Subject 50:   Low textual competence, prudent, persistent
Subject 43:   Low textual competence, prudent, capitulating

There was no subject who was judged to be of high textual competence, risk-taking and capitulating.

Note that square brackets in the text samples denote deletions [DEL], insertions [INSERT] and obvious gaps, where the subject left some material unwritten [GAP]. Where the deletion or insertion could be clearly read in the handwritten originals, the deleted or inserted material is included in the brackets. Where it is unclear, the approximate number of letters is indicated by 'x's: [DEL xx].

Subject 45:   High textual competence, risk-taking, persistent

Finance

As predicted, the years scheduled for the exhaustion of the American reserves have passed, and no sign of (catastrophe). But the price of petrol has declined and the exporting countries could lose its ability to resist this decline. How did that happen, and what future changes will occur on the role played by [DEL pet] petrol asa source of energy; and what [DEL 's] are the plans [DEL to] for the development of the sources of energy in the future, and it's effects between the nations? During the fifties and the sixties occupied countries gained their independence and started their economic and national growth with great enthusiasm and activity, accompanied with the projection of the [DEL economic – social] [INS socioeconomic] crisis in the capitalistic countries. With the loss of these countries to solve it's [DEL problem] crisis [DEL with] economically. the policy to activate it's internal demands by spending [GAP]. All it's resources were exhausted therefore this economic liberation which was refused by the third world countries revolutions, and their voices were raised requesting changes in the [INS international] economic systems in order to minimize the gap between themselves and the advanced countries. [DEL which] This was a pessimistic cry for the capitalist countries who wish to develop new methods of economic [DEL sovrei] supremacy

It's a great fault to explain figures as they are [GAP] as numbers, they need to be explained and it's impossible to understand it's meaning unless the changes of the [DEL social] international life is understood.

Africa

Whilst life is choking in the African continent under the pressures of hunger, locusts, poisonous gases and the civil wars (Sudan – Angola), the sylos of the affluent countries are overflowing with surplus grains.

So why don't the lucky countries distribute it's surplus to the hungry nations? The logical answer to these severe contradictions as seen by these nations, is that they can't give away such precious gifts without losing their popularity within their societies, although the specialists regard[DEL s] that such assistance does not solve the third world countries' problems.

What's required is [DEL xx] agricultural development in those countries.

In August, the American president, Ronald Raegen granted the Soviet Union a concession of 13 dollars per ton, in order to encourage them to purchase the American wheat, that would total to 52 million dollars for the 4 million tons agreed to be sold to Moscow. That prompted the minister of Foreign Affairs George Schultz to declare that it's not just for the American citizen to purchase his wheat at a higher price [DEL that] than that paid by the Soviet citizen. Days after this event at the conference held at Sans Francisco (at the defence league's meeting between America – Australia – New Zealand) Washington was faced by the Australians criticism accusing the Americans by ruining the international markets suppliers with their concessions to the Soviets. Also it was clarified by the Australians that such an agreement will tend to reduce the American imports.

And whilst the economic situation is awaiting the crystallization of the complications caused at the beginning of the year, the sylos are filled with millions of tons from the surplus of wheat, [DEL what] which it's cost of storage is increasing to 400 million dollars per annum, that exceeds the amount of aid given to the victims of famine.

Subject 19: High textual competence, prudent, persistent

Finance

The years fixed for the drainage of American reserve might have ended and the symptoms of the 'crisis' are not apparent yet. As for the price of oil, it is decreasing and oil exporting countries are almost loosing power to stop and resist this decline. How did this happen and what changes will take place in the role of oil [DEL in] as a source of power, in the future and what are the new plans to develop sources of energy in the world of tomorrow, and the impact of all this on the states and nations of the world?

During the fifties and sixties the people of the colonies were able to achieve political independence and national economic construction began with such vigour and enthusiasm, together with the [DEL appe] emergence of the economic social crisis in the advanced capitalist countries while these countries were lacking power to deal with this crisis through their own economic means.

The present policies based on encouragement of local demand artificially by government spending to ensure full utilisation of the material [DEL ly] [INS and human] productive apparatus, have consumed their potential and their negative accumulations began to change to wide social upheavals [DEL inside] within the capitalist countries. For this reason, [DEL xx] the [DEL aim] target of economic liberation which was rejected by the [INS national] governments and revolutions of the third world, and the emergence of voices demanding the introduction of basic changes in the world economic system to compensate countries liberated from colonialism, for the long plunder [DEL j] which they were subjected to, and to consolidate their efforts to reduce the gap between themselves [DEL and] and the advanced countries. are all considered as a bad omen for the capitalist countries which are looking for new means of economic control.

It is a great error to [DEL change] transfer changes taking place to dead silent figures, because figures do not explain themselves alone, and many times it happens that facts behind them are [DEL oppos] contrary to what they say at a glance. Figures themselves need explanation and they cannot be understood and [DEL xx] their meanings realised except through the essence of changes currently taking place in the social and international life.

Africa

While life [INS in Africa suffocates] under the pressure of famine, locusts, volcanic poisonous gases and the flames of national wars (Sudan – Angola), stores in rich countries are flooded with surplus grain.

Why unfortunate countries take the initiative to distribute their surplus to hungry people? The justified answer to this sharp contradiction is confined to the fact that concerned governments cannot, in their view, hand over such valuable gifts without raising the level of their own performance, which make them lose the popularity of their societies. While experts on their part, explain that such assistance does not solve the problems of the Third World and what is needed is development of [DEL the] basic agriculture in these countries.

On world market level, President Ronald Reagan took, during early last August, the initiative to offer an encouraging subsidy to the Soviet Union which wanted to purchase American wheat, and earmarked a support fund of 13 dollars for each ton of grain, which rais[DEL ed] [INS es] the total fund alloted to [INS the] more than 4 million tons to be sold to Moscow, to 52 million dollars. This [DEL made] [INS prompted] the minister of sate, Jeorge Scholtz to announce that it was not fair for the American citizen to buy for the sale of his wheat, more than what the Soviet citizen pays.

A few days after this incident, Washington faced (during the defence alliance meeting between U.S.A., Australia and New Zealand) in San Francisco, the Australian criticisms accusing the Americans because of their support for the Soviet side, that they were trying to defeat other suppliers on the world trade front, and [DEL cause] cause their extinction. The Australian side also explained that loss resulting from such competition might lead to decrease of Australian imports from the United States of America. While waiting for the trade situation, which had been complicated at the beginning of this year, to cristallize, stores of exporting countries are flooded with millions of tons of surplus wheat, with the cost of storage rising to 400 million dollars annually – which is more than the value of contributions of the concerned countries to the Food relief Fund for the victims of the famines.

Subject 28:   High textual competence, prudent, capitulating

Finance

Perhaps, the years set up for American oil reserve [INS drought] as per expectation has finished, without seeing any symptoms of a (catastrophe). But the price of oil has fallen again and it seems that exporting countries are loosing power to stop or defend this price fall.

So how did this happen? And what are the changes that will occur on future role of oil amongst [DEL resources of] energy resources and what are the new policies to develop energy in the world of tomorrow? And the effect of all that on relations between countries and people of the world?

In fifties and sixties, people of colonies achieved political independence and started – actively and enthusiastically – to build their national economy. In the same time that advanced countries faced social and economical crisis, and they [DEL lacked] failed to solve the crisis by their special economic methods. Therefore, their current policies aimed – mecanically – to [DEL achieve] activate internal demand by government expenditure to achieve full employment of both resouce and workforce in the production system, have lost power, and it's negative accumulation began to convert into large social crisis in thees capitalist countries. Therefore they aimed for economic liberation, refused by national movements and revolutions of third world. And the appearance of voices, calling on basical changes in the international economic system to compensate liberated countries from longtime [DEL theft] theft they faced and supporting their efforts to fill in the gap between these countries and advanced ones, which they regard this move in a pessimistic feeling because they are [DEL loocki] looking for new ways to economic control.

Converting changes occuring in the world to dead numbers is very wrong. Numbers cannot explain themselves by themselves and so often realities behind thees numbers contradict what they say on [DEL su] surface. Numbers themselves need to be explained and what they mean can not be understood other than through the essence of current changes in social and international life.

Africa

When African continent dies from hangar and volcanic gaz and national wars (Sudan, Angola) the rich countries warehouse are [DEL full of] flooded with grains reserves and surpluses.

So why theese lucky countries don't harry up and distribute their surpluses on starving people? A response to that sharp contradiction is that governments concerned can't – in their views – give theese precious gifts without raising performance symptoms wich make them loose their popularities in their societies. In other hand experts believe that theese aids do not solve the crisis in the third world. And what's needed is to develop agriculture in theese countries in international market, president ronald reagen took an incentive to subsidise American wheat selling to U.S.S.R. in August 1986, by [DEL $ 13 US] 13 dollars per tonne, which makes to total subsidy on a m. tonnes to be sold to U.S.S.R. 52 million dollars. This decision made the minister for external affairs Mr G. Shultz, saying that he can't see the equality that [DEL the] [INS an] american citizens [DEL been bein] have to pay more that the soviet's for his wheat.

Days after, Wachington faced (in an UNZUS meeting between [DEL am] U.S.A. Australia and New Zealand) in San Francisco, the Australian comment that U.S.A. by [DEL subsidin] subsidising the wheat deals is trying to push other suppliers out of the market, the Australian delegation explained that losses will occur from compeeting, will result in minimising imports to Australia from the U.S.A. untill the trade situations clear up after complication in the [DEL biggini] biginning of this year, the warehouses of countries exporting grains are full with millions of tonnes which the maintenance of them costs $400 million dollars per year which more over then theese governments assistance to needy countries and victims of starvation.

Subject 8:   Low textual competence, risk-taking, persistent

Finance

It may be expected that the years the American storage have come an end. However the beginning the (crisis) has not appeared yet.

However The price of petroleum is still decreasing, and the Exporting Petroleum Countries are about to lose the ability to stop and resist this. How did this take place? and what are the changes that will occur the part played by Petroleum in the future among Energy resources? What will be the new steps to develop the resources power in the world of future?

During the fifties and sixties many imperialized countries could achieve their Political dependence. And the scheme of national and economic building has begun with actively and enthousiastically. This happened side by side with the beginning of the Economic Social Crisis in the advanced Capitalism countries. And because these countries have lacked the ability to remedy this crisis through their own Economic means, therefore the present artificial policies for activating the interior demand through the government expenditure to fulfill the full work of the material and human productive organisation have exhausted all their energy and its passive accumulations began to face vast social explosions in the capitalism countries. Therefore the aim the Economic freedom which was rejected by the movements and revolutions of the third world and the appearance of the loud voices claiming for radical changes to the Universal Economic system to make up what the liberated countries from imperialism have lost for a long time to which they have been exposed, and to approve their efforts to lessen the deep distance between them and the developing countries. all this is a bad alarm to the Capitalism countries which tries to find new means of Economic dominion

It's a big mistake to consider the the changes that take place in the world mere numbers. It's a fact that numbers can not be a commentary for themselves. It happens many times that the facts hiding behind them are contrary to what they say from the surface. Numbers themselves should be interpreted. And they could not be understood or rekoned without the understanding the major changes that take place in the social and universal life.

Africa

While life in the African Continent is over suffering under the burdain of starvation and the creeping litus and the poisons of [DEL Ear] Volcano[DEL s] gases and the burning Civil War (The Sudan-Angola), The stores of the rich countries are flooding with extra grains.

Therefore why don't the lucky countries quickly distribute their extra grains amongst the starving peoples? The expected answer to this extreme contraversy is that the [DEL meant] [INS envolved] governments cannot, according to their point of view, deliver these [DEL gifts] expensive gifts without raising their doings-signals which may cause, losing their popularity among their communities. While the experts declare, on their parts, that th[DEL e]is[DEL e] assist[INS ance] would not solve the problem of the Third World.

[DEL On the first of August of last year [INS The American] President Regan The American declared, according to the universal Market, The initialy of giving The Soviet Union an encouraging privilage]

According to the Universal Market, the American President Ronald Regan declared on the first of August of the last year the initiati[INS ve][DEL ly] of giving the Soviet Union who is about to buy the American Wheat (corn) an encouraging privilage. That is devoting [INS a support] [DEL an assistance] of $13 for each ton of corn which will [DEL reach] raise the whole encouraging sum on 4M. Ton which is intended to sell to Mosqu[DEL e]o to $52M.. This compelled the exterior minister [INS Mr] George Shoultz to declare that it is not out of Justice a all to let the American Citizin [DEL pay] when buying his corn more than what the Soviet Citizen pays.   .

Some day later after this speech, Washigton (in the conference of Defence Allies between America, Australia and Newzeland) which was held in Sanfrancsico, faced the Australian criticism which accuses the Americans in their support to the Soviet part. That is; they are [DEL tryng] trying to demolish the other delivers in the [DEL w] universal Trade to make an end of them. The Australian part showed that the loses that will result according to this mistreat may decrease the Australian imports from the USA.

While, Waiting for reaching a focus point of the [INS complicated] commercial [DEL sit] conditions [DEL that has been complicated] at the beginning of this year, we see that the stores of the exporting countries are over crowded with millions of extra corn which cost to preserve, $400 M anually. That is extremely more [DEL than] valued than the shares of the [DEL mean] [INS involved] countries in the nourishing help for the [DEL starvating] [INS starving] victims

Subject 9:   Low textual competence, risk-taking, capitulating

Finance

[DEL The years [DEL for] as predicted for the American resource, might have elapsed]

The years for usage of the American reserve, as predicted, might have been elapsed and no sign of the catastrophe has appeared. As for the petrol price, it has come down and the countries which export the oil can do nothing and can not control the price decrease. How did this happen, and what changes will affect the oil among the other energy sources, and what new plans to develop the oil sources in the future, and what impact will be among the world?

In the fifties and sixties, the people of the colonies could obtain the political independence, and enthusiastically started to build for the national economy, while the [DEL crise] [DEL st] started among the developed capitalist countries.

and so thes countries failed to cure the crise by their own means. The current Idoligical ways is to develope the national industrial, by spending to [DEL achied] achieve full production, whether [DEL materialistc] materialistic or humaine. the exhusted all their reserve and revelutions bursted. For that the aim of freeing the economy which has been refused [DEL f] by the nations of the third world. and the appearence of new ideas to introduce basic changes to the international economical sistem to compensate the indepent countries for the loss which they excersied during the occupation, trying to shorten the gap beteen them and the developed coutries, all this indicates bad luck to the capitalist countries who are trying to find new methods to dominate the international economy.

It is a big mistake to interpret the changes which happen in the world to just stone figures. this figures do not interpret themselves, and sometimes the truth hidden behind opposit to a theory, the figures themselves need to be [DEL interpreted] [INS explained] and can not be understood except by looking at the constant changes in the social and international lives.

Africa

While [DEL Africa] life [DEL ??] [INS in] Africa is suffering from lack of food [INS and famine] and from volcanic [DEL poisounous] [INS poisonous] gasses and from civil war (Sudan-Angola). The grain stores of the rich countries are full of excess of the reserve of [DEL the] grains. Why the lucky countries do not hasten and distribute their excess on the hungry people? The answer to this contradiction lies in that the con-cerned governments can not, as they think, deliver these precious presents without increasing the price, which makes [DEL he] them loose the popularity of their people. While the experts explain that this kind of help will not solve the problem of the [DEL countries] [DEL ?] third world countries, but the required is to develope the basic agriculture of these countries.

On the international market, the American [DEL pred] president Ronald Regan on first of last August, he offered [DEL encourgingly] [INS encouragement] preference to the soviet union to buy the American wheat and alocated a compensation of $13 American dollars for each ton, which makes the total compensation alocated for the 4 million tons [DEL which] to be sold to Moscow $52 Million dolars. [DEL Because] [INS because] of that Mr George Schultz the foreign Minsiter said that it is not fair that the American citizen payes to buy his own wheet more than the soviet citizen pays.

After few days of this [DEL ???] incident, while the [DEL conference] defence conference between (America, Australia and NewZealand) was held in San Francesco, Washington attacked the Australira currency which [DEL acused] [INS accused] the [DEL Amercians] Americans, by selling the wheet cheap to the soviet, they causing [DEL grievuous] [INS grievious damage] to othher suppliers in the international market. The Australian Party has declared that the loss to be incurred due to this [DEL competion] competition, will lead the decrease of imports from the United States of America.

While waiting for the outcome of the trading situations which has been complecated in the [DEL beging] begining of this year, the stores of the export countries are full of [DEL x] million of tons of grain which costs them [DEL more] more than 400 million dollars to store it every year, and that exceeds the contributions of the concerned countries.

Subject 50:   Low textual competence, prudent, persistent

Finance

As it has been predicted, the definite few years for the American reserved oil has consumed, and still there is no sign of a disaster. Once again the oil price has been reduced and the oil producer countries are nearly incapable to stop and resist its declination. How did this happen, and what are the changes that may occur to the role of [DEL the] oil in the future, among the other power sources, What are the new plans to de-velop the power sources in the future. and the effect of all these on the relations of the people and the countries of the world?

In the 50's and 60's the people of the colonization could achieve their political independence, the operation of the national economy building started [DEL ens] [INS actively and] enthusiastically it occured with the rise of the soci[DEL al][INS o] – economy crisis in the advanced capital-ized countries. and with these countries being incapable to deal with the crisis in her own special ways. So the current policies of activating the industrial home demand, through the government expenditure to achieve the full action of the human and material productive system. All her capacities have been worn out and her negative piling ups began to change into a wide social explosions inside the capatilist countries.

For these reasons there [DEL had been] [INS was] the [DEL eco freedom of the economy] economical freedom which had been enforced by the third world national movement and revolutions and the rise of the voices that demanded to emplement the radical changes to the international system of the economy to compensate the countries that had been freed from colonizing her long term [DEL of] [INS in] stealing which had been exposed to., and to support its effort to reduce the gap between herself and the advanced countries. All these are considered to be a pessimistic sign to capitalist countries [DEL that are] looking for new methods to have economy control.

It is a big mistake to transfer these changes, that are taking place in the countries into [DEL figures] numbers because numbers do not explain themselves and often the potential fact behind it is opposite to it because it is superficial. The numbers in themselves need to be explained. It is not easy to understand them, only through the essence of the current changes in the social and international life.

Africa

When [INS the] Africa[DEL n] continent are suffering from starvation locus attacks, posinous volcanoe gases, civil war fires (Sudan & Angola) the rich countries' stores are surplus of a huge reserved quantity of grains.

So why don't these countries rush to distribute their surpluses among the hungry people?

The justifiable answer for this severe contradiction is that the relevant government – in their opinion – ca not give these precious gifts without removing the signs of giving which make her lose her popularity in her own society; While some other specialists that this kind of help does not solve the problem of the third world countries. but the development of the basic agriculture in these countries is the answer.

On the international market level, and at the beginning of last August, the [DEL pres] American president Ronald Regean initiated to give the Soviet Union an encouraging prevelege for his intention to buy the American wheat, allocating a fund of 13 dollar for every ton of grain and this raise the whole encouraging [DEL for] [DEL of the] [INS for] 4m ton that is intended to be sold to [DEL Mo] Mosko to 52 million dollar. This made the foreign minister Mr George Sholtz to declare that [DEL it is not ju] he sees no justice making the American citizen to pay for his own wheat more than the soviet citizen.

After few days of this happening. Washington faces (in a meeting of the defence pact [DEL bet] among America, Australia & New Zealand) which was held in San Fransisco, the Australian criticism that accused [DEL the] American of supporting the soviets, because they are trying to defeat the other suppliers on the international trade stage and that threatens them of destruction. The Australian side declaired the losses that [DEL may] result out of this compitition and this lead to the reduction of the Australian exports from the U.S.A.

Waiting for the clearance of the trading situations which has been complicated at the beginning of this year, the stores of the producer countries are full with millions of tons of the surplus of wheat which their costs of [DEL it] keeping are more than 400 m dollars each year. it is more than the [DEL relevant countries] shares of the relevant countries in the [DEL helping box aids] [DEL food helping box] [INS Nurishment subsidizes box] for the victims of the starvation.

Subject 43:   Low textual competence, prudent, capitulating

Finance: Subject A43

The expected number of years for the recovery of the [DEL A] american economy are over. Despite the drop in petrol world price. How this happened. And the [DEL pro] countries they produce the petrol cannot stop this decline. and they cannot predict with the changes that could happen in the future. And what are the new [DEL developing] developments [DEL to] as another source of energy and what this could effect on the relationship between different countries

In the fifties & the sixties the undeveloped countries achived there [INS political] independence, and [GAP] building there national economy with great enthusiasm. Unfortunately they could not solve there economic problems. [DEL There was exciting way] There [DEL polical] political [DEL regime] [INS system] to increase there demands through the industry by [DEL be] forcing the [DEL gov] government to spent more to encourage the productivity and the human power were not [DEL successful] successful in these countries which led to internal social problems.

That is why the main purpose for these third world wars [DEL is] in the developed countries is for changes in the economic world system to compensate for there [DEL losess] losses during the occupation of there land and the long plundering they were exposed to. In the meantime this could [DEL led] lead to decrease the distance [DEL w] between the developed and capitalist countries. This all considered as a [DEL warn] warning to the capitalist contries which searching [DEL w] for new methods to [DEL economi] [INS find differand] economic controls.

It is the biggest mistake to look [DEL to] only to figures. Figures does not mean a lot and [DEL doe] does not explain it self. Some times facts are more reliable than figures. Some time figures need more exexplanations and cannot be understood. Unless it is understood from the current international social lives.

Africa: Subject G43

While live is very harsh in Africa because of famine dies to invasion of loctus, [DEL and] poisonous volcanic gases and national wars. In [DEL Oth] other parts of the world silos have excess of grain for human consumption. The question is why these lucky countries starts to distribute the excess of these stored grains to the [DEL faimine] [INS famine] countries.

To justify this question [DEL rely] [INS depends] on these countries that they cannot donate these valuable [DEL assets] [INS assets] unless [DEL it] [INS they] increase[DEL s] [DEL its] [INS their] support to these people to increase its popularity.

Besides the experts indicates that these donations will not solve the third world problems, what is needed is the new develoments in agricultural methods in these countries.

From the international point of view last August Mr Ronald Reagen President of the United States of America gave the previlage to the Soviet Union to buy the American wheat, and they supported this by giving 13 dollars for each ton, which will increase the total supported amount of money on 4 million tons will sell to Moscow to 52 million dollars.

This issue forced Mr George Shaults the minister of foreign affairs of USA in his statment that it is unjustifiable to the [DEL Americans] American citizen to pay more in wheat price than the soviet citizen. A few days later [DEL in a] after this speach Washington faced (during the defence meeting between America, Australia, New Zealand) which was held in San franciscow.

The Australian criticism against America to support the Soviet Union [GAP]

Besides the Australians indicated that this may decrease the exports of goods to the United States of America.

Due to these commercial problems which [DEL rising] arise at the begining of this year [INS to be solved], in the mean time there are in excess of stored grains available which costes more than 400 million dollars to store [DEL which] this amount of money exceeds the amount of money [DEL doned] [INS donated] to the international help foundation to the famine countries.

APPENDIX 2: Real-time edited texts

E1: Unemployment

Unemployment is one of the worse problem faced by the world. It is rare (unusual) to find a country ~~w~~ dosnot face this problem in the present time. Although ~~many~~ people ~~believe before~~ not long time ago, believe that some countries dont ~~have en~~ unemployed people, either because of their richness or because ~~of thei~~ they economic policies that they follow. The social results ~~for~~ of the unemployment is deadly (worse) effect more than the unemployment. ~~While At the time~~ we see government of the ~~advance~~ deloped countries provide allowances to unemployed til they find a suitable job, ~~at the same time,~~ in the other han we find a group (set) of psycholgical & social diseases, ~~cannot which is difficult~~ (~~that~~ by ~~specialist cannot estimate its cost on the~~) long run specialllist ~~find face~~ find it difficult to estimate its costs on the long run. ~~Auth~~ Responables assure ~~that people regions which~~ residence ~~who~~ live ~~in a ver~~ high social & economic levels, in a region, these regions definetely ~~willbe~~ be effected by problem resulted of unemployment in the other regions.

E2: Unemployment

Unemployment ~~con~~ is considered the worst problem the world faces, Because at the ~~tim~~ present time, it is unique to find a country that doesn't suffer from this problem.

That inspite of many people who think ~~,that~~ untill recently that ~~some countries~~ unemployed people can not be found in some countries, either because those countries are rich or ~~be~~ as a result of the economic system ~~that~~ which they follow.

The social results of unemployment is more effective from unemployment itself. While we see ~~that~~ that the ~~progressed~~ governments of the progressed countries, give allowances to help unemployed people to succeed in findinf suitable jobs, On the other hand we find group of ~~mental~~ psychological ~~diseases~~ and social diseases, which the specialist find it hard to estimate its cost on a long time.

(confirm that the ~~regions~~ with residents in x)

Responsibles confirm that the regions ~~that which~~ that the residents ~~enjoy~~ ~~a~~ live a high ~~le~~ social and economic level, should influence by the results arise from unemployment in the other regions.

E3: Unemployment

Enemployment is considered one of the worse problems encountring the world. Since ~~it~~ it is rare to finde a country not suffering from this problem, at our presente time, in spite of the believe of many till recently, that ~~some countries~~ it is imposible to find unemployed people in some countries. Either because of its wealth, or of its economique systeme pursued.

The social consequences of unemployment are more effective than the unemployment itself. While we see governments of developed countries give help to help unemployed people till they find suitable positions, we find in ~~the~~ other side a serie of psychlogical and social disease, which ~~the~~ specialists can not evaluate its ~~costs~~ at a long time. Officials confirm that regions <in> which <people> enjoy <of> a high ~~a~~ social and economique level ~~is inevitable that they~~ will be affected, inevitably, by the consequences issued from the unemployment existing in the other regions.

E1: Lady Di

It is truely <to believe> what has been said about Lady Diann that she is pregnant and preoccupied people. She ~~loved~~ fell in loved, <got> engaged, got married, traveled, stood up, sat down, slept, dreamed, got pregnant and deliverd. The ~~Prince crown prince~~ succesor of the great British ~~Crown~~ throne has come. The days have passed and Lady Dian the wife of Prince Chalre who is waiting to take over ~~the~~ the ~~British Crown~~ throne of British in very short time, ~~She~~ remained, number one person ~~who~~ has large popularity in all Europe.The ~~subject~~ matter is not ~~only~~ <~~the~~ a matter of> poupularity ~~only~~ only, but it is a matter of growing attention that she received from (~~psychological doctor~~) psychiatrists who said ~~i~~ that it would better for prince william to be ~~not the~~ not his parents' only son, and <the> time has come, so that Lady Diann can have another child. It was said, and this saying is related to the editor of social section

E2: Lady Di

I beleive what is said about lady Diana, she is pregnant and making the people busy. She <fell in> ~~loved~~ engaged, ~~g~~ got married, travelled, <stood up> got up sat down, slept, ~~dreamted~~, got pregnant, gave birth. The ~~crown prince~~ successor has come to the noble British ~~crown~~ throne. The days passed, and lady Diana, ~~the Prince Charles~~ <the> wife <of prince charles> who is waiting ~~to~~ for accession to the throne ~~nearly~~ soon, ~~Diana stayed~~ <remained> ~~had~~ the ~~popularity~~ <person> number one in all ~~Europpe~~ Europe. The subject is not only a <a matter of popularity> ~~subject of popularity subject~~, but it is the matter of the increased care of the psychologists who said that it is better for <young> prince williams ~~to have~~ not to be the only child. The time has come for lady Di to have another baby. It has been said ~~and~~ and that saying is related to the editor of the social subject in the <British> Daily night-~~news~~ newspaper, and he is counted as a friend of the ~~cas~~ palace.

E3: Lady Di

It is prooved what is said about laidy Diana that she is pregnant and preoccupies people. She was in love, ~~fianced~~ engaged, married, travelled, ~~woke~~ <stood> up, sat down, slept, dreamed, got pregnant, give birth. The successor of the <noble> British throne came. Days passed on, but laidy ~~Diana~~, the <wife of> ~~<Prince's wife still>~~ Prince Charle's ~~wife~~ who is waiting the accession to the <British> throne in the near future, still the first popular person in all Europe. The probleme is not <the popularity> only, but is the ~~ps~~ increased interest from psychologists who say that it is better that the prince William should not be the only child. It is time to the laidy Di to give birth to another . . . . It is said ~~which~~ and this say is attributed to the editor of the social part in the <British> 'Daily life', which is considered as one of the palace friends.

References

Ahlsvad, K.-J. (1978) 'Translating into the translator's non-primary language', in Paul A. Horguelin (ed.) *Translating, A Profession*. *Proceedings of the Eighth World Congress of the International Federation of Translators*. Paris: Federation Internationale des Traducteurs. Ottawa: Conseil des traducteurs et interprètes du Canada, pp. 183–8.

Amos, F.R. (1973) *Early Theories of Translation*. New York: Octagon Books.

Anderson, J.R. (1985) *Cognitive Psychology and Its Implications* (2nd edn). New York: Freeman.

Ba'albaki, M. (ed.) (1980) *Al-Mawrid. A Modern English–Arabic Dictionary* (14th edn). Beirut: Dar El-Ilm Lil-Malayen.

Bachman, L. (1990) *Fundamental Considerations in Language Testing*. Oxford: Oxford University Press.

Bell, R. (1991) *Translation and Translating: Theory and Practice*. London: Longman.

Ben Zeev, S. (1977) 'The influence of bilingualism on cognitive strategies and cognitive development', *Child Development* 48: 1009–18.

Berry, V. (1993) 'Personality characteristics as a potential source of language test bias', in A. Huhta, K. Sajavaara and S. Takala (eds) *Language Testing: New Openings*. Jyväskylä: Institute of Education Research, University of Jyväskylä, pp. 115–24.

Biber, D. (1986) 'Spoken and written textual dimensions in English: resolving the contradictory findings', *Language* 62: 384–414.

Biber, D. (1988) *Variation Across Speech and Writing*. New York: Cambridge University Press.

Blau, J. (1981) *The Renaissance of Modern Hebrew and Modern Standard Arabic: Parallels and Differences in the Revival of Two Semitic Languages*. Near Eastern Studies Vol. 18. Berkeley, CA: University of California Press.

Börsch, S. (1986) 'Introspective methods in research on interlingual and intercultural communication', in J. House and S. Blum-Kulka (eds) *Interlingual and Intercultural Communication*. Tübingen: Gunter Narr Verlag, pp. 195–209.

Campbell, S. (1983) 'A rule of thumb for rendering Arabic measure V Verbs in English', *TEAM* 44 (Autumn): 19–21.

Campbell, S., Dyson, B., Karim, S. and B. Rabie (1993) *Unlocking Australia's Language Potential. Profiles of 9 Key Languages in Australia. Vol. 1 – Arabic*. Canberra: National Languages and Literacy Institute of Australia.

Canale, M. and M. Swain (1980) 'Theoretical bases of communicative approaches to second language teaching and testing', *Applied Linguistics* 1 (1): 1–47.

Cascallar, E., Cascallar, M.I., Lowe Jr., P. and J.R. Child (1996) 'Development of new proficiency-based skill level descriptors for translation: theory and practice', in M. Milanovic and N. Saville (eds) *Performance Testing, Cognition and*

Assessment: Selected Papers from the 15th Language Testing Research Colloquium (LTRC), Cambridge and Arnhem. Cambridge: University of Cambridge, Local Examinations Syndicate, pp. 292–313.

Catford, J.C. (1965) *A Linguistic Theory of Translation.* London: Oxford University Press.

Chafe, W. and D. Tannen (1987) 'The relation between written and spoken language', *Annual Review of Anthropology* 16: 383–407.

Clyne, M., Fernandez, S., Chen, I. and R. Summo-O'Connell (1997) *Background Speakers: Diversity and Its Management in LOTE Programs.* Belconnen: Language Australia.

Corder, S.P. (1967) 'The significance of learners' errors', *International Review of Applied Linguistics* 4: 161–9.

Cummins, J. (1979) 'Cognitive/academic language proficiency, linguistic interdependence, the optimum age question and some other matters'. *Working Papers on Bilingualism,* No. 19, pp. 121–9.

Cummins, J. (1981) 'Age on arrival and immigrant second language learning in Canada: A reassessment.' *Applied Linguistics* 2, 132–49.

Cummins, J. (1991) 'Conversational and academic language proficiency in bilingual contexts', in J.H. Hulstijn and J.F. Matter (eds) *Reading in Two Languages.* Amsterdam: AILA (AILA Review 8), pp. 75–89.

Delisle, J. (1980) *L'analyse du discours comme méthode de traduction.* Ottawa: University of Ottawa Press (Cahiers de traductologie No. 2).

Duff, A. (1981) *The Third Language: Recurrent Problems of Translation into English.* Oxford: Pergamon Press.

Dulay, H. and M. Burt (1974) 'Natural sequences in child second language acquisition', *Language Learning* 24: 37–53.

Ellis, R. (1992) *Second Language Acquisition and Language Pedagogy.* Clevedon: Multilingual Matters.

Ely, C. (1986) 'An analysis of discomfort, risk-taking, sociability and motivation in the L2 classroom', *Language Learning* 36: 1–25.

Faerch, C. and G. Kasper (eds) (1987) *Introspection in Second Language Research.* Clevedon and Philadelphia: Multilingual Matters.

Farahzad, F. (1992) 'Testing achievement in translation classes', in C. Dollerup and A. Loddegaard (eds) *Teaching Translation and Interpreting. Training, Talent and Experience.* Amsterdam: John Benjamins, pp. 271–8.

Fau, S. (1990) 'A statistical method for translation quality assessment', *Target* 2 (1): 43–67.

Felix, S.W. (1977) 'Interference, interlanguage and related issues', in C. Molony, H. Zobl and W. Stölting (eds) *German in Contact with Other Languages.* Kronberg: Scriptor Verlag, pp. 237–58.

Fried, L. (1983) 'On the validity of language tests', in K. Hyltenstam and M. Pienemann (eds) *Modelling and Assessing Second Language Development.* Clevedon: Multilingual Matters, pp. 349–71.

Galambos, S.J. and S. Goldin-Meadow (1983) 'Learning a second language and metalinguistic awareness', in *Papers from the Regional Meetings, Chicago Linguistic Society* 19: 117–33.

Gerloff, P. (1987) 'Identifying the unit of analysis in translation: some uses of think-aloud protocol data', in C. Faerch and G. Kasper (eds) *Introspection in Second Language Research.* Clevedon and Philadelphia: Multilingual Matters, pp. 135–58.

196   *Translation into the Second Language*

Halliday, M.A.K. (1993) *Language in a Changing World*. Canberra: Applied Linguistics Association of Australia (Occasional Paper No. 13).

Hatim, B. (1989) 'Text linguistics in the didactics of translation: the case of the verbal and nominal clause types in Arabic', *International Review of Applied Linguistics* 27 (2): 137–44.

Hatim, B. and I. Mason (1990) *Discourse and the Translator*. London and New York: Longman.

Hayes, J.R., Flower, L., Schriver, K.A., Stratman, J.F. and L. Carey (1987) 'Cognitive processes in revision', in S. Rosenberg (ed.) *Advances in Applied Psycholinguistics, Vol. 2. Reading, Writing and Language Learning*. Cambridge: Cambridge University Press, pp. 176–240.

Hewson, L. and J. Martin (1991) *Redefining Translation. The Variational Approach*. London: Routledge.

Hölscher, A. and D. Möhle (1987) 'Cognitive plans in translation', in C. Faerch and G. Kasper (eds) *Introspection in Second Language Research*. Clevedon and Philadelphia: Multilingual Matters, pp. 113–34.

Hosington, B. and P. Horguelin (1980) *A Practical Guide to Bilingual Revision*. Montréal: Linguatech.

Kachroo, B. (1984) 'Textual cohesion and translation', *Meta* 29 (2): 128–34.

Kalina, S. (1992) 'Discourse processing and interpreting strategies – an approach to the teaching of interpreting', in C. Dollerup and A. Loddegaard (eds) *Teaching Translation and interpreting. Training, Talent and Experience*. Amsterdam: John Benjamins, pp. 251–7.

Kiraly, D. (1990) 'A role for communicative competence and the acquisition–learner distinction in translator training', in B. Van Patten and J.F. Lee (eds) *Second Language Acquisition – Foreign Language Learning*. Clevedon: Multilingual Matters, pp. 207–15.

Krashen, S. (1977) 'The monitor model for adult second language performance', in Burt, M., Dulay, H. and M. Finocchiaro (eds) *Viewpoints on English as a Second Language*. New York: Regents, pp. 152–61.

Krings, H. (1986) 'The translation strategies of advanced German learners of French', in J. House and S. Blum-Kulka (eds) *Interlingual and Intercultural Communication*. Tübingen: Gunter Narr Verlag, pp. 263–76.

Krings, H.P. (1987) 'The use of introspective data in translation', in C. Faerch and G. Kasper (eds) *Introspection in Second Language Research*. Clevedon and Philadelphia: Multilingual Matters, pp. 157–76.

Kuepper, K. (1984) 'Coreference in translation', in Wolfram Wilss and Gisela Thome (eds) *Translation Theory and Its Implementation in the Teaching of Translating and Interpreting*. Tübingen: Gunter Narr Verlag, pp. 145–53.

Larsen-Freeman, D. and M. Long (1991) *An Introduction to Second Language Acquisition Research*. London: Longman.

Larson, M.L. (1984) *Meaning-based Translation: A Guide to Cross-cultural Equivalence*. Lanham, NY and London: University Press of America.

Lindquist, H. (1989) *English Adverbials in Translation: A Corpus Study of Swedish Renderings*. Lund: Lund University Press.

Lise, W. (1997) 'Machine translation – is it working in Japan?' *Language International* 9 (1): 27–35.

Lörscher, W. (1986) 'On analyzing translation performance', in J. House and S. Blum-Kulka (eds) *Interlingual and Intercultural Communication*. Tübingen: Gunter Narr Verlag, pp. 277–92.

Malone, J.L. (1988) *The Science of Linguistics in the Art of Translation: Some Tools from Linguistics for the Analysis and Practice of Translation*. Albany, NY: State University of New York.

Mareschal, G. (1989) 'Repérage d'unités terminologiques dans la contexte de l'enseignement de la traduction spécialisée', *Meta* 34 (3): 377–80.

McAlester, G. (1992) 'Teaching translation into a foreign language – status, scope and aims', in C. Dollerup and A. Loddegaard (eds) *Teaching Translation and Interpreting. Training, Talent and Experience*. Amsterdam: John Benjamins, pp. 291–7.

Mohanty, A.K. (1983) 'Bilingualiam and metalinguistic ability among Kond tribals in Orissa, India', *Journal of Social Psychology* 121 (1): 15–22.

Mossop, B. (1982) 'A procedure for self-revision', *Terminology Update* 15 (3): 6–9.

NAATI (1993) *Manual for Interpreter and Translator Examiners*. Canberra: National Accreditation Authority for Translators and Interpreters.

Neubert, A. (1981) 'Translation, interpreting and text linguistics', *Studia Linguistica* 35 (1–2): 133–45.

Nida, E. and C. Taber (1969) *The Theory and Practice of Translation*. Leiden: E.J. Brill.

Nord, C. (1992) 'Text analysis in translator training', in C. Dollerup and A. Loddegaard (eds) *Teaching Translation and Interpreting. Training, Talent and Experience*. Amsterdam: John Benjamins, pp. 39–48.

O'Malley, J.M. and A.U. Chamot (1990) *Learning Strategies in Second Language Acquisition*. Cambridge: Cambridge University Press.

Ozolins, U. (1991) *Interpreting Translating and Language Policy*. Melbourne: National Languages and Literacy Institute of Australia.

Picht, H. (1985) 'The terminology component in translation training programs', in H. Bühler (ed.) *Xth World Congress of FIT: Proceedings*. Vienna: Wilhelm Braumüller, pp. 338–42.

Pienemann, M. (1983) 'Learnability and syllabus construction', in K. Hyltenstam and M. Pienemann (eds) *Modelling and Assessing Second Language Development*. Clevedon: Multilingual Matters, pp. 23–75.

Pienemann, M. and M. Johnston (1986) 'An acquisition-based procedure for second language acquisition', *Australian Review of Applied Linguistics* 9: 92–122.

Pienemann, M. and M. Johnston (1987) 'Factors influencing the development of language proficiency', in D. Nunan (ed.) *Applying Second Lanuguage Acqustion Research*. Adelaide: National Curriculum Resource Centre, pp. 45–141.

Plimer, D. and C.N. Candlin (1996) *Language Services for Non-English-speaking-background Women*. Canberra: Australian Government Publishing Service.

Pym, A. (1992) 'Translation error analysis and the interface with language teaching', in C. Dollerup and A. Loddegaard (eds) *Teaching Translation and Interpreting. Training, Talent and Experience*. Amsterdam: John Benjamins, pp. 279–88.

Sa'addedin, M. (1987) 'Target-word experiential matching: the case of Arabic/English translating', *Quinquereme* 10 (2): 137–64.

Selinker, L. (1969) 'Language Transfer', *General Linguistics* 9 (2): 67–92.

Selinker, L. (1992) *Rediscovering Interlanguage*. London: Longman.

Snell-Hornby, M. (1988) *Translation Studies: An Integrated Approach*. Amsterdam and Philadelphia: John Benjamins.

Snow, C.E., Cancino, H., De Temple, J. and S. Schey (1991) 'Giving formal definitions: a linguistic or metalinguistic skill?', in E. Bialystok (ed.) *Language Processing among Bilingual Children*. London: Cambridge University Press, pp. 90–112.

Stern, C.M. (1984) 'The accreditation program of the American Translators Association', in Patricia E. Newman (ed.) *Proceedings of the 25th Annual Conference of the ATA*. Medford, NJ: Learned Information Inc., pp. 19–23.

Tannen, D. (1982) 'Oral and written strategies in spoken and written narratives', *Language* 58: 1–21.

Tirkonnen-Condit, S. (1985) *Argumentative Text Structure and Translation*. Jyväskylä: University of Jyväskylä.

Tommola, J. (1986) 'Translation as a psycholinguistic process', in L. Wollin and H. Lindquist (eds) *Translation Studies in Scandinavia. Proceedings from the Scandinavian Symposium on Translation Theory, Lund, 14–15 June 1985*. Malmö: Liber Förlag, pp. 140–9.

Toury, G. (1984) 'The notion of "Native Translator" and translation teaching', in Wolfram Wilss and Gisela Thome (eds) *Translation Theory and Its Implementation in the Teaching of Translating and Interpreting*. Tübingen: Gunter Narr Verlag, pp. 186–95.

Valdés, G. and R.A. Figueroa (1994) *Bilingualism and Testing: A Special Case of Bias*. Norwood, NJ: Ablex.

Vitale, G., Sparer, M. and R. Larose (1978) *Guide de la traduction appliquée. Tome premier*. Paris: Librairie Vuibert. Montréal: Les Presses de l'université du Québec.

Wilkinson, R. (1987) 'Information structure variability: translating into the foreign language', in G.M. Anderman and M.A. Rogers (eds) *Translation in Teaching and Teaching Translation. Translation in Language Teaching and for Professional Purposes. Vol. III*. Guildford: University of Surrey, pp. 71–85.

Wilss, W. (1976) 'Perspectives and limitations of a didactic framework for the teaching of translation', in R.W. Brislin (ed.) *Translation Applications and Research*. New York: Gardner Press Inc., pp. 117–37.

Woods, A., Fletcher, P. and A. Hughes (1986) *Statistics in Language Studies*. London: Cambridge University Press.

Index

abstractness, 85, 101
Abu Dhabi, 39, 40
academic grading, 163
accreditation
  authority, 172, 173
  examinations, 73, 76, 161
  of translation skills, 2, 28
  testing, 171
  tests, 173, 174
accrediting
  authorities, 168, 169
  bodies, 171
accuracy, 9, 57
  grammatical, 8
  technical translation, 27
adjectival constructions, 59
Ahlsvad, 27, 28, 57
American Translators Association, 173
Amos, 3
Anderson, 127
anisomorphism, 112
Arab communities, 30
Arabic, 25, 26, 27, 32, 36, 37, 39, 45, 46, 47, 49, 51, 61, 73, 80, 93, 132, 135, 136, 137, 160
  candidates, 34, 42–5
  discourse structure, 10
  -English translation, 10, 103, 129, 138
  -English translators, 2, 94
  Form V verbs in, 94, 159
  immigration to Australia, 32
  native speakers, 10
  prose, 160
  religious use, 43
  speakers, 25
  Standard, 92, 176
Arabic/French candidates, 35
Argentina, 39, 40
Armenian, 25

Asia, 23
assessment
  of equivalence, 11
  quality, 9, 163
  student, 8, 166, 168
  techniques, 18
Australia, 22, 28, 39, 40, 43, 52, 53, 54, 57, 58, 73, 160, 173
  history of translation in, 23
  immigrant community, 23
  multicultural, 26
average word length, 61, 64, 67

Bachman, 60, 61
Bell, 4, 21, 128
Ben Zeev, 137
Berry, 104
Biber, 72, 73, 74, 75, 76, 89, 92, 97, 98, 102
bidialectalism, 27
bilingual
  and interlingual ability, 4
  education, 40, 42, 43, 45, 48, 51
  homes, 41, 42, 43, 47, 50, 52
  Italian-English primary education, 46
  primary education, 49, 52, 53
  profiles, 31, 36, 38
  schooling, 42
  secondary education, 52, 53
  selection test, 31
  skills, 163
  social life, 41, 42, 50, 52
  work, 43, 45, 48
bilingualism, 12, 20, 22, 25, 26, 129, 161
  balanced, 45, 51, 54
  child, 137
  circumstantial, 25, 26
  compound, 137
  coordinate, 137

development of, 4
elective, 25, 26
immersion, 42
one language, one parent, 42
bilinguals
    balanced, 25, 57
    perfect, 3
    receiving, 25
Blau, 176
Börsch, 19
bracketed alternative, 138, 142, 143, 145

Campbell, 159, 161
Canada, 22, 39, 161
Canadian Language Quality Measurement System, 170, 172
Canadian Translators and Interpreters Council, 169
Canale and Swain, 5
capitulating, 104, 107, 108, 109, 110, 124, 125
capitulation, 3, 103, 156, 162
carelessness, 162
Cascallar, 8, 21
Catford, 3, 19
Chafe and Tannen, 59
Child, 21
Chile, 25, 39, 40
Chinese, 45, 50, 52
choice networks, 110–22
citation form, 105
cognitive
    load, 20
    model, 127
    processing, 153
    skills development, 20
cognitive science, 128
coherence, 9
cohesion, 9, 159
collocation, 113
Colombia, 39, 40
colonialism, 30
committee reports, 162
communication relations, 11
competence
    acquired linguistic, 5
    approaches to investigating translation, 6
    bilingual, 137

communicative, 5
discourse, 5
dissimilative, 5
general language, 67, 94
global, 157, 174
grammatical, 5
ideal bilingual, 5
innate translation, 4
language, 28, 30, 36, 137
levels of, 56, 68, 71, 72, 175
levels of language, 2, 22
lexico-grammatical, 124
linguistic and cultural, 5
matching, 159
monitoring, 153, 154, 157, 158
pretextual, 3, 68, 69, 72, 89, 156
research, 5
sociolinguistic, 5, 61
strategic, 5
substandard, 3, 68, 69, 89, 156, 159, 167
target language, 70, 81, 159, 162
text production, 5
text reception and analysis
textual, 2, 3, 11, 18, 20, 56, 57, 60, 61, 67, 68, 69, 70, 72, 76, 89, 93, 94, 96, 101, 102, 103, 104, 109, 122, 124, 125, 148, 152, 153, 154, 155, 156, 157, 158, 159, 160, 161, 167, 173, 175
transfer, 4, 5
transferred, 5
translation, 1, 2, 3, 4, 6, 7, 11, 12, 13, 14, 16, 20, 21, 28, 58, 59, 60, 63, 72, 109, 125, 126, 141, 150, 158, 160, 163, 166, 176
translation quality assessment, 5
translational, 6
translator, 4, 5, 21
components of translation
    competence, 9, 18, 70, 152, 166, 167, 173
composition, 59, 127, 167, 170
concord, 72
concord error, 15
concreteness, 85
conference interpreting, 23
congruity, 9
    judgements, 9
    scale, 9

connotation, 104, 112, 123
construction stage, 127
content words, 59, 64, 67, 69, 87
content/function words, 61, 66, 67,
    89, 92
context-independent reference, 75
contexts of use, 41, 47, 50
contrastive analysis, 12, 14, 15, 20
conversational analysis, 18
Corder, 15
coreference, 10
correction, 16, 138, 139, 140, 142,
    143, 145, 146, 148, 149, 150, 162
criterion-referenced, 168
cross-linguistic influence, 13
C-test, 31, 32, 34, 36, 37, 131, 137
Cuba, 39, 40
Cummins, 38, 76
curriculum
    design, 163
    models, 28
    objectives, 18

Danish, 45
data
    analysis, 19
    cross-sectional, 70
    empirical, 7
    linguistic, 20
    pseudo-empirical, 10
    verbal, 20
decision-making, 7
decontextualized and contextualized,
    60, 76
deletion, 126, 127, 138, 142, 143, 145,
    149, 165
Delisle, 10
denser text, 59, 63, 89
determiner system, 15
developmental
    hypothesis, 70
    pathway, 18, 102, 157
    sequence investigations, 17
diagnosis of student problems, 166
dictation, 31, 32, 34, 36, 37, 131, 137
direct equivalent, 65
direct translations, 65, 67
discourse, 15, 56, 57
    academic nominal, 96
    analysis, 1, 10, 18

approach, 158
domain, 14
equivalence, 171
function, 18
nominal, 101
of administration and commerce, 161
technical, 161
disposition, 3, 17, 91, 96, 101, 103,
    104, 105–9, 125, 153, 154, 155,
    156, 157, 159
grid, 107, 109, 110, 158, 162, 166
profile, 104
dissimilarity
    matrix, 105
    scores, 107
Duff, 13
Dulay and Burt, 156
Dutch, 13

Eco, 60
editing
    economy, 138, 142, 148, 150
    effectiveness, 138, 140, 141, 142,
        146, 147, 148, 149, 150
    frequency, 138, 142, 148, 150
    level, 138, 142, 148
    purpose, 138, 139, 142
    real-time, 16, 126, 127, 129, 138–50
    strategy, 138, 142
edits
    clause-level, 145, 147, 148, 150
    phrase-level, 145, 147, 148
    word-level, 145, 149, 150
educational measurement theory, 9, 171
Egypt, 39, 40
Ellis, 17
Ely, 17
empirical
    data, 128
    procedures, 9
    studies, 17
English
    adverbials, 19
    as a foreign language, 27, 45
    as a Second Language teaching, 27
    genres of, 101
    in Australia, 54
    non-native, 27
    second language speakers of, 27
    spoken and written, 73, 74

text types, 73
to Spanish translation, 130
translation from Dutch into, 13
well-formed, 156
equivalence
  paradigm, 5
  semantic, 139
equivalent forms, 171, 172
error
  analysis, 16
  processing, 167
  types, 8, 157
errors, 1, 14, 16, 72, 159, 162, 164, 169, 174
  binary, 15
  grammatical, 57
  motivation for, 15
  non-binary, 15
  spelling, 8
  stylistic, 16
  target language, 68
ethnic communities, 24
evaluation of teaching, 166, 168
execution stage, 127
experienced and inexperienced writers, 127
expert system, 5, 170
expression, 9

face-to-face conversation, 76, 84, 92, 93, 96, 101
factor analysis, 73
Faerch and Kasper, 6
false start, 138, 142, 145, 148, 149
Farahzad, 6
Farsi, 43, 49
Fau, 8, 170, 172
Federal Bureau of Investigations, 8
Felix, 16
Finland, 22, 27, 28
Finnish, 28, 57, 175
Finnish Translators' and Interpreters' Association
first generation
  Italian candidates, 38
  speakers, 25
first language
  defining, 30
  father's and mother's, 41
  identifying, 71

speakers of Italian, 46
writers, 57
writing, 148
formulaic
  transfers, 17
  utterances, 17
frame incompatibility, 175
freelancers, 25
French, 11, 15, 22, 25, 32, 35, 36, 37, 43, 45, 52, 53, 54, 159
  candidates, 34
  grammar, 15
French / Vietnamese, English trilinguals, 35
Fried, 174
function words, 59, 60, 64, 66, 67, 69, 89, 90, 91
functional standpoint, 158
fuzzy logic, 170, 172
fuzzy-restricted values, 170
fuzzy values, 172

Galambos and Goldin-Meadow, 137
genre, 1, 2, 20, 72, 77, 102, 152, 153, 156, 160, 161, 162
  distinctions, 75
  variation, 73, 74
genres, 76, 84
  encountered by professional translators, 56
  written, 2, 27
Gerloff, 7
German, 26, 32, 36, 37, 39, 45, 46, 51, 58, 131, 132
  candidates, 34, 45–6
  -English translation, 129
  migration to Australia, 32
  -speaking community in New South Wales, 46
Germanic words, 64
Germany, 46
grade averages, 167
grammatical
  category, 65, 105
  shifts, 68, 69, 96, 105
  structure, 16
Guatemala, 40

Halliday, 161
Hatim, 10

Hatim and Mason, 4
Hayes, 127, 148
Hebrew, 176
Hewson and Martin, 4
Hölscher and Möhle, 7
Hosington and Horguelin, 8, 157,
    168, 169, 170
Hungarian candidates, 46

ideational meaning, 77, 85
IL Hypothesis, 12
immigrant
    first and second generation, 25, 41
    language professionals, 24
    students, 23
immigration, 2, 12, 22, 24, 30
implicational scale, 94
indirect equivalent, 65
Indonesian, 45
inference mechanism, 5
inflectional morphology, 72
Informational Production, 74
insertion, 126, 127, 138, 142, 143,
    145, 149
insurance policies, 162
integrating information, 85
interference, 10, 13, 15, 117, 160
interlanguage, 1, 2, 12, 13, 14, 16, 20,
    22, 28, 70, 175
    continuum, 160
    universals, 14
interlingual identification, 14
inter-marker method, 171
interpersonal meaning, 77
interpreter/translator education, 39
interpreting, 128
interpreting and translation, 129
    community, 23
    degree programmes, 23
    free, 23
    subprofessional courses, 31
    training, 23
    undergraduate programme in
        Australia, 30
interpretive information, 9
intertextuality, 10
introspection, 19
Involved Production, 74
involved versus detached, 60, 76
Iran, 39, 40, 43

Iranian candidates, 46
irony, 160
Italian, 25, 26, 27, 32, 37, 38, 39, 47,
    49, 50, 51, 54, 132, 135, 136,
    137
-Australians, 25
    candidates, 46–8
    dialect speakers, 136
-English translation, 129
    migration to Australia, 32
Italy, 39, 40

Japan, 27
Japan Association of Translators, 27
Japanese, 45, 46

Kachroo, 159
Kalina, 128
Kiraly, 5
knowledge base, 5
Krashen, 127, 128
Krings, 128, 158
Kuder-Richardson formulae, 171, 172
Kuepper, 10
Kurdish, 50
Kuwait, 39, 45

language
    acquisition, 26, 153
    acquisition theory, 14
    asymmetry, 22
    community, 58
    development, 1, 20, 58, 152
    ethnic, 25
    everyday and specialized, 11
    first, 24, 25, 26
    host, 12
    loss, 24, 42
    maintenance, 38, 49, 137, 161
    non-standard varieties, 24, 27
    of power, 161
    production models, 127
    second, 24, 25, 26
    service agencies, 23
    services, 21, 32
    shift, 24, 58
    spoken, 3
    status, 22
    substandard varieties, 25
    test performance, 104

tests, 30
third, 13
transfer, 14
universals, 14
written and spoken, 59, 192
written versus spoken, 56
Larsen-Freeman and Long, 14, 15
Larson, 11
Latin, 45
Latin American
    communities, 30
    immigrants, 32
learnability hypothesis, 156
learning theory, 157
Lebanese
    dialect, 25
    education system, 35
    students, 25
Lebanon, 39, 40, 42, 43, 45
levels
    of linguistic analysis, 57
    performance, 9
    structural, 17
lexical
    choice, 9
    diversity, 59
    specificity, 92
    transfer, 103, 104, 106, 109, 110,
        122
    variety ratio, 60, 61, 63, 68
lexicalization, 59, 63, 66, 67, 69
lexicon, 11
lexis, 3, 15, 125, 153
Lindquist, 19
linguistic
    analysis, 15
    level, 14
    structure, 3
    transfer paradigm, 5
linguistics
    applied, 1, 2, 20, 167
    suprasentential, 28
Lise, 27
literalness, 8
Lörscher, 7

Malone, 19
Malta, 39, 40, 46
Maltese, 47, 48
Mareschal, 11

marked translations, 163, 164, 166,
    168
marking
    error model of, 157
    of student texts, 15
    scales, 170
    scheme, 8
matching, 17, 159
McAlester, 28
mediopassive, 94
Melbourne, 25
memory, 171
mental
    constructs, 6, 7
    processes, 19, 127, 158
metalinguistic ability, 137
metaphor, 17, 87, 111, 112, 113, 115,
    116, 121, 123, 138, 160, 176
migration, 38, 43, 136
mis-estimation of translation
    competence, 134–7
misspellings, 8
mistakes, 16
mistranslations, 8
model
    of competence, 8
    of learning, 8, 12
    of planning, 7
    of translation assessment, 8
    of translation competence, 31, 54,
        152
    of the translation process, 7, 158
    of translating, 4, 158
    of translation competence, 12, 154,
        157, 158, 173
Mohanty, 137
Monitor Model, 128
monitoring, 7, 127, 128, 138–50, 159,
    162, 166, 167
    of translation output, 16, 126
    of translation performance, 3
    plan, 140
    production, 139
    self-, 128
    strategies, 3, 128, 158
    strategy, 140
    style, 140
monolingual
    education, 54
    homes, 41, 43, 45, 50, 52

primary education, 42
social life, 41, 43, 46, 47, 50
more verbs analysis, 61, 66, 67
morpheme, 17
studies, 156
morphosyntax, 15
Mossop, 128
multicultural policies, 31
multiculturalism, 23
multiple choice tests, 171, 174

NAATI, 8, 57, 157, 169, 170, 173
Narrative Concerns, 74
native speaker, 3, 26
neo-Cartesian standpoint, 158
Neubert, 10, 57
Nicaragua, 39
Nida and Taber, 3
nominal constructions, 100
nominalization, 66, 80, 81, 84–8, 101
Non-Narrative concerns, 74
non-native
    readers of English, 57
    speaker, 26
    style, 10
non-target language systems, 16
Nord, 5, 13
norm-referenced, 164, 171
normative lexical choices, 125
Norway, 27

objective testing, 172
O'Malley and Chamot, 127, 128, 139
omissions, 8, 65, 100, 103, 107, 110
oral / literate dimensions, 75, 76
overestimation of translation
    competence, 134–7

parallelism, 160
partial switch, 138, 142, 145
passive, 59, 75, 87
    agentless, 80, 81, 84, 93–6, 101,
    159
patent applications, 162
Pearson product-moment, 130, 131
peer assessment, 168
performance analysis, 17
persistence, 3, 103
persistent, 107, 108, 110, 124, 125,
    155, 156

personality, 104, 155, 158
Peru, 39,40
Picht, 11
Pienemann, 156
Pienemann and Johnston, 17, 128, 157
planning, 127
Plimer and Candlin, 29
polysemy, 11
Portugal, 39, 40
Portuguese, 49
practice factor, 171
prefabricated patterns, 17
prepositional phrases, 80, 81, 84,
    96–101
press editorials, 76, 84, 91, 92, 93, 96,
    101
private verb, 77, 102
processing constraints, 17
production monitoring, 139
professional certification, 8
proficiency
    Academic versus Conversational, 76
    development of, 9
    pre-professional, 9
    professional, 9
    transitional, 9
proof-reading, 167
propositional structure, 11
prudence, 3, 104
prudent, 107, 108, 109, 110, 116, 124,
    125
psychological
    approaches, 7
    aspects of translation competence
    modelling, 9
    motivation, 103
Pym, 6, 15

quantitative feedback, 164

reading and writing ability, 8
real-world knowledge, 159
redundancy, 164
relative clauses, 75, 77, 96
reliability, 36, 157, 165, 166, 171, 172
retrieval, 7
revision, 16, 127, 138, 139, 140, 142,
    143, 145, 146, 148, 149, 150, 162
    self-, 128
rhetorical devices, 160

risk-taking, 3, 17, 96, 104, 107, 108, 110, 115, 124, 125, 155, 156
Romance words, 64

Sa'addedin, 10
sampling instrument, 164
second generation
  candidates, 27
  German candidates, 38
  Italian candidates, 38
  speakers, 25
  speakers of languages other than English, 58
  students, 24
second language
  ability, 67
  acquisition, 1, 12, 16, 18, 20, 22, 28, 72, 126, 128, 156, 160, 175
  acquisition analysis, 14
  acquisition research, 2, 55, 128, 159
  identifying, 71
  learners, 2
  learning, 1, 128
  output, 1
  proficiency, 58, 59
  repertoire, 58
  translator education, 12
  translator output, 1
  writers, 57
  writing, 58, 60, 148
self-assessment, 126
Selinker, 12, 15, 16
semantic
  discursiveness, 90
  field, 116
semilingualism, 38
shaping, 9
situation-dependent reference, 75
skills
  comprehension, 58
  linguistic and cognitive, 4
  productive, 58, 65
  reading and writing, 9
  textual, 2, 16, 27
Snell-Hornby, 4
Snow, 60, 76
social services, 23
source text
  analysis, 11
  comprehending, 57

Soviet Union, 27
Spain, 39, 40
Spanish, 17, 24, 25, 26, 32, 37, 39, 47, 49, 50, 130, 131, 132, 135, 136, 137
  candidates, 34, 49–51
  -English translation, 129
spelling, 69, 104
split-halves, 171, 172
stamina, 159
standard equivalent, 108
Stern, 173
strategies
  cognitive, 7
  learner, 17
  practical translation, 10
  teaching and learning, 166, 167
  textual, 104
  training and learning, 14
  transfer, 11
  translation, 7
structural asymmetry, 93
student-centred approach, 167
style, 13, 125
  decontextualized, 93
  detached, 93
  microlinguistic exponents of, 13
  nominal, 66
  verby, 66, 69
stylistic
  aspects of lexis in translation, 77
  difficulties of students, 1
  dimensions, 74
  judgements, 123
  norms, 76
  variation, 73, 153
stylistics, 2
subordination, 164
supply demand paradox, 25, 26, 30, 32
Swedish, 19, 28
Sydney, 25
syntactic
  shift, 66
  structure, 65
system-centred approach, 2

table of specifications, 174
Tannen, 60, 76

target
  genre, 101
  language competence, 155
  language error, 138
  language lexical repertoire, 65, 69
  language genres, 159
  language grammar, 72
  language norm, 28
  language system, 72
  norms, 16
teacher-centred approach, 167
teaching and learning
  theories of, 9
terminology
  in translator education, 11
  technical, 11
test-retest, 171, 172
test-wiseness, 38
testing procedures, 11
text
  analysis, 5, 10
  -centred approach, 2
  corpus, 10
  extract, 171
  grammatically dense, 67
  length, 8, 61
  modes, 9
  nominal, 100, 101
  quality, 8
  syntactically strung-out, 67
  syntactically substandard, 66
  telegraphic, 67, 90, 91, 156
  type, 73, 102, 171
  verbal, 100, 101
textlinguistics, 1, 9, 10
texts, 11
  authentic-looking, 17
  evaluative, 9
  forestry, 27
  grading translated, 8
  instructive, 9
  journalistic, 173
  natural-looking, 57
  orientational, 9
  primary, 58
  projective, 9
  specialized, 173
  stylistically authentic, 1
  target, 4
  technical, 57

telegraphic, 64
typology of, 9
writing of, 2
textual meaning, 77
textuality, 164, 171
think-aloud
  data, 7, 128
  experimenters, 19
  methodologists, 6
  protocols, 127
  verbalizations, 127
thought conveyance, 8
Tirkonnen-Condit, 171, 175
tokens misspelt, 61, 64, 68
Tommola, 151
tone, 9, 104, 114
Toury, 4
transfer in second language learning,
  15
transformation stage, 127
translation
  back-, 11
  Bible, 11
  bureau quality control, 127
  community, 24
  competence assessment, 157
  competence profile, 165, 167, 172,
    175
  competence studies, 2
  curriculum, 14, 18
  didactics, 10
  difficulties, 11
  education, 25, 26, 27, 163
  fullness of, 6
  indirect, 69
  into the first language, 2, 4, 22, 57,
    152, 160, 161, 162
  into the second language, 1, 2, 4,
    10, 20, 26, 27, 54, 56, 57, 157,
    163, 176
  literary, 60
  market, 2, 25
  marking scales, 169
  oral, 7
  output quality, 3
  pedagogy, 6, 9, 10, 11, 28, 56, 163
  performance, 8
  poor reputation of, 13
  process of, 3, 4, 6, 20, 155, 170
  product of, 3

project, 11
quality assessment, 6, 7
research, 152
studies, 1, 2, 3, 6, 12, 19, 20, 54,
    72, 122, 127, 128, 157
    task of, 1
    teachers of, 16
    teaching, 5, 11
    tests, 157, 169
    units, 170
Translation Operator, 4
translational equivalent, 113, 115,
    120, 121, 122
translator
    accredited, 161, 169, 172
    -centred approach, 2
    educators, 2
    services, 38
translators
    Bible, 3
    first generation, 25
    into the second language, 101, 102,
        103, 125, 150, 159, 162
    labour market-place, 24
    medieval, 3
    non-native, 28
    professional, 9
    second generation, 25
    student, 7, 10, 13
    supply of, 24
trilingual
    education, 40, 42, 43, 51
    homes, 42, 43, 47, 50
    primary education, 49
    secondary education, 52
    social lives, 42, 50
trilingualism, 35
T-scores, 130, 131, 134, 151
Tunisia, 39, 40
type/token ratio, 59, 80, 81, 84,
    88–92, 101, 102

underestimation of translation
    competence, 134–7
unit of analysis, 7
United Arab Emirates, 40, 45
universal order of acquisition, 156
University of Western Sydney
    Macarthur, 30, 126
unmarked equivalent, 107, 117

Uruguay, 39, 40
USA, 40

Valdés and Figueroa, 25
validity, 157
    concurrent, 173
    construct, 8, 166, 173, 174
    ecological, 173
    face, 165, 173, 174, 175
    predictive, 173, 174
Variational Approach, 4
verbal constructions, 100
verbal data
    experimenters, 19
    methods, 19
    protocol method, 139
verbal reports, 19
verbalization, 20, 139
verby, 71
Vietnam, 39, 40, 52, 53, 54
Vietnamese, 26, 30, 32, 37, 38, 39,
    51, 52, 54, 58, 131, 132
    candidates, 34, 51–4
    -English translation, 129
    immigration to Australia, 32
Vitale, 11
vocabulary
    choice, 3, 57
    diverse, 59
    repertoire, 63

Weaver, 60
Wilkinson, 13
Wilss, 11
Woods, 105, 106
word
    length, 74, 80, 84, 90, 92, 101
    order, 72
words
    directly translated, 61, 64, 65
    Germanic-derived, 77
    omitted, 61, 65
    Romance-derived, 77
    shifted, 61, 65, 67
working languages, 35
writing plans, 128

Yugoslav candidates, 46

z-scores, 63, 107, 110